Winning Arguments

From Aristotle to Obama –
Everything You Need to Know About
the Art of Persuasion

Jay Heinrichs

PENGUIN BOOKS

PENGUIN BOOKS

Published by the Penguin Group
Penguin Books Ltd, 80 Strand, London WC2R ORL, England
Penguin Group (USA) Inc., 375 Hudson Street, New York, New York 10014, USA
Penguin Group (Canada), 90 Eglinton Avenue East, Suite 700, Toronto, Ontario, Canada M4P 2Y3
(a division of Pearson Penguin Canada Inc.)
Penguin Ireland, 25 St Stephen's Green, Dublin 2, Ireland (a division of Penguin Books Ltd)
Penguin Group (Australia), 250 Camberwell Road, Camberwell, Victoria 3124, Australia
(a division of Pearson Australia Group Pty Ltd)
Penguin Books India Pvt Ltd, 11 Community Centre, Panchsheel Park, New Delhi – 110 017, India
Penguin Group (NZ), 67 Apollo Drive, Rosedale, North Shore 0632, New Zealand
(a division of Pearson New Zealand Ltd)
Penguin Books (South Africa) (Pty) Ltd, 24 Sturdee Avenue, Rosebank,
Johannesburg 2196, South Africa

Penguin Books Ltd, Registered Offices: 80 Strand, London WC2R ORL, England

www.penguin.com

First published in the USA by Three Rivers Press 2007
First published in Great Britain by Allen Lane as *Thank You for Arguing* 2008
This revised edition published by Penguin as *Winning Arguments* 2010
008

Copyright © Jay Heinrichs, 2007, 2010
All rights reserved

The moral right of the author has been asserted

Set in New Baskerville
Printed in England by Clays Ltd, St Ives plc

ISBN: 978-0-141-03258-0

www.greenpenguin.co.uk

Penguin Books is committed to a sustainable
future for our business, our readers and our planet.
This book is made from Forest Stewardship
Council™ certified paper.

To Dorothy Junior and George:

You win.

▲

CONTENTS

PREFACE xi

INTRODUCTION

1. Open Your Eyes 3
THE INVISIBLE ARGUMENT

OFFENSE

2. Set Your Goals 15
CICERO'S LIGHTBULB

3. Control the Tense 27
ORPHAN ANNIE'S LAW

4. Soften Them Up 38
CHARACTER, LOGIC, EMOTION

5. Get Them to Like You 46
EMINEM'S RULES OF DECORUM

6. Make Them Listen 56
THE LINCOLN GAMBIT

7. Show Leadership 66
THE BELUSHI PARADIGM

8. Win Their Trust 72
QUINTILIAN'S USEFUL DOUBT

9. Control the Mood 79
   THE AQUINAS MANEUVER

10. Turn the Volume Down 91
    THE SCIENTIST'S LIE

11. Gain the High Ground 98
    ARISTOTLE'S FAVORITE TOPIC

12. Persuade on Your Terms 108
    WHAT "IS" IS

13. Control the Argument 121
    HOMER SIMPSON'S CANONS OF LOGIC

DEFENSE

14. Spot Fallacies 137
    THE SEVEN DEADLY LOGICAL SINS

15. Call a Foul 155
    NIXON'S TRICK

16. Know Whom to Trust 171
    PERSUASION DETECTORS

17. Find the Sweet Spot 181
    MORE PERSUASION DETECTORS

ADVANCED OFFENSE

18. Speak Your Audience's Language 191
    THE RHETORICAL APE

19. Make Them Identify with Your Choice 200
    THE MOTHER-IN-LAW RUSE

20. Get Instant Cleverness 208
    MONTY PYTHON'S TREASURY OF WIT

21. Seize the Occasion 226
    STALIN'S TIMING SECRET

22. Use the Right Medium 237
    THE JUMBOTRON BLUNDER

ADVANCED AGREEMENT

23. Give a Persuasive Talk 247
    THE OLDEST INVENTION

24. Wow Your Audience 260
    THE OBAMA IDENTITY

25. Use the Right Tools 271
    THE BRAD PITT FACTOR

26. Run an Agreeable Country 284
    RHETORIC'S REVIVAL

APPENDICES

  I. The Tools 297
 II. Glossary 307
III. Chronology 313
IV. Further Reading 317

    ACKNOWLEDGMENTS 319
    INDEX 321

▲

PREFACE

Few people can say that John Quincy Adams changed their lives. Those who can are wise to keep it to themselves. Friends tell me I should also avoid writing about my passion for rhetoric, the three-thousand-year-old art of persuasion.

John Quincy Adams changed my life by introducing me to rhetoric.

Sorry.

Years ago, I was wandering through Dartmouth College's library for no particular reason, flipping through books at random, and in a dim corner of the stacks I found a large section on rhetoric, the art of persuasion. A dusty, maroon-red volume attributed to Adams sat at eye level. I flipped it open and felt like an indoor Coronado. Here lay treasure.

The volume contained a set of rhetorical lectures that Adams taught to undergraduates at Harvard College from 1805 to 1809, when he was a United States senator commuting between Massachusetts and Washington. In his first class, the paunchy, balding thirty-eight-year-old urged his goggling adolescents to "catch from the relics of ancient oratory those unresisted powers, which mould the mind of man to the will of the speaker, and yield the guidance of the nation to the dominion of the voice." To me that sounded more like hypnosis than politics, which was sort of cool in a *Manchurian Candidate* way.

In the years since, while reading all I could of rhetoric, I came to realize something: Adams's language sounded antique, but the powers he described are real. Rhetoric means more than grand oratory, more than "using words . . . to influence or persuade," as Webster's defines it. It teaches us to argue without anger. And it offers a chance to tap into a source of social power I never knew existed.

You could say that rhetoric talked me into itself.

Concordia discors
Harmony in discord

—HORACE

INTRODUCTION

1. Open Your Eyes

▲

THE INVISIBLE ARGUMENT
A personal tale of unresisted persuasion

Truth springs from argument among friends.
— DAVID HUME

I t is early in the morning and my seventeen-year-old son eats breakfast, giving me a narrow window to use our sole bathroom. I wrap a towel around my waist and approach the sink, avoiding the grim sight in the mirror; as a writer, I don't have to shave every day. (Marketers despairingly call a consumer like me a "low self-monitor.") I do have my standards, though, and hygiene is one. I grab toothbrush and toothpaste. The tube is empty. The nearest replacement sits on a shelf in our freezing basement, and I'm not dressed for the part.

"George!" I yell. "Who used all the toothpaste?"

A sarcastic voice answers from the other side of the door. "That's not the point, is it, Dad?" George says. "The point is how we're going to keep this from happening again."

He has me. I have told him countless times how the most productive arguments use the future tense, the language of choices and decisions.

"You're right," I say. "You win. Now will you please get me some toothpaste?"

"Sure." George retrieves a tube, happy that he beat his father at an argument.

Or *did* he? Who got what he wanted? In reality, by conceding his point, I persuaded *him*. If I simply said, "Don't be a jerk and get me some toothpaste,"

> **TRY THIS IN A MEETING**
> Answer someone who expresses doubt over your idea with "Okay, let's tweak it." Now focus the argument on revising your idea as if the group had already accepted it. This move is a form of *concession*—rhetorical jujitsu that uses your opponent's moves to your advantage.

George might stand there arguing. Instead I made him feel triumphant, triumph made him benevolent, and that got me exactly what I wanted.

I achieved the height of persuasion: not just an agreement, but one that gets an audience—a teenaged one at that—to do my bidding.

No, George, *I* win.

The Matrix, Only Cooler

What kind of father manipulates his own son? Oh, let's not call it manipulation. Call it *instruction*. Any parent should consider rhetoric, the art of argument, one of the essential R's. Rhetoric is the art of influence, friendship, and eloquence, of ready wit and irrefutable logic. And it harnesses the most powerful of social forces, argument.

▸ **Useful Figure**
The *syncrisis* (Greek for "alternative judgment") reframes an argument by redefining it. "Not manipulation—instruction." You'll find a whole chapter on figures later on, as well as a glossary in the back.

Whether you sense it or not, argument surrounds you. It plays with your emotions, changes your attitude, talks you into a decision, and goads you to buy things. Argument lies behind political labeling, advertising, jargon, voices, gestures, and guilt trips; it forms a real-life Matrix, the supreme software that drives our social lives. And rhetoric serves as argument's decoder. By teaching the tricks we use to persuade one another, the art of persuasion reveals the Matrix in all its manipulative glory.

▸ **Persuasion Alert**
It's only fair to show my rhetorical cards—to tell you when I use devices to persuade you. The Matrix analogy serves as more than a pop culture reference; it also appeals to the reader's acceptance of invisible wheels within wheels in modern existence, from computer software to quantum physics. Rhetoric calls this shared attitude a "commonplace"; as you shall see, it is one of the building blocks of persuasion.

The ancients considered rhetoric the essential skill of leadership—knowledge so important that they placed it at the center of higher education. It taught them how to speak and write persuasively, produce something to say on every occasion, and make people like them when they spoke. After the ancient Greeks invented it, rhetoric helped create the world's first democracies. It trained Roman orators like Julius Caesar and Marcus Tullius Cicero and gave the Bible its finest language. It even inspired William Shakespeare. Every one of America's founders studied rhetoric, and they used its principles in writing the Constitution.

Rhetoric faded in academia during the 1800s, when social scientists dismissed the notion that an individual could stand up to the inexorable forces of history. Who wants to teach leadership when academia doesn't believe in leaders? At the same time, English lit replaced the classics, and ancient thought fell out of vogue. Nonetheless, a few remarkable people continued to study the art. Daniel Webster picked up rhetoric at Dartmouth by joining a debating society, the United Fraternity, which had an impressive classical library and held weekly debates. Years later, the club changed its name to Alpha Delta and partied its way to immortality by inspiring the movie *Animal House*. To the brothers' credit, they didn't forget their classical heritage entirely; hence the toga party.

▸ **Persuasion Alert**
Here I yank you from Webster to *Animal House,* not just to encapsulate rhetoric's decline but to make you unconsciously vote for my side of the argument. Whose side are you on, Webster's or John Belushi's? The technical term for this shotgun marriage of contrasting thoughts is *antithesis,* meaning "opposing idea."

Scattered colleges and universities still teach rhetoric—in fact, the art is rapidly gaining popularity among undergraduates—but outside academia we forgot it almost entirely. What a thing to lose. Imagine stumbling upon Newton's law of gravity and meeting face-to-face with the forces that drive the universe. Or imagine coming across Freud for the first time and suddenly becoming aware of the unconscious, where your Id, Ego, and Superego conduct their silent arguments.

I wrote this book for that reason: to lead you through this ill-known world of argument and welcome you to the Persuasive Elect. Along the way you'll enhance your image with Aristotle's three traits of credible leadership: virtue, disinterest, and practical wisdom. You'll find yourself using logic as a convincing tool, smacking down fallacies and building airtight assertions. Aristotle's principles will also help you decide which medium—e-mail? phone? skywriting?—works best for each message. You will discover a simple strategy to get an argument unstuck when it bogs down in accusation and anger.

TRY THIS IN A PRESENTATION
The Romans were using the "But wait, there's more" pitch a couple of millennia before infomercials. They gave it a delectable name: *dirimens copulatio,* meaning "a joining that interrupts." It's a form of *amplification,* an essential rhetorical tactic that turns up the volume as you speak. In a presentation, you can amplify by layering your points: "Not only do we have this, but we also . . ."

And that's just the beginning. The pages to come contain more than a hundred "argument tools" borrowed from ancient texts and adapted to modern situations, along with suggestions for trying the techniques at home, school, work, or in your community. You will see when logic works best, and when you should lean on an emotional strategy. You'll acquire mind-molding figures of speech and ready-made tactics, including Aristotle's irresistible **enthymeme**, a neat bundle of logic that I find easier to use than pronounce.

By the end of the book you will have mastered the rhetorical tricks for making an audience eager to listen. People still love a well-delivered talk; the top professional speakers charge more per person than a Rolling Stones concert. I devote a whole chapter to Cicero's elegant five-step method for constructing a speech—invention, arrangement, style, memory, and delivery—a system that has served the greatest orators for the past two thousand years.

Great argument does not always mean elaborate speech, though. The most effective rhetoric disguises its art. And so I'll reveal a rhetorical device for implanting opinions in people's heads through sheer sleight of tongue.

Besides all these practical tools, rhetoric offers a grander, metaphysical payoff: it jolts you into a fresh new perspective on the human condition. After it awakens you to the argument all around, the world will never seem the same.

I myself am living proof.

Ooh, Baby, Stir Harder

To see just how pervasive argument is, I recently attempted a whole day without persuasion—free of advertising, politics, family squabbles, or any psychological manipulation whatsoever. No one would persuade me, and I would avoid persuading them. Heck, I wouldn't even let myself persuade myself. Nobody, not even I, would tell me what to do.

If anyone could consider himself qualified for the experiment, a confirmed hermit like me could. I work for myself; indeed, having dropped out of a career in journalism and publishing, I work *by* myself, in a cabin a considerable distance from my house. I live in a tiny village in northern New England, a region that boasts the most persuasion-resistant humans on the planet. Advertisers have nightmares about people like me: no TV, no cell phone, no BlackBerry, dial-up Internet. I'm commercial-free, a walking NPR, my own individual, persuasion-immune man.

As if.

My wristwatch alarm goes off at six. I normally use it to coax myself out of bed, but now I ignore it. I stare up at the ceiling, where the smoke detector blinks reassuringly. If the smoke alarm detected smoke, it would *alarm,* rousing the heaviest sleeper. The philosopher Aristotle would approve of the smoke detector's rhetoric; he understood the power of emotion as a motivator.

For the time being, the detector has nothing to say. But my cat does. She jumps on the bed and sticks her nose in my armpit. As reliable as my watch and twice as annoying, the cat persuades remarkably well for ten dumb pounds of fur. Instead of words she uses gesture and tone of voice—potent ingredients of argument.

I resist stoically. No cat is going to boss me around this morning.

The watch beeps again. I wear a Timex Ironman, whose name comes from a self-abusive athletic event; presumably, if the watch works for a masochist who subjects it to two miles of swimming, a hundred miles of biking, and 26.2 miles of running all in one day, it would work for someone like me who spends his lunch hour walking strenuously down to the brook to see if there are any fish. The ancient Romans would call the Ironman's brand appeal *argumentum a fortiori,* "argument from strength." Its logic goes like this: If something works the hard way, it's more likely to work the easy way. Advertisers favor the argument from strength. Years ago, Life cereal ran an ad with little Mikey the fussy eater. His two older brothers tested the cereal on him, figuring that if Mikey liked it, anybody would. And he liked it! An *argumentum a fortiori* cereal ad. My Ironman watch's own argument from strength does not affect me, however. I bought it because it was practical. Remember, I'm advertising-immune.

> **TRY THIS IN A PROPOSAL**
>
> If your idea has been used elsewhere, describe its success in vivid detail as though the audience itself had accomplished it. Show how much more skill and resources your plan dedicates to the idea. Then feel free to use your favorite cliché, e.g., "It's a slam dunk."

But its beeping is driving me crazy. Here I'm not even up yet and I already contemplate emotional appeals from a cat and a smoke detector along with a wristwatch argument from strength. Wrenching myself out of bed, I say to the mirror what I tell it every morning: "Don't take any crap from anyone."

The cat bites me on the heel. I grab my towel and go fix its breakfast.

Five minutes later I'm out of toothpaste and arguing with my son. Not a good start to my experiment, but I'll chalk it up to what scientists euphemistically call an "artifact" (translation: boneheaded mistake) and move on. I make coffee, grab a pen, and begin writing ostentatiously in a notebook. This does little good in the literary sense—I can barely read my own scribble before coffee—but it produces wonderful rhetorical results; when my wife sees me writing, she often brings me breakfast.

Did I just violate my own experiment? Shielding the notebook from view, I write a grocery list. There. That counts as writing.

TRY THIS AT HOME
If you're appalled at the notion of manipulating your loved ones, try using pure logic—no emotions, no hidden tactics, no references to your authority or the sacrifices you make. Do it for a whole day, and you may be surprised by a rising level of anger in your family. Seduction is a great pacifier.

Dorothy returned to full-time work a year and a half ago, after I quit my job. The deal was that I would take over the cooking, but she loves to see her husband as the inspired author and herself as the able enabler. My wife is a babe, and many babes go for inspired authors. Of course, *she* might be persuading *me:* by acting as the kind of babe who goes for inspired authors, she turns me on. Seduction underlies the most insidious, and enjoyable, forms of argument.

Seduction is not just for sex, either. Writer Frederick Kaufman recently showed in *Harper's Magazine* how the Food Network uses techniques identical to that of the porn industry—overmiked sound, very little plot, good-looking characters, along with lavish close-ups of firm flesh and flowing juices.

RACHAEL RAY: Lentils poof up big when you cook 'em. They just suck up all the liquid as they get nice and tender.

EMERIL LAGASSE: In go the bananas. Oh, yeah, babe. Get 'em happy right now.

We live in a tangled, dark (I almost added "moist") world of persuasion. A used car salesman once seduced me out of fifteen grand. My family and I had just moved to Connecticut, and I needed cheap transportation. It had been a tough move; I was in ill sorts. The man at the car lot had me pegged before I said a word. He pointed to a humble-looking Ford Taurus sedan,

▶ Tips from the Ancients
WHEN JUSTICE WASN'T BLIND: Aristotle said that emotion trumps logic. A famous Roman orator proved this by using strategic pornography to defend a beautiful priestess of the Temple of Aphrodite charged with prostitution. When the trial appeared to be going badly, the orator made the young woman stand in the middle of the Roman Forum, where he tore off her clothes. It worked. Moved by this zaftig agent of the goddess of love, the (all-male) jury acquitted her. The same technique helped Sharon Stone get away with murder in *Basic Instinct*.

suggested a test drive, and as soon as I buckled in he said, "Want to see P. T. Barnum's grave?" Of course I did.

The place was awesome. We had to stop for peacocks, and brilliant-green feral Peruvian parrots squawked in the branches of a huge fir tree. Opposite Barnum's impressive monument stood Tom Thumb's marker with a life-sized statue of the millionaire midget. Enthralled by our test drive, I did everything else the salesman suggested, and he suggested I buy the Ford. It was a lemon.

He sized me up and changed my mood; he *seduced* me, and to tell you the truth, I enjoyed it. I had some misgivings the next morning, but no regrets. It was a consensual act.

Which leads us to argument's grand prize: the consensus. It means more than just an agreement, much more than a compromise. The consensus represents an audience's commonsense thinking. In fact it *is* a common sense, a shared faith in a choice—the decision or action you want. And this is where seduction comes in. As Saint Augustine knew, faith requires emotion.

Seduction is manipulation, manipulation is half of argument, and therefore many of us shy from it. But seduction offers more than just consensual sex. It can bring you consensus. Even Aristotle, that logical old soul, believed in the curative powers of seduction. Logic alone will rarely get people to do anything. They have to *desire* the act. You may not like seduction's manipulative aspects; still, it beats fighting, which is what we usually mistake for an argument.

TRY THIS AT WORK You can use seduction—the nonsexual kind—in a presentation. Will your plan increase efficiency? Get your audience to lust after it; paint a vision of actually taking lunch hours and seeing their families more.

Birds Do It . . .

Meanwhile my experiment gets more dubious by the moment. I'm leaving the bathroom when Dorothy puts a plate of eggs on the table, shrugs into her suit jacket, and kisses me good-bye. "Don't forget, I'll be home late— I'm having heavy hors d'oeuvres at the reception tonight," she says, and leaves for her fund-raising job at a law school. (Fund-raising and law. Could it get more rhetorical?)

I turn to George. "So, want to have dinner with me or on campus tonight?" George attends a boarding school as a day student. He hates the food there.

"I don't know," he says. "I'll call you from school."

I want to work late and don't feel like cooking, but I'm loath to have George think my work takes priority over him. "Okay," I say, adding with as much enthusiasm as I can fake, "we'll have stew!"

TRY THIS AFTER
YOU'RE PUT ON HOLD
This works with most
bureaucrats. Pretend
you have all the time
in the world, and
present your choice
as the lesser of two
evils. They either cut
you a break, or waste
more time with you.
Functionaries, like
water, follow the path
of least resistance.

"Ugh," says George, right on cue. He hates my stew even more than school food. The odds of my cooking tonight have just gone way down.

Oops, as that fine rhetorician Britney Spears put it. I did it again.

And so goes my day. In my cabin office, I e-mail editors with flattering explanations for missing their deadlines. (I'm just trying to live up to their high standards!) I put off calling Sears to complain about a $147 bill for replacing a screw in our oven. When I do call eventually, I'll take my time explaining the situation. Giving me a break on the bill will cost less than dealing with me any further.

At noon, I grab some lunch and head outside for a walk. A small pile of fox scat lies atop a large granite rock. "Mine," the fox says with the scat. "This spot belongs to me." Territorial creatures, such as foxes and suburbanites, use complicated signals to mark off terrain and discourage intruders—musk, fences, scat, marriage licenses, footprints, alarm systems . . . Argument is in our nature, literally.

A mockingbird sings a pretty little tune that warns rivals off its turf. Without a pause it does the same thing in reverse, rendering a figure of speech called **chiasmus.** This crisscross figure repeats a phrase with its mirror image: "You can take a boy out of the country, but you can't take the country out of a boy." "I wasted time, and now time doth waste me." Our culture underrates figures, but only because most of us lack the rhetorical savvy to wield them. They can yield surprising power. John F. Kennedy deployed a chiasmus during a televised address—"Ask not what your country can do for you, ask what you can do for your country"—and thousands joined the Peace Corps. I fell in love with figures, and even launched

TRY THIS IN A PRESENTATION
Present a decision with a
chiasmus by using a mirror
image of your first choice:
"Either we control expenses
or let expenses control us."

a Web site, Figarospeech.com, devoted to them. Figures add polish to a memo or paper, and in day-to-day conversation they can supply ready wit to the most tedious conversations.

The phone is ringing when I get back to my cabin. It's George calling to say he plans to eat at school. *(Yes!)* So I work late, rewarding myself now and then by playing computer pinball. I find I can sit still for longer stretches with game breaks. Is this persuasion? I suppose it is. My nonrhetorical day turned out to be pretty darn rhetorical, but nonetheless agreeable.

▸ **Persuasion Alert**
Whoa, there. A presidential chiasmus drove people into the Peace Corps? I use one of the more persuasive ways to cheat in logic—because B follows A, A caused B. I call it the Chanticleer fallacy, after the rooster who thought his crowing made the sun come up.

I finally knock off work and head back to the house for a shower and shave, even though this isn't a shaving day. My wife deals with a lot of good-looking, well-dressed men, and now and then I like to make a territorial call, through grooming and clothing, to convince her she did not marry a bum. I pull on a cashmere sweater that Dorothy says makes my eyes look "bedroomy" and meet her at the door with a cold gin and tonic.

Let the seduction begin.

OFFENSE

2. Set Your Goals

▲

CICERO'S LIGHTBULB
Change the audience's mood, mind, or willingness to act.

Aphrodite spoke and loosened from her bosom the embroidered girdle of many colors into which all her allurements were fashioned. In it was love and in it desire and in it blandishing persuasion which steals the mind even of the wise. — HOMER

Back in 1974, *National Lampoon* published a parody comic-book version of Plato's *Republic*. Socrates stands around talking philosophy with a few friends. Each time he makes a point, another guy concedes, "Yes, Socrates, very well put." In the next frame you see an explosive "POW!!!" and the opponent goes flying through the air. Socrates wins by a knockout. The *Lampoon's Republic* has some historical validity; ancient Greeks, like argumentative nerds throughout the ages, loved to imagine themselves as fighters. But even they knew the real-life difference between fighting and arguing. We should, too. We need to distinguish rhetorical argument from the blame-shifting, he-said-she-said squabbling that defines conflict today. In a fight, each disputant tries to win. In an argument, they try to *win over* an audience—which can comprise the onlookers, television viewers, an electorate, or each other.

> ▶**Meanings**
> "Debate" and "battle" share the same Latin root. Typical of those pugnacious Romans.

This chapter will help you distinguish between an argument and a fight, and to choose what you want to get out of an argument. The distinction can determine the survival of a marriage, as the celebrated research psychologist John Gottman proved in the eighties and nineties. Working out of his "love lab" at the University of Washington, he and his assistants videotaped hundreds of married couples over a period of nine years, poring over every tape and entering every perceived emotion and logical point into a database. They watched hours and days and months of arguments, of couples glaring at each other and revealing embarrassing things in front of the camera. It was like a bad reality show.

When Gottman announced his findings in 1994, though, rhetoricians around the country tried not to look smug, because the data confirmed what rhetoric has claimed for several millennia. Gottman found that couples who stayed married over those nine years argued about as much as those who ended up in divorce. However, the successful couples went about their arguments in a different way, and with a different purpose. Rhetoricians would say they instinctively followed the basic tenets of argument.

When some of the videotapes appeared on network television, they showed some decidedly uncomfortable moments, even among the happy couples. One successfully married husband admitted he was pathologically lazy, and his wife cheerfully agreed. Nonetheless, the couples who stayed married seemed to use their disputes to solve problems and work out differences. They showed faith in the outcome. The doomed couples, on the other hand, used their sessions to attack each other. Argument was a problem for them, not a means to a solution. The happy ones argued. The unhappy ones fought.

Much of the time, I'm guessing that the happy ones also *seduced*—they manipulated one another. That's a good thing. While our culture tends to admire straight shooters, the ones who follow their gut regardless of what anyone thinks, those people rarely get their way in the end. Sure, aggressive loudmouths often win temporary victories through intimidation or simply by talking us to exhaustion; but the more subtle, eloquent approaches lead to long-term commitment. Corporate recruiters will confirm this theory. There are a few alpha types in the business world who live to bully their colleagues and stomp on the competition; but if you ask headhunters what they look for in executive material, they describe a persuader and team builder, not an aggressor.

TRY THIS WITH YOUR CAREER
The growing profession of "leadership branding coaches" teaches CEO wannabes how to embody their company. The ideal trait? Not aggression, not brains, but the ability to tell a compelling life story and make yourself desirable. Later on, you'll see how storytelling is critical to emotional persuasion.

You succeed in an argument when you persuade your audience. You win a fight when you dominate the enemy. A territorial dispute in the backseat of a car fails to qualify as argument, for example, unless each child makes the unlikely attempt to persuade instead of scream. ("I see your point, sister. However, have you considered the analogy of the international frontier?")

At the age of two, my son, George, became a devotee of what rhetoricians call "argument by the stick"; when words failed him, he used his fists. After every fight I would ask him: "Did you get the other kid to agree with you?" For years he considered that to be a thoroughly stupid question, and maybe it was. But eventually it made sense to him: argument by the stick—fighting—is no argument. It never persuades, it only inspires revenge or retreat.

In a fight, one person takes out his aggression on another. Vice President Dick Cheney was fighting when he urged U.S. senator Pat Leahy to commit an autoerotic act on the Senate floor. Cheney said this spleen venting made him "feel better," but it wasn't an argument. (It *would* have been one if Cheney really wanted Leahy to do what he suggested, God forbid.)

On the other hand, when George Foreman tries to sell you a grill, he makes an argument: persuasion that tries to change your mood, your mind, or your willingness to do something.

Homer Simpson offers a legitimate argument when he demonstrates our intellectual superiority to dolphins: "Don't forget—we invented computers, leg warmers, bendy straws, peel-and-eat shrimp, the glory hole, *and* the pudding cup."

Mariah Carey pitches an argument when she sings, "We belong together," to an assumed ex-boyfriend; she tries to change his mind (and judging by all the moaning in the background, get some action).

Daughter screaming at her parents: *fight.*
Business proposal: *argument.*
Howard Dean saying of Republicans, "A lot of them have never made an honest living in their lives": *fight.*
Yogi Berra saying, "It's not the heat, it's the humility": *argument.*

The basic difference between an argument and a fight: an argument, done skillfully, gets people to want to do what you want. You fight to win; you argue to achieve agreement.

That may sound wimpy. Under some circumstances, though, argument can take a great deal of

▶ **Persuasion Alert**
The ancients hated arguing through books, partly because an author cannot see his audience. If I could speak to you personally, I probably wouldn't veer from my son to Dick Cheney to George Foreman to Homer Simpson to Mariah Carey. I would know which case appeals to you the most. Still, the wildly varied examples make a point all their own: You can't escape argument.

courage. It can even determine a nation's fate. Ancient rhetoricians dreaded most the kind of government led by a demagogue, a power-mad dictator who uses rhetorical skills for evil. The last century shows how right the ancients were. But the cure for the dark side of persuasion, they said, is the other side. Even if the stakes aren't quite as high—if the evildoer is a rival at work or a wacky organization on campus—your rhetorical skills can balance the equation.

TRY THIS IN A POLITICAL ARGUMENT
If you actually get someone to agree with you, test her commitment to your point. Ask, "Now what do you think you'll say if someone brings up this issue?"

But rhetoric offers a more selfish reason for arguing. Learn its tools and you'll become the face to watch, the rising star. You'll mold the minds of men and women to your will, and make any group yield to the dominion of your voice. Even more important, you'll get them to *want* to yield, to *commit* to your plan, and to consider the result a consensus. You will make them desire what you desire—seduce them into a consensual act.

How to Seduce a Cop

A police patrol stops you on the highway and you roll your window down.

> YOU: What's wrong, Officer?
> COP: Did you know that the speed limit here is fifty?
> YOU: How fast was I going?
> COP: Fifty-five.

The temptation to reply with a snappy answer is awful.

> YOU: Whoa, lock me up!

And indeed the satisfaction might be worth the speeding ticket and risk of arrest. But rewind the scene and pause it where the cop says "fifty-five." Now set your personal goal. What would you like to accomplish in this situation?

Perhaps you would like to make the cop look like an idiot. Your snappy answer accomplishes that, especially if you have passengers for an audience. Good for you. Of course, the cop is unlikely to respond kindly, the result will be a fight, and you are the likely loser. How about getting him to apologize for being a martinet bastard? Sorry. You have to set a realistic goal. F. Lee Bailey and Daniel Webster combined could not get this cop to apologize. Instead, suppose we set as your personal goal the avoidance of a ticket. Now, how are we to do that?

> **Argument Tool**
> THE GOAL: Ask yourself what you want at the end of an argument. Change your audience's mind? Get it to do something or stop doing it? If it works, then you've won the argument, regardless of what your opponent thinks.

To win a deliberative argument, don't try to outscore your opponent. Try instead to get your way.

It's unlikely that your opponent knows any rhetoric, however. He probably thinks that the sole point of an argument is to humiliate you or get you to admit defeat. This cognitive dissonance can be useful; your opponent's aggressiveness makes a wonderful argument tool. Does he want to score points? Let him score points. All you want to do is win—to get your audience to accept your choice or do what you want it to do. People often win arguments on points, only to lose the battle. Although polls showed that people thought John Kerry won the presidential debates against President Bush, the president's popularity actually

> **Meanings**
> Rhetoric has a name for debating that seeks to win points: *eristic.*

improved. The audience liked Kerry's logic, but they preferred Bush—not the words but the man. Kerry won on points; Bush won the election.

Even if your argument includes only you and another person, with no one else looking on, you still have audience: the other person. In that case, there are two ways to come out on top: either by winning the argument—getting your opponent to admit defeat—or by "losing" it. Let's try both strategies on your cop.

1. Win the argument with a bombproof excuse.

> YOU: My wife's in labor! I need to get her to the hospital stat!
> COP: You're driving alone, sir.
> YOU: Oh my God! I forgot my wife!

Chances are, this kind of cop won't care if your wife is having triplets all over the living room floor. But if the excuse works, you win.

2. Play the good citizen you assume the cop wants you to be. Concede his point.

> ▸ **Argument Tool**
> *CONCESSIO,*
> the formal
> name for
> concession.
> Concede your
> opponent's
> point in order
> to win what
> you want.

> YOU: I'm sure you're right, Officer. I should have been watching my speedometer more.

Good. You just let the cop win on points. Now get him to let you off easy.

> YOU: I must have been watching the road too closely. Can you suggest a way for me to follow my speedometer without getting distracted?

This approach appeals to the cop's expertise. It might work, as long as you keep any sarcasm out of your voice. But assume that the appeal needs a little more sweetening.

> COP: You can start by driving under the speed limit. Then you won't have to watch your speedometer so much.
> YOU: Well, that's true, I could. I've been tailgated a lot when I do that, but that's their problem, isn't it?
> COP: Right. You worry about your own driving.
> YOU: I will. This has helped a lot, thanks.

Now what do you think is most likely to happen? I can tell you what *won't* happen. The cop won't order you out of the car. He won't tell you to stand spread-eagled against it while he pats you down. He won't call for backup, or even yell at you. You took the anger out of the argument, which these days is no mean accomplishment. And if he actually does let you off with a warning, congratulations. You win. The cop may not recognize it, but you have just notched the best kind of win. He leaves happy, and so do you.

TRY THIS IN A POLITICAL ARGUMENT
Practice your rhetorical jujitsu with a variation on the rhetorical question "With friends like that, who needs enemies?" Opponent: "The Democrats are now the reform party." You: "With reformers like that, who needs crooks?"

The easiest way to exploit your opponent's desire to score points is to let him. Concede a point that will not damage your case irreparably. When your kid says, "You never let me have any fun," you say, "I suppose I don't." When a coworker says, "That'll never work," you say, "Hmm, maybe not." Then use that point to change her mood or her mind.

In other words, one way to get people to agree with you is to agree with them—tactically, that is. Agreeing up front does not mean giving up the argument. Instead, use your opponent's point to get what you want. Practice rhetorical jujitsu by using your opponent's own moves to throw him off balance. Does up-front agreeing seem to lack in stand-up-for-yourself-ishness? Yes, I suppose it does. But wimps like us shall inherit the rhetorical earth. While the rest of the world fights, we'll argue. And argument gets you what you want more than fighting does.

> ▶ **Persuasion Alert**
> Pretty agreeable of me, yes? The ancient Greeks gave a name to this kind of anticipatory concession, agreeing in advance to what the other person is likely to say: *prolepsis,* meaning "anticipation."

How to Manipulate a Lover

Having decided what you want out of an argument, you can determine how your audience must change for you to achieve that goal. Maybe all you need to do is alter a person's mood, as in, say, seduction. Or you want to change someone's mind—to promote you instead of a rival, for instance. Or you want your audience to do something concrete for you.

> ▶ **Tips from the Ancients**
> The playwright Aristophanes said that persuasion can make "the lesser side appear the greater." Plato thought that was a bad thing; but throughout history, ninety-pound weaklings have applauded.

Actually, the seductive argument often entails more than just a mood change. Suppose your goal is a little lovemaking. If both of you are in the mood already, then you need no persuasion. As Lord Nelson said, never mind maneuvers, go straight at 'em.

> ▶ **Persuasion Alert**
> I risk offending some readers with talk of sex. But like an actor performing a nude scene, I do it for art. Seduction is the rhetorical opposite of fighting; and it's a wonderful tool for teaching rhetoric. Some of the standard topics for practicing speeches in Roman schools were extremely racy.

YOU: *Voulez-vous couchez avec moi?*

If your partner-to-be shows reluctance, however, the direct approach is unlikely to succeed. You would have a better chance with a mild argument:

YOU: Know what would really liven things up,

relationship-wise? If we did that role-playing game. Which one of us should wear the maid's costume?

But easiest of all would be to change your audience's mood.

> YOU: Let me pour you some more wine. The music? Oh, just Barry White. Wow, by candlelight you look like a movie star.

That, at least, is how history's greatest orator, Marcus Tullius Cicero, would say to do it. He came up with three goals for persuading people, in order of increasing difficulty:

Stimulate your audience's emotions.
Change its opinion.
Get it to act.

Sometimes it takes all three goals to get some action. For some reason this reminds me of the tired old joke "How many psychiatrists does it take to screw in a lightbulb?"

First, the punch line says, *the bulb has to want to change.* How inefficient! How long will *that* take? Twenty years of therapy? And once the bulb decides to change, what will compel it to carry out the job? A rhetorician would go about this much more simply—by *persuading* the lightbulb. The task would require three persuasive steps:

> Start by changing its **mood.** Make the bulb feel how scary it is to sit in the dark. This turns it into a receptive audience, eager to hear your solution.
> Then change its **mind.** Convince the bulb that a replacement is the best way to get some light in here.
> Finally, fill it with the **desire to act.** Show the bulb that changing is a cinch, and inspire

> **Classic Hits**
> BARELY LEGAL BRIDE: Cicero may have been more seductive in the forum than in bed. After divorcing his wife of thirty years, the sixty-year-old wedded a teenager. When asked what he was doing marrying a young girl, Cicero smirked. "She'll be a woman tomorrow." Citizens throughout the republic were heard to say, "Ick."

> TRY THIS IN A SPEECH
> You don't need a strong emotion to get an audience to change its mind; attentiveness may be the best mood for a rational talk. Instead of a joke, use mild surprise. "I brought some prepared remarks, but after meeting some of you today I've decided to speak from the heart."

it with a vision of lightness. This requires stronger emotions that turn a decision into a commitment.

Stimulating emotions puts the other goals within range. When Frank Capra directed *It's a Wonderful Life,* he had a problem persuading a shy Jimmy Stewart to kiss Donna Reed. Stewart kept making excuses to put off the scene. Capra finally threw away the script, which had the two actors listening over separate extensions to the girl's asinine boyfriend. Instead, the director made the couple share the same phone. The physical contact did the trick; you can almost see a hormonal miasma hanging over the World War II vet and the lovely young actress. Stewart did his duty with obvious pleasure, completing in a single take one of the great screen kisses of all time. Capra won over his audience—Stewart—through surrogate seduction. In the resulting consensus, everybody made out very well (so to speak).

The Seduction Diet

Changing the mood is the easiest goal, and usually the one you work on first. Saint Augustine, a onetime rhetoric professor and one of the fathers of the Christian Church, gave famously boffo sermons. The secret, he said, was not to be content merely with seizing the audience's sympathetic attention. He was never satisfied until he made them cry. (Augustine could not have been invited to many parties.) As one of the great sermonizers of all time, he converted pagans to Christianity through sheer emotional pyrotechnics. By changing your audience's emotion, you make them more vulnerable to your argument—put them in the mood to listen.

Wringing tears from an audience is easy compared to goal number two, making them *decide what you want.* Henry Kissinger used a classic persuasive method when he served as Nixon's national security adviser. He would lay out five alternatives for the president to choose from, listing the most extreme choices first and last, and putting the one Kissinger preferred in the middle. Nixon inevitably chose the "correct" option, according to Kissinger. (Not

TRY THIS AT HOME
To see whether people actually do the thing you ask them to—whether they desire the acts—create a "commitment ratio": divide the number of "Okays" and "Yes, dears" by the number of times they followed through. I achieved a 70 percent rate over three days—a passing grade. (You may do better if you don't have children.)

TRY THIS IN A STORE
Like Kissinger, retailers
use the Goldilocks
technique all the time,
offering lower-priced
junk and high-end
goods to make their
best-selling items
seem just right. Next
time you buy, say, an
electronic gadget, ask
the sales staff to show
you the midpriced
version first. Then go
up or down in price
depending on your
desires and budget.

exactly the most subtle tactic, but I've seen it used successfully in corporate PowerPoint presentations.)

Usually, since most arguments take place between two people, most of the time you deal with just two choices—yours and your opponent's. My daughter, Dorothy Junior, makes an especially difficult adversary. Although she enjoys argument much less than her brother does, she can be equally persuasive. She launches an argument so gently you fail to realize you're in one.

I recently visited her in London, where she was spending a term as a college student. My first evening there, she proposed dinner at a low-price Indian restaurant. I wanted to play the generous dad and take her someplace fancier. Guess who won.

ME: We could still eat Indian, but someplace more upscale.

DOROTHY JR.: Sure.

ME: So do you know of any?

DOROTHY JR.: Oh, London's full of them.

ME: Uh-huh. So do you know of any in particular?

DOROTHY JR. [*vaguely*]: Oh, yeah.

ME: Any near here?

DOROTHY JR.: Not really.

ME: So you'd rather eat at your usual place.

DOROTHY JR.: If you want to, sure.

ME: I don't want to!

And then I felt guilty about losing my patience, which, though she denies it, may have been Dorothy Junior's strategy all along. We ate at her usual place. She won, using my guilt as her emotional goal. Dorothy couldn't have done better if she had prepared a Ciceronian speech in advance. Cicero might even approve: the most effective rhetoric disguises itself, he said. Dorothy knew this instinctively. She has a biting tongue but knows how to restrain it to win an argument. Still, Dorothy had it relatively easy. We were going to dinner one way or another. All she had to do was pull me toward her choice.

Goal number three—in which you get an audience to *do something or to stop doing it*—is the most difficult. It requires a different, more personal level of emotion. Suppose I didn't want to go to dinner at all. Dorothy would have had a lot more arguing to do to get me out the door. That's like getting a horse to drink, to use an old expression. You can give the horse salt to stimulate its desire for water (arousing its emotions, if you will); you can persuade it to follow you to a stream (the choice part); but getting it to commit to drinking poses the toughest rhetorical problem.

Get-out-the-vote campaigns for young people are notoriously bad at this. The kids flock to rock concerts and grab the free T-shirts; they get all charged up and maybe even register as Democrats or Republicans— a triumph of persuasion, as far as emotions and choice are concerned. But showing up at the polls on election day is something else altogether. Youth turns stubborn at the getting-to-drink part. (I meant that metaphorically.)

TRY THIS IN A WRITTEN PROPOSAL
After you outline the document, jot down a two-part inventory of your goal: (1) Have you thought of all the benefits and weighed them against the alternatives? (2) How doable is it? How cheap or easy compared to the other choices? Now check off those points in your outline. Did you cover everything?

Besides using desire to motivate an audience, you need to convince it that an action is no big deal—that whatever you want them to do won't make them sweat. A few years ago, when I was an editorial director at the Rodale publishing company, I heard that some people in another division were working on a diet book. *God, I thought, another diet,* as if there weren't enough already. Plus, the title they planned for the book made no sense to me. It referred to a particular neighborhood in a major city, a place most Americans probably had never heard of. The author, a cardiologist, happened to live there. But who would buy a book called *The South Beach Diet?*

▸ **Persuasion Alert**
Self-deprecating humor is an acceptable way to brag. Mentioning a moment of boneheadedness at my former company beats the far more obnoxious "I was a high-level manager at a publishing company that had twenty-three million customers the year I left." But I'm still bragging.

So I'm a lousy prognosticator of best sellers; but in retrospect I can explain why the title was not such a bad idea after all. "South Beach" conjures an image of people—*you*—in bathing attire. It says vacation, one of the chief reasons people go on a diet. The Rodale editors stimulated an emotion by making readers picture a desirable and highly personal goal: you, in a bathing suit, looking great. So much for the desire part. The book's subtitle employs the no-big-deal tactic: *The Delicious, Doctor-Designed, Foolproof Plan for Fast and Healthy Weight Loss.* No suffering, perfectly safe, instant results . . . they hit all the buttons except for *So You Can Eat Like a Glutton and Get Hit on by Lifeguards.* People took action in droves. At this writing, the book has sold nearly five million copies.

The Tools

This chapter gave you basic devices to determine the outcome of an argument:

- Set your personal goal.
- Set your goals for your audience. Do you want to change their **mood,** their **mind,** or their **willingness** to carry out what you want?

3. Control the Tense

▲

The three basic issues of rhetoric have to do with time.

MARGE: *Homer, it's very easy to criticize . . .*
HOMER: *And fun, too!*

—*THE SIMPSONS*

You have your personal goal (what you want out of the argument) and your audience goals (mood, mind, action). Now, before you begin arguing, ask yourself one more question: *What's the issue?* According to Aristotle, all issues boil down to just three (the Greeks were crazy about that number):

Blame

Values

Choice

> ▸ **Argument Tool**
> THE THREE CORE ISSUES:
> blame, values, choice.

You can slot any kind of issue involving persuasion into one of these categories.

Who moved my cheese? This, of course, is a
   blame issue. Whodunit?

Should abortion be legal? **Values.** What's
   morally right or wrong about letting a
   woman choose whether or not to end the
   budding life inside her own body? (My
   choice of words implies the values each
   side holds—a woman's right to her own
   body, and the sanctity of life.)

Should we build a plant in Oaxaca? **Choice:** to
   build or not to build, Oaxaca or not
   Oaxaca.

> ▸ **Persuasion Alert**
> What's missing from
> my list? How about
> capital-T Truth? Can't
> you argue about truth
> and falsity? You can,
> but that wouldn't be
> persuasion. Absolute
> Truth demands a dif-
> ferent kind of argu-
> ment, one the
> philosophers called
> "dialectic." It seeks to
> discover things, not
> talk people into them.

Should Brad and Jen have split up? **Values**—not moral ones, necessarily, but what you and your interlocutor value. Were they just too
cute to separate?

Did O.J. do it? **Blame.**

Shall we dance? **Choice:** to dance or not to dance.

Why should you care which question slots into which core issue? It matters because you will never meet your goals if you argue around the wrong
core issue. Watch a couple in their living room, reading books and listening
to music:

SHE: Can you turn that down a little?

HE: You're the one who set the volume last.

SHE: Oh, really? Then who was it blasting "Free Bird" all over
the place this afternoon?

HE: So that's what this is about. You hate my music.

What does she want out of this argument? Quiet. It's a choice issue. She
wants him to choose to turn the music down. But instead of choices, the argument turns to blame, then values.

Blame: You're the one who set the volume last.

Values: So that's what this is about. You hate my music.

It's hard to make a positive choice about turning the volume knob when
you argue about a past noise violation and the existential qualities of
"Free Bird."

The examples I gave of the core issues—blame, values, and choice—
show a certain pattern. The blame questions deal with the past. The values
questions are in the present tense. And the choice questions have to do
with the future.

Blame = *Past*
Values = *Present*
Choice = *Future*

If you find an argument spinning out of control, try switching the tense.
To pin blame on the cheese thief, use the past tense. To get someone to
believe that abortion is a terrible sin, use the present tense. The future,
though, is the best tense for getting peace and quiet in the living room.

Aristotle, who devised a form of rhetoric for each of the tenses, liked the future best of all.

The rhetoric of the *past,* he said, deals with issues of justice. This is the judicial argument of the courtroom. Aristotle called it "forensic" rhetoric, because it covers forensics. Our music-challenged couple uses the past tense for blaming each other.

> HE: You're the one who set the volume last.
> SHE: Then who was it blasting "Free Bird"?

If you want to try someone on charges of volume abuse (not to mention bad taste), you're in the right tense. Forensic argument helps us determine whodunit, not who's-doing-it or who-will-do-it. Watch *Law and Order* and you'll notice that most of the dialogue is in the past tense. It works great for lawyers and cops, but a loving couple should be wary of the tense. The purpose of forensic rhetoric is to determine guilt and mete out punishment; couples who get in the habit of punishing each other suffer the same fate as the doomed marriages in Dr. Gottman's love lab.

How about the *present* tense? Is that any better? It can be. The rhetoric of the present handles praise and condemnation, separating the good from the bad, distinguishing groups from other groups and individuals from each other. Aristotle reserved the present for describing people who meet a community's ideals or fail to live up to them. It is the communal language of commencement addresses, funeral orations, and sermons. It celebrates heroes or condemns a common enemy. It gives people a sort of tribal identity. (We're great, terrorists are cowards). When a leader has trouble confronting the future, you hear similar tribal talk.

Aristotle's term for this kind of language is "demonstrative" rhetoric, because ancient orators used it to demonstrate their fanciest techniques. Our argumentative couple uses it to divide each other.

> HE: So that's what this is about. You hate my music.

TRY THIS AT WORK
Most office back-stabbing uses the past or present tense. ("He's the one who screwed up that bid." "She's a total jerk.") If you find yourself a victim, refocus the issue on future choices. "How is blaming me going to help us get the next contract?" "Whether you think I'm a jerk or not, let's figure out a way for you and me to get along."

▶ **Persuasion Alert**
If this seems to hint at an agenda, you're right. The Democrats and Republicans love the present tense. It's a great way to stir up the base, and a lousy way to conduct a democracy. More on this in the last chapter.

▶ Meanings
Aristotle's Greek word for demonstrative rhetoric is *epideictic,* but the only people who use that unpronounceable term are academic rhetoricians. They're just being demonstrative.

TRY THIS IN A PITCH
If you're competing against a superior company or candidate (or suitor of any kind), use the future tense against your opponent. "You've heard a lot of bragging about past accomplishments and how great my opponent is, but let's talk about the future: what do you want done?"

You might say that the man bears sole blame for switching tenses from past to present. But let's not get all forensic on each other, okay? The man may be right, after all; perhaps the argument has to do with the guy's thing for Lynyrd Skynyrd and not the volume knob. In any case, their dialogue has suddenly turned tribal: I like my music, you hate it. If the man happened to be a politician he would find it hard to resist adding, "And that's just wrong!" We use the present tense to talk about values: That is wrong. This is right. Detesting "Free Bird" is morally wrong.

If you want to make a joint decision, you need to focus on the future. This is the tense that Aristotle saved for his favorite rhetoric. He called it "deliberative," because it argues about choices and helps us decide how to meet our mutual goals. Deliberative argument's chief topic is "the advantageous," according to Aristotle. This is the most pragmatic kind of rhetoric. It skips right and wrong, good and bad, in favor of expedience.

Present-tense (demonstrative) rhetoric tends to finish with people bonding or separating.
Past-tense (forensic) rhetoric threatens punishment.
Future-tense (deliberative) argument promises a payoff. You can see why Aristotle dedicated the rhetoric of decision making to the future.

Our poor couple remains stranded in the present tense, so let's rewind their dialogue and make them speak deliberatively—in the future tense, that is.

SHE: Can you turn that down a little?
HE: Sure, I'd be happy to.

Wait. Shouldn't he say, "*I'll* be happy to"? I *will*, not I *would*? Well, sure, you're probably right. He could. But by using the conditional mood—"would" instead of "will"—he leaves himself an opening.

HE: But is the music too loud, or do you want me to play
   something else?
SHE: Well, now that you mention it, I'd prefer something a
   little less hairbandy.

Ouch! He plays nice, and she insults the entire classic rock genre. That makes him feel justified to retaliate; but he does it moderately.

HE: Something more elevatorish, you mean? That doesn't
   really turn me on. Want to watch a movie?

By turning the argument back to choices, the man keeps it from getting too personal—and possibly keeps her off balance, making her a bit more vulnerable to persuasion.

SHE: What do you have in mind?
HE: We haven't seen *Terminator 2* in ages.
SHE: *Terminator 2*?! I hate that movie.

As he well knows. This is a little off topic, but I can't resist giving you another rhetorical trick: propose an extreme choice first. It will make the one you want sound more reasonable. I used the technique myself in getting my wife to agree to name our son after my uncle George. I proposed lots of alternatives—my personal favorite was Herman Melville Heinrichs—until she finally said, "You know, 'George' doesn't really sound that bad." I kissed her and told her how much I loved her, and notched another argument on my belt.

▶ **Persuasion Alert**
I presumably didn't dash this book off in one draft, so what excuse do I have for straying off topic? Cicero used digressions to change the tone and rhythm of an argument, and so do I. By describing a persuasive trick in the middle of my description of tenses, I hope to show how these tools work on all sorts of occasions.

Back to our couple.

HE: Well, then, how about *Lawrence of Arabia*?

He knows she would prefer a different movie—the desert just isn't her thing—but it doesn't sound that bad after the first choice.

SHE: Okay.

Lawrence it is. Which happens to be the movie he wanted in the first place. The distinctions between the three forms of rhetoric can determine the success of a democracy, a business, or a family. Remember the argument I had with my son, George?

> ME: Who used all the toothpaste?
>
> GEORGE: That's not the question, is it, Dad? The question is, how are we going to keep it from happening again?

Sarcasm aside, the kid deserves credit for switching the rhetoric from past to future—from forensic to deliberative. He put the argument in decision-making mode. What choice will give us the best advantage for stocking an endless supply of toothpaste?

TRY THIS WHEN ARGUING TURNS TO FIGHTING
Consider "What should we do about it?" and "How can we keep it from happening again?" as rhetorical versions of WD-40 lubricant. The past and present can help you make a point, but any argument involving a decision eventually has to turn to the future.

Annie's Pretty Sure Bet

▶ **Persuasion Alert**
A good persuader anticipates the audience's objections. Ideally, you want to produce them even before the audience can think to. The technique makes your listeners more malleable. They begin to assume you'll take care of all their qualms, and they lapse into a bovine state of persuadability. (Oh, wait. You're the audience here. Scratch "bovine.")

Hold on. The future sounds lovely, but isn't civil discourse supposed to be about sticking to the facts? The future *has* no facts, right? Doesn't it simply speculate?

Correct. Facts do not exist in the future. We can know that the sun came up yesterday, and that it shines now; but we can only *predict* that the sun will come up tomorrow. When Little Orphan Annie sings that godawful *Tomorrow* song, she doesn't make a fact-based argument, she *bets*. Like a proper Aristotelian, Annie even admits the case.

> *Bet your bottom dollar*
> *That tomorrow*
> *There'll be sun!*

Annie concedes that the sunrise has not yet become a fact. Call it Orphan Annie's Law: The sun only *may* come up tomorrow. A successful argument, like anything about the future, cannot stick to the facts.

Deliberative argument can *use* facts, but it must not limit itself to them. While you and I can disagree about the capital of Burkina Faso, we're not arguing deliberatively; we simply dispute a fact. Neither of us can decide to make it Ouagadougou. We merely look it up. (I just looked it up.)

All we have for the future is conjecture or choices, not facts. When Homer Simpson argues with his wife in the future tense of deliberative argument, facts have nothing to do with it:

> MARGE: Homer, I don't want you driving around in a car you built yourself.
>
> HOMER: You can sit there complaining, or you can knit me some seat belts.

Instead of helping us to find some elusive truth, deliberative argument *deliberates,* weighing one choice against the other, considering the circumstances.

Choices:

> Beach, or mountains, this summer?
> Should your company replace its computers, or hire a competent tech staff?
> Will Frodo come out as a gay Hobbit?
> Should we invade Iraq?

When you argue about values, you use demonstrative rhetoric, not deliberative. If you rely on a cosmic authority—God, or Bono—then the audience has no choice to make.

Eternal truths will answer these:

> Is there a God?
> Is homosexuality immoral?
> Is capitalism bad?
> Should all students know the Ten Commandments?

In each case the argument has to rely on morals and metaphysics. And it takes place mostly in the present tense, the language of demonstrative rhetoric. It can be particularly maddening in a marital dispute, because it comes across as preachy. (Demonstrative rhetoric is the rhetoric of preachers, after all.) Besides, it is far more difficult to

---

▶ **What's Wrong with This Argument?**

Caller: I don't know much about the Democrats, but George Bush is a jerk!

Next Caller: I'm unbelievably angry at that caller. If she saw what Bush is doing for our boys in Iraq, she'd shut her mouth!

Host: Put her in a burkha, baby.

WHAT'S WRONG: The host could have turned this into a political argument by asking whether Bush's policies will get what we want in Iraq. Instead, he went all tribal. She's not one of us! Tribal talk deals with present questions—who's in and who's out? Political talk deals with the future: what's to our best advantage?

change someone's values than to change her mind. After all, eternal truths are supposed to be . . . eternal.

Practical concerns, on the other hand, are open to deliberative debate. Because deliberation has to do with choices, everything about it *depends*—on the circumstances, the time, the people involved, and whatever "public" you mean when you talk about public opinion. Deliberative argument relies on public opinion to resolve questions, not a higher power.

The audience's opinion will answer these:

> Should the state legislature raise taxes to fund decent schools?
> Should you raise your kid's allowance?
> When should your company release its newest product?

If you reply, "That's just wrong!" to an argument, you use demonstrative, values rhetoric. If you reply, "On the other hand," then your argument has a chance of making a choice.

> FATHER: Our kid could break her neck on those old monkey
> bars.
> MOTHER: On the other hand, she may not. Besides, the coordination she learns might prevent future accidents.

And it might not. Choices are full of these what-if scenarios, and deliberative discourse deals with their probabilities. In *The Simpsons*—an endless source of rhetorical material—Ned Flanders, a born-again Christian, attacks Moe the bartender with demonstrative, present-tense rhetoric, and Moe makes a weak attempt at the conjectural language of deliberative rhetoric.

> NED FLANDERS: You ugly, hate-filled man.
> MOE: Hey. I may be ugly, and I may be hate-filled, but . . .
> uh . . . what was the last thing you said?

Deliberation is the rhetoric of choice, literally. It deals with decisions, and decisions depend on particular circumstances, not eternal truths and cold facts. If life were free of contingencies, then we could live by a few rules written in stone that would apply to all our decisions. Every baby would come with an operating manual, the same guide that worked for her older brother. Every rule of thumb would apply to every situation. The early bird would always catch the worm, *everything* would be cheaper by the dozen, and the world would come in two colors: black and white. But alas, it doesn't. Sometimes, under some circumstances (say, jumping out of an airplane for the first time), it's a very bad idea to look before you leap. Sometimes the enemy of your enemy makes a terrible friend.

Girl Versus Turkey

A husband and wife debate over whether to invest more in stocks, or in bonds.

> HE: Let's get aggressive with growth stocks.
> SHE: The experts predict the market will tank this year. I say we stay conservative.

Why argue? Because they can't predict the economic future. They can only take their best guess today. What would that argument look like in the present tense?

> HE: My dad always said blue chips are the way to go. That's the right kind of investment.
> SHE: Well, that's just wrong. My astrologer says blue chips are evil.

The same couple argues over whether to provide orthodontia for their ten-year-old.

> SHE: Straight teeth will be good for his self-esteem.
> HE: Yeah, but if we put the money into a college fund, we'll have a debt-free college graduate.
> SHE: A bucktoothed college graduate.

Is there a right choice? Maybe. But they don't know what it is and have to make a decision nonetheless. These questions deal with probabilities, not facts or values.

Suppose your uncle Randy decides to divorce your

TRY THIS IN A MEETING
Hold your tongue until well into the discussion. If an argument bogs down in the past or present tense, switch it to the future. "You're all making good points, but how are we going to . . . ?" Make sure that question defines the issue in a way that's favorable to your side.

aunt on their thirtieth anniversary so he can marry a surfing instructor he met at Club Med. You have two issues here, one moral and the other practical. The moral issue is inarguable by our definition. Your uncle is either wrong or right. You could remind him that he is breaking a wonderful woman's heart, but you would be sermonizing, not arguing. You could threaten to bar him from Thanksgiving dinner, but that would be coercion, not argument—assuming he would prefer your turkey to a cruise buffet with his Club Med hottie.

The practical, debatable issue in your uncle's case deals with the likely consequences of ditching your aunt for the trophy wife.

> YOU: She'll leave you within the year, and you'll be lonely and miserable forever.
>
> UNCLE: No she won't. And a young woman will make me feel younger, which means I'll live longer.

▸ **Argument Tool**
SPOT THE INARGUABLE: It's what is permanent, necessary, or undeniably true. If you think your opponent is wrong—if it ain't necessarily so—then try to assess what the audience believes. You can challenge a belief; but deliberative argument prefers to use beliefs to persuasion's advantage.

Which prediction is true? Neither of you has a clue. But Uncle might persuade you that he has good practical reasons for remarrying. Will he ever convince you that he is morally in the right? Not a chance. Morals are inarguable in deliberative rhetoric.

Argument's Rule Number One: **Never debate the undebatable.** Instead, focus on your goals. The next chapter will tell you how to achieve them.

The Tools

We expect our arguments to accomplish something. You want a debate to settle an issue, with everyone walking away in agreement—with you. This is hard to achieve if no one can get beyond who is right or wrong, good or bad. Why do so many arguments end up in accusation and name-calling?

The answer may seem silly, but it's crucial: most arguments take place in the wrong tense. Choose the right tense. If you want your audience to make a choice, focus on the future. Tenses are so important that Aristotle assigned a whole branch of rhetoric to each one. We'll get into tenses in much greater detail in the chapters to come. You'll see how you can use values to win an argument about choices, and how tribal speech can help mightily in an otherwise rational debate. Meanwhile, remember these tools:

> **Control the issue.** Do you want to fix **blame?** Define who meets or abuses your common **values?** Or get your audience to make a **choice?** The most productive arguments use choice as their central issue. Don't let a debate swerve heedlessly into values or guilt. Keep it focused on choices that solve a problem to your audience's (and your) advantage.
>
> **Control the clock.** Keep your argument in the right tense. In a debate over choices, make sure it turns to the future.

4. Soften Them Up

▲

CHARACTER, LOGIC, EMOTION

The strangely triumphant art of agreeability

Audi partem alteram.
Hear the other side.

—SAINT AUGUSTINE

....

At the age of seven, my son, George, insisted on wearing shorts to school in the middle of winter. We live in icy New Hampshire, where playground snow has all the fluffy goodness of ground glass. My wife launched the argument in the classic family manner: "You talk to him," she said.

So I talked to him. Being a student of rhetoric, I employed Aristotle's three most powerful tools of persuasion:

Argument by character
Argument by logic
Argument by emotion

In this chapter you will see how each of these tools works, and you'll gain some techniques—the persuasive use of decorum, argument jujitsu, tactical sympathy—that will put you well on the way to becoming an argument adept.

The first thing I used on George was argument by character: I gave him my stern father act.

> ME: You have to wear pants, and that's final.
> GEORGE: Why?
> ME: Because I told you to, that's why.

But he just looked at me with tears in his eyes. Next, I tried reasoning with him, using argument by logic.

ME: Pants will keep your legs from chapping. You'll feel a lot
    better.

GEORGE: But I want to wear *shorts*.

So I resorted to manipulating his emotions. Following Cicero, who claimed that humor was one of the most persuasive of all rhetorical passions, I hiked up my pant legs and pranced around.

ME: Doh-de-doh, look at me, here I go off to work wearing
    shorts . . . Don't I look stupid?

GEORGE: Yes. *(Continues to pull shorts on.)*

ME: So why do you insist on wearing shorts yourself?

GEORGE: Because I don't look stupid. And they're my legs. I
    don't mind if they get chaffed.

ME: Chapped.

Superior vocabulary and all, I seemed to be losing my case. Besides, George was making his first genuine attempt to argue instead of cry. So I decided to let him win this one.

ME: All right. You can wear shorts in school if your mother
    and I can clear it with the authorities. But you have to put
    your snow pants on when you go outside.
    Deal?

GEORGE: Deal.

He happily fetched his snow pants, and I called the school. A few weeks later the principal declared George's birthday Shorts Day; she even showed up in culottes herself. It was mid-February. Was that a good idea? For the sake of argument, and agreement, I believe it was.

▸ **Useful Figure**
These two sentences ("Good idea? I believe it was.") form a figure of speech called a *hypophora*, which asks a rhetorical question and then immediately answers it. The *hypophora* allows you to anticipate the audience's skepticism and nip it in the bud.

Aristotle's Big Three

I used my best arguments by character, logic, and emotion. So, how did George still manage to beat me? By using the same tools. I did it on purpose, and he did it instinctively. Aristotle called them *logos, ethos,* and *pathos;*

and so will I, because their meanings are richer than the English versions. Together they form the three basic tools of rhetoric.

Logos is **argument by logic.** If arguments were children, *logos* would be the brainy one, the big sister who gets top grades in high school. It doesn't just follow the logical rules; instead, its techniques use what the audience itself is thinking.

> ► **Argument Tool**
> LOGOS: argument by logic.

Ethos, or **argument by character,** employs the persuader's personality, reputation, and ability to look trustworthy. (While *logos* sweats over its GPA, *ethos* gets elected class president.) In rhetoric, a sterling reputation is more than just good; it's persuasive. I taught my children that lying isn't just wrong, it's *un*persuasive. An audience is more likely to believe a trustworthy persuader, and to accept his argument. "A person's life persuades better than his word," said one of Aristotle's contemporaries. This remains true today. Rhetoric shows how to shine a flattering light on your life.

> ► **Argument Tool**
> ETHOS: argument by character.

Then you have *pathos,* or **argument by emotion,** the sibling the others disrespect but who gets away with everything. Logicians and language snobs hate *pathos,* but Aristotle himself—the man who *invented* logic—recognized its usefulness. You can persuade someone logically, but as we saw in the last chapter, getting him out of his chair to act on it takes something more combustible.

> ► **Argument Tool**
> PATHOS: argument by emotion. *Pathos* forms the root of the word "sympathy"; a successful persuader must learn how to read the audience's emotions.

Logos, ethos, and *pathos* appeal to the brain, gut, and heart of your audience. While our brain tries to sort the facts, our gut tells us whether we can trust the other person, and our heart makes us want to do something about it. They form the essence of effective persuasion.

George instinctively used all three to counter my own arguments. His *ethos* put mine in check:

> **TRY THIS BEFORE AN IMPORTANT MEETING**
> If you want to get a commitment out of the meeting, take stock of your proposal's *logos, pathos,* and *ethos:* Do my points make logical sense? Will the people in the room trust what I say? How can I get them fired up for my proposal at the end?

> ME: You have to wear pants because I told you to.
>
> GEORGE: They're my legs.

His *logos* also canceled mine out, even if his medical terminology didn't:

ME: Pants will make your legs feel better.
GEORGE: I don't mind if they get chaffed.

Finally, I found his *pathos* irresistible. When he was little, the kid would actually stick his lower lip out when he tried not to cry. Cicero *loved* this technique—not the lip part, but the appearance of struggling for self-control. It serves actually to amplify the mood in the room. Cicero also said a genuine emotion persuades more than a faked one; and George's tears certainly were genuine. Trying not to cry just made his eyes well up more.

I wish I could say my *pathos* was as effective, but George failed to think it funny when I hiked my pants up. He just agreed that I looked stupid. I had been studying rhetoric pretty intensively at that point, and to be thrown to the mat by a seven-year-old was humiliating. So was facing my wife afterward.

DOROTHY: So did you talk to him?
ME: Yeah, I handled it.

George picked that moment to walk into the room with his shorts on.

DOROTHY: Then why is he wearing shorts?
GEORGE: We made a deal!
DOROTHY: A *deal*. Which somehow allows him to wear shorts to school.
ME: I told you, I handled it.

So what if his legs looked like rhubarbs when he came home? While I was moderately concerned about the state of his skin, and more apprehensive about living up to Dorothy's expectations, neither had much to do with my personal goal: to raise persuasive children. If George was willing to put all he had into an argument, I was willing to concede. That time, I like to think, we both won. (Today he expresses his individuality in the opposite way: he wears ties to school. And pants, even.)

Logos, pathos, and *ethos* usually work together to win an argument, debates with argumentative seven-year-olds excepted. By using your opponent's logic and your audience's emotion, you can win over your audience with greater ease. You make them happy to let you control the argument.

Logos: Use the Logic in the Room

Later on, we'll get into rhetoric's more dramatic logical tactics and show how to bowl your audience over with your eloquence. First, though, let's master the most powerful *logos* tool of all, concession. It seems more Jedi knight than Rambo, involving more self-mastery than brute force, but it lies closer to the power center of *logos* than rhetoric's more grandiloquent methods. Even the most aggressive maneuvers allow room for the opponent's ideas and the audience's preconceptions. To persuade people—to make them desire your choice and commit to the action you want—you need all the assets in the room, and one of the best resources comes straight from your opponent's mouth.

Calvin concedes effectively in the comic strip *Calvin and Hobbes* when his dad tries to teach him to ride a bike:

> DAD: Look, Calvin. You've got to relax a little. Your balance will be better if you're loose.
> CALVIN: I can't help it! Imminent death makes me tense! I admit it!

Clever boy. Perched atop a homicidal bike, he still manages to gain control of the argument. By agreeing that he's tense, he shifts the issue from nerves to peril, where he has a better argument.

Salespeople love to use concession to sell you stuff. I once had a boss who came from a sales background. He proved that old habits die hard. The guy never disagreed with me, yet half the time he got me to do the opposite of what I proposed.

> ME: Our research shows that readers love beautiful covers without a lot of type.
> BOSS: Beautiful covers. Sure.
> ME: I know that clean covers violate the usual rules for selling magazines on the newsstand, but we should test dual covers: half of them will be crammed with the usual headlines, and half of them with a big, bold image—very little type.

TRY THIS AT HOME Aristotle said that every point has its flip side. That's the trick to concession. When a spouse says, "We hardly ever go out anymore," the wise mate does not spew examples of recent dates; he says, "That's because I want you all to myself." This response will at least buy him time to think up a credible change in tense: "But as a matter of fact, I was going to ask if you wanted to go to that new Korean restaurant."

BOSS: Clean covers. Great idea. How'll that affect your budget?

ME: It'll cost a lot. I'm gambling on selling
more magazines.

BOSS: So you haven't budgeted for it.

ME: Uh, no. But I tell you, boss, I'm pretty
confident about this.

BOSS: Sure. I know you are. Well, it's a great
idea. Let's circle back to it at budget time.

ME: But that's nine months from—

BOSS: So what else is on your agenda?

My covers never got tested. If a circle in Hell is reserved for this kind of salesman, it's a pretty darn
pleasant one. And despite myself, I never stopped lik-
ing the guy. Arguments with him never felt like arguments; I would leave his office in a good mood after
losing every point, and he was the one who did all the
conceding.

**TRY THIS IN A
POLITICAL ARGUMENT**
Politics makes an ex-
cellent test of conces-
sion, in part because
the tactic is so refresh-
ing. See if you can go
through an entire dis-
cussion without overtly
disagreeing with your
opponent. She: "I'm
willing to give up a
little privacy so the
government can keep
me safe." You: "Safety's
important." She: "Not
that they're going to
tap *my* phone." You:
"No, you'd never rock
the boat." She: "Of
course, I'll speak up if
I disagree with what's
going on." You: "I know
you will. And *let* the
government keep a file
on you."

Pathos: Start with the Audience's Mood

Sympathize—align yourself with your listener's *pathos*. You don't have to
share the mood; when you face an angry man, it doesn't help to mirror that
anger. Instead, rhetorical sympathy shows its con-
cern, proving, as George H. W. Bush put it, "I care."
So when you face that angry man, look stern and
concerned; do not shout, "Whoa, decaf!" When a little girl looks sad, sympathy means looking sad, too; it does not mean chirping, "Cheer up!"

▶ **Argument Tool**
SYMPATHY: Share your
listeners' mood.

This reaction to the audience's feelings can serve as a baseline, letting
them see your own emotions change as you make your point. Cicero hinted
that the great orator transforms himself into an emotional role model,
showing the audience how it should feel.

LITTLE GIRL: I lost my balloon!

YOU: Awww, did you?

(Little Girl cries louder.)

YOU (*still trying to look sad while yelling over the crying*): What's
    that you're holding?

LITTLE GIRL: My mom gave me a dinosaur.

YOU (*cheering up*): A dinosaur!

Being a naturally sympathetic type, my wife is especially good at conceding moods. She has a way of playing my emotion back so intensely that I'm embarrassed I felt that way. I once returned home from work angry that my employer had done nothing to recognize an award my magazine had won.

DOROTHY: Not a thing? Not even a group e-mail congratulating you?

ME: No . . .

DOROTHY: They have no idea what a good thing they have in you.

ME: Well . . .

DOROTHY: An e-mail wouldn't be enough! They should give you a bonus.

ME: It wasn't *that* big an award.

She agreed with me so much that I found myself siding with my lousy employers. I believe her sympathy was genuine, but its effect was the same as if she had applied all her rhetorical skill to make me feel better. And I did feel better, if a bit sheepish.

And then there's the concession side of *ethos*, called *decorum*. This is the most important jujitsu of all, which is why the whole next chapter is devoted to it.

TRY THIS AT WORK
Oversympathizing makes someone's mood seem ridiculous without actually ridiculing it. When a staffer complains about his workspace, say, "Let's take this straight to the top." Watch his mood change from whiny to nervous. Of course, you could have an *Alice's Restaurant*–style backfire. Arlo Guthrie yelled, "I wanna kill! Kill!" when he registered for the draft, and they pinned a medal on him. You'll see more of this technique, called the "backfire," later on.

The Tools

"Thus use your frog," Izaak Walton says in *The Compleat Angler.* "Put your hook through his mouth, and out at his gills . . . and in so doing use him as though you loved him." That pretty much sums up this chapter, which teaches you to use your audience as though you loved it. All of these tools require understanding your opponent and sympathizing with your audience.

> **Logos:** Argument by *logic*. The first logical tactic we covered was **concession,** using the opponent's argument to your own advantage.
>
> **Pathos:** Argument by *emotion*. The most important pathetic tactic is **sympathy,** registering concern for your audience's emotions and then changing the mood to suit your argument.
>
> **Ethos:** Argument by character. Aristotle called this the most important appeal of all—even more than *logos*.

Argument by logic, emotion, and character are the megatools of rhetoric. You're about to learn specific ways to wield each one. Read on.

5. Get Them to Like You

▲

He who is unable to live in society, or who has no need because he is sufficient for himself, must be either a beast or a god.   —ARISTOTLE

An agreeable *ethos* matches the audience's expectations for a leader's tone, appearance, and manners. The ancient Romans coined a word to describe this kind of character-based agreeability: **decorum.** The concept is far more interesting than the mandatory politesse of Emily Post and Miss Manners. Rhetorical decorum is the art of fitting in—not just in polite company but everywhere, from the office to the neighborhood bar. This is why salespeople wear terrific shoes, and why a sixteen-year-old girl will sneak out of the house to get a navel ring. She fits herself into a social microhabitat that happens to exclude her mortified parents.

▶ **Argument Tool**
DECORUM: Your audiences find you agreeable if you meet their expectations.

Actually, the Latin word *decorum* meant "fit," as in "suitable." In argument, as in evolution, survival belongs to the fittest. The elite of every society large and small, from the playground to the boardroom, are the product of survival of the decorous.

▶ **Meanings**
Ethos in Greek originally meant "habitat"—the environment animals and people live in. This makes no sense until you think about the meaning of "ethics" (a direct etymological descendant of *ethos*). An ethical person fits her audience's rules and values the same way a penguin fits the peculiar habitat of an iceberg. *Ethos* has to do with a person's ability to fit in with a group's expectations.

Decorum tells the audience, "Do as I say *and* as I do." The speaker should sound like the collective voice of his audience, a walking, talking consensus. To show proper decorum, act the way your audience *expects* you to act—not necessarily like your audience. Parents sometimes make this mistake when they deal with groups of children. Talking baby talk to a three-year-old does not just look idiotic to fellow adults; the three-year-old also sees you as an idiot. The ultimate fashion crime is to dress like your own teenager. Whenever I spot a do-rag or baggy pants on someone over forty, I want to shoot them and put them out of their kids' misery.

We think of decorum as a fussy, impractical art, but the manuals the ancients wrote on decorum—covering voice control, gestures, clothing, and timing, as well as manners—touted the same themes as a modern best seller, combining the contents of *How to Dress for Success,* Martha Stewart, Emily Post, and *The One-Minute Manager.* A couple of thousand years after the Romans invented it, modern rhetorician Kenneth Burke declared that decorum is "perhaps the simplest case of persuasion." He went on to offer a good inventory of decorous skills:

> *You persuade a man only insofar as you can talk his language by speech, gesture, tonality, order, image, attitude, idea, identifying your ways with his.*

Burke wrote that in 1950, by the way—back when it was perfectly decorous to refer to a person as "a man," a usage that most people today would consider rude. Does that mean we grow more polite every year? Few people over eighteen seem to think so. But that doesn't mean we have grown ruder, either. Every era has its rules; humans continuously adapt those rules to changes in the social environment. Men used to wear coat and tie to the movies, but they also smoked in them.

Speaking of movies, my mother was fourteen when *Gone with the Wind* came to the local theater in Wayne, Pennsylvania. Rhett Butler's profanity was all the buzz back then. Mom was looking forward to hearing someone actually curse in a movie, but when the time came for "Frankly, my dear, I don't give a damn," the audience gasped and whispered so much that she never heard it. "The line was quite a shocker," she said many years later.

These days every middle school student talks like a sailor. Score one for the superior politeness of my mother's generation. On the other hand, when Mom watched *Gone with the Wind,* she had to sit in the balcony; she went with the family's cook, who was black. Even in suburban Philadelphia, back in 1939, while *Gone with the Wind* reminisced about the chivalrous South, theaters banned "coloreds" from the good seats.

What are manners but the ways we treat one another? People who complain about "political correctness" may just be lamenting inevitable change in the social environment. Sure, some people love to enforce manners; every culture has its bluenoses who take decorum to the point of rudeness—bluenoses on the left who get offended at an ethnic joke, and bluenoses on the right who practically faint when someone wishes them "Happy Holidays" instead of "Merry Christmas." But more than manners are at stake here. We're talking about a critical persuasive tool.

TRY THIS IN AN INVASION
It may seem obvious that discretion is the better part of decorum, but someone should have told the Pentagon. It didn't begin training substantial numbers of officers in Iraqi decorum until three years after the Iraq invasion. Force let us win on points, but it failed to win native commitment.

Decorum follows the audience's rules. If you find yourself in a fundamentalist church, you do not lecture the parishioners about the etymology of "holiday"; you wish them a Merry Christmas. If you attend a faculty meeting on an Ivy League campus, you do not roll your eyes and snort when somebody refers to "people of color." You sit there and look pious. Of course, no law says you have to be decorous. Away from talk radio and the more diversity-mad college campuses, it's a free country. Go ahead and tell it like it is. But you cannot be indecorous and persuasive at the same time. The two are mutually exclusive.

Deliberative argument is not about the truth, it's about choices, and persuasive decorum changes to match the audience. When in Rome, do as the Romans do; but when you're not in Rome, doing as the Romans do might get you in trouble. Decorum can make the difference between persuading an audience and getting thrown out by it.

One of the greatest decorum scenes in movie history graces the climax of *8 Mile*, Eminem's semiautobiography. He gets talked into a competition at a dance club in downtown Detroit where hip-hop artists (orators, if you will) take turns insulting each other. The audience chooses the winner by applause. Eventually, the contest comes down to two people: Eminem and a sullen-looking black guy. (Well, not as sullen as Eminem. Nobody can be that sullen.) Enimem wears proper attire: stupid skullcap, clothes a few sizes too big, and as much bling as he can afford. If he showed up dressed like Cary Grant, he would look terrific—to you and me. But the dance club crowd would find him wildly indecorous.

Clothing is the least of his decorum problems, though. He happens to be white, and everyone else in the room is black. Eminem nonetheless manages to devastate his adversary by revealing a nasty little secret: this putative gangbanger *attended a prep school!* All the poor guy's hip-hop manners are pointless, because the audience finds them phony. Eminem, that foul-mouthed master of decorum, blends in better with an inner-city crowd than his black opponent does.

Was My Fly Down?

As Cicero said, decorum that works for one persuader may not work for another, even in front of the same people. Before you begin to argue, ask yourself, What do they expect?—and mean it. To move people away from their current opinion, you need to make them feel comfortable with you.

This is more difficult than it sounds. When I worked in Greensboro, North Carolina, I carried a coffee mug with large black type that said "Piss Off." People loved it in New York, but it didn't get the same reception in Greensboro. No one said anything until I started gesturing with it in a meeting with potential clients. Luckily they thought it was funny, but my boss told me to switch cups. Not so funny was the bumper sticker of an entry-level editor I hired right out of college. The sticker advertised a local rock band by claiming that it violated "Your Honor Student." Some employees complained. When I casually advised the young woman to ditch the bumper sticker, her reaction surprised me.

TRY THIS WITH A STRANGE CROWD
Before you walk in front of people of a different culture or social group, try to reach a member of the audience a few days before. Ask, "What are the five stupidest things you'd expect a person like me to do?" If they expect a badly dressed faux pas spewer, then you might try the unexpected. A white woman, for example, would win propers—respect—in a traditional black church if she wore a great hat. Traditionalist African-American women love high-class headgear.

NEW EDITOR: I can't believe they complained about it!

ME: Yeah, I know. But you've been living in the South for years. You know the culture better than I do.

N.E.: It's a freedom of speech issue!

ME: No, actually, it's not . . .

N.E.: I have the right to put anything I want on my car.

ME: That's true.

N.E. *(uneasily):* Right.

ME: But if you can't get along with people here, the company

> has the right to fire you. You own the car, but it owns
> your job.

She never removed the sticker. She didn't have to; someone removed it for her that afternoon.

It isn't always easy to adapt your decorum to the circumstances, even if you want to. Back when I was single and living in D.C., my younger brother came to visit me. One evening in Georgetown, center of Washington's nightlife, we crossed M Street to hit a few bars when a Hare Krishna approached us with some scraggly-looking roses for sale. John bought one and gave it to the first pretty woman he saw, saying, "Here you go, doll."

Here you go, doll? Who did he think he was, Dean Martin?

Instead of smacking him, the woman said, "Oh, thank you!" She looked as if she wanted to kiss him, but her girlfriends dragged her across the street.

I stared at John in astonishment.

> JOHN: What?
> ME: How did you do that?
> JOHN: Do what? Give a girl a flower?
> ME: You called her *"doll."*
> JOHN: Yeah. She was cute.

TRY THIS IN A NEW JOB
When my wife resumed her career, she asked me what she should wear on casual Fridays. "Does anyone above you dress casually?" I asked. "No," she said. "Then don't go casually," I said. "Always dress one step above your rank." It worked. Within eighteen months she was promoted to vice president.

Maybe he was onto something. "Wait here," I told him, and I jaywalked back across the street and bought another rose from the Hare Krishna just as the light changed and a crowd of bar hoppers came toward me, including several young women. I picked out a stunning blond and thrust the rose at her just as John had done. I even tried to imitate his tone.

> ME: Here ya go, doll.
> WOMAN: Go to hell.

She said it matter-of-factly, without any apparent rancor, the way one might say, "No thanks," to a Hare Krishna. I've never stopped wondering what happened. John and I look alike—same build, same hair. At any rate, it couldn't have been my looks, because she never looked at me. Did John have a homing instinct for the type of female who liked being called "doll"?

More likely, the one I approached sensed my embarrassment. John is the kind of irony-free, straight-ahead guy who attracts women. I'm not, apparently. Cicero would nod his head. He taught that you can't assume a character that strays too far from your own. What works for one can wreak disaster for the other. "Indeed," said Cicero, "such diversity of character carries with it so great significance that suicide may be for one man a duty, for another (under the same circumstances) a crime."

Speak for yourself, C-man. But we get the point.

▶ **Persuasion Alert**
We have been taught that a successful persuader never admits ignorance, but the Romans saw doubt as a rhetorical device. They called it *aporia*: wonder openly or admit you cannot fathom a reason, and the audience will unconsciously start reasoning for you. Without even knowing it, they comfortably get inside your head.

Decorum is the art of the appropriate, and an *ethos* that fails to fit your actual personality is usually indecorous. People pick up on it.

Captain Kangaroo's Fashion Tip

Romans wore togas, so Cicero offers little relevant advice for us on how to dress decorously. But the decorum rule of thumb applies to dress as well as everything else: look the way you think your audience will want you to look. When in doubt, use camouflage. Dress the way the average audience member dresses. Is black the common color in your office? Wear black. You want to dress slightly above your rank—wearing a jacket on a casual Friday, for instance—but not too far above (a Friday tie makes you look like a jerk in many offices). And if you're in a persuasive situation, don't let your clothes make a statement unless your audience will agree with it. A camo tie might be a witty fashion accessory in the offices of the People for the Ethical Treatment of Animals, but the PETA people may not enjoy your indecorum.

In all honesty, I'm not the best one to give fashion advice. I once found myself in a job that had me

TRY THIS WHEN YOU RUN FOR OFFICE
If you find it difficult to blend in with your audience, delight in it. Because Jimmy Carter's presidency didn't go so well, we forget what a great campaigner he was. He would wear conservative suits and sweeten them with his broad smile. Decorum is an aspect of sympathy. You don't have to be your audience; just be deeply sympathetic to it.

speaking in front of business execs as well as fellow editors. Up to that point I considered corduroy the height of male fashion. So I went to the best men's store I could afford in New Hampshire and introduced myself to a salesman named Joe, a natty dresser who looked like the businessmen I was meeting. I said I wanted to equip myself minimally—enough for a two-day trip—but that I'd be back once I had observed enough successful men and got a clue about what I was supposed to wear.

As it happened, Joe had the wisdom of a Zen master. He told me to look for guys wearing the most expensive-looking shoes—not so I could imitate the shoes, mind you; I couldn't afford them. Their suits would also be out of my reach. But he said I could mimic the colors and patterns in their shirts and ties.

Actually, I'm paraphrasing. Joe put it more cryptically.

> JOE: Look for the guy with the best shoes, but don't buy the shoes. Buy the colors.

> **▸ Useful Figure**
> The this-not-that figure is called a *dialysis:* "Don't buy the shoes. Buy the colors." People take your wisdom more seriously if you put it cryptically; it's the idiot savant approach. But perhaps you don't wish to *be* an idiot savant.

Every man should have a clothier like Joe. He became my fashion consultant for years, even though he rocked my confidence by including Captain Kangaroo among his clients. I'm not joking. While looking at a suit in the mirror, I saw Bob Keeshan—the Captain—enter the store. He had *the* kids' show when I was little, and he hadn't changed much in forty years. Same bad haircut, even. Bad hair is decorous on a kiddie show, but not in a clothing store.

> CAPTAIN KANGAROO: Wondering whether to buy it?
> *(I nod, suddenly feeling five.)*
> CAPTAIN: Well, if you'd be willing to wear that suit every single day for a year without getting tired of it, then buy it.

> **TRY THIS IN A PRESENTATION**
> If you have to address more than one audience, make two outlines: one for the contents, and the other for the occasions. List the people who should be at each one, with a chart for what they believe and expect. Adjust your speech accordingly.

I bought it. But when I gave Joe my credit card I looked down at the Captain's shoes. They were terrible—some sort of loafer deal. The suit turned out okay, but I never wanted to wear it daily. The Captain was wrong. So was the comte de Buffon, the man who first said, "Style makes the man." It doesn't. Style makes the *occasion*.

Basketball Decorum in Afghanistan

Besides knowing how to dress, a decorous persuader has to know how to adapt her language to the particular occasion. This is especially important in business. A PowerPoint presentation needs a sophisticated sense of decorum, because the speaker may be delivering versions of it to several different audiences.

First, she might give it to her department head, while sitting on the edge of the conference table and talking blue, with phrases like "If this doesn't work, we're screwed" or "The bleeps in accounting need to support us on this."

Next comes the presentation to the vice president. Some blunt or even crude language might be appropriate, but sitting on the edge of the table isn't. She sits *at* the table, establishing eye contact before looking up at the screen and hitting the buttons of her remote.

When she speaks to the COO, she stands, wearing her best suit and speaking as though she doesn't see the big boss check messages on his cell phone and flip through the paper "leave-behind" version of the presentation.

On each occasion she behaves appropriately, the way the people in the room expect her to behave—not necessarily the way the audience itself behaves. If our presenter acted as rudely as the COO, she would get pink-slipped in no time.

Naturally, the same adaptive rule applies to politics. A good politician changes his language, behavior, and even his dress to suit the expectations of particular audiences. But decorum is a lot trickier in politics than in business. A businesswoman can keep her life private, while for a politician the personal is definitely political. The public doesn't expect the president of the United States to canoodle with an intern; up until recently, it was scandalous even to get a divorce.

TRY THIS WITH YOUR WRITING
Besides checking your spelling and grammar, go over your e-mails and memos for decorum. Are you meeting your audience's expectations? Exceeding them? In later chapters, you'll learn specific ways to size up those expectations.

Senator Bob Packwood learned the personal-is-political lesson the hard way, with a decorum disaster that wrecked his career. One of the most effective feminists on Capitol Hill, the Oregon Republican championed women's rights legislation. But in 1992 word got out that he was chasing female staff around his desk; the civil rights hero turned out to be a total horn dog. Although he was a great public servant for women, his lack of decorum showed how he really felt about them. Persuasion requires sympathy. His rotten behavior made him unpersuasive. In politics, persuasion is power; so, bereft of political capital, he eventually resigned. Packwood may have been true to himself. Maybe, deep down, he was a horn dog. But persuasion doesn't depend on being true to yourself. It depends on being true to your audience.

That may sound dishonest and cynical, especially in our society. We celebrate indecorous behavior. Because we undervalue persuasion, decorum seems to put us at a disadvantage. When everyone around us acts like a jerk, why should *we* behave? As we have seen, though, decorum—rightly understood—is a source of rhetorical strength, not weakness. It gives people a sense of group identity, a resource that rhetoric loves to exploit. Get the group to identify with *you* and you have won half the persuasive battle.

Besides, being true to your audience can be downright noble. Decorum counts even more in the Senate than it does in other places, because so much is at stake. When one person addresses the other as "the distinguished senator from the commonwealth of Massachusetts," he is not merely following tradition; he is maintaining a high state of decorum so that a minor violation won't end up in a political squabble or—what the founders feared most—civil war.

You will find exceptional decorum in places where the consequences of indecorous behavior are the most dire. Anthropologists say that basketball in the more remote parts of Afghanistan, where missionaries introduced it long ago, may be the politest game on earth. Personal fouls are virtually unheard of, because touching another man could lead to a blood feud.

▶ **Persuasion Alert**
I risk sounding preachy here, which would be extremely indecorous. But I need to counter the attitude most of us bring to persuasion. "The last thing we need these days is manipulation," people often say to me. So I throw Afghans and senators into the mix to show argument's civic virtue. It results in peace, love, freedom, and mastery of your fellow beings. What more could you want?

In short, people who stick to their guns are the ignoble ones. Decorum is the better part of valor.

The Tools

We now get to the meat of *ethos*—the tools that turn you into a credible leader. In the next chapter, you'll learn how to define your character for an audience. But the first step is fitting in.

> **Decorum:** Argument by character starts with your audience's love. You earn it through decorum, which Cicero listed first among the ethical tactics.

6. Make Them Listen

▲

THE LINCOLN GAMBIT
Converting character into a tool of persuasion

The argument which is made by a man's life is of more weight than that which is furnished by words.
— ISOCRATES

icero said you want your audience to be **receptive**—sitting still and not throwing anything at you. Beyond that, they should be **attentive**—willing to listen closely to what you have to say. And most important of all, they should **like and trust** you. All three require argument by character. This chapter will delve deeper into the techniques of *ethos*.

> ▸ **Argument Tool**
> THE PERFECT AUDIENCE: receptive, attentive, and well disposed toward you

According to Aristotle, people have to be able to trust your judgment as well as your essential goodness. They may think you're a terrific person, but they won't follow you if they think you will lead them off a cliff. Likable knuckleheads make bad leaders. Your audience also has to consider you a good person who wants to do the right thing and will not use them for your own nefarious purposes.

All of which boils down to Aristotle's three essential qualities of a persuasive *ethos:*

> ▸ **Argument Tool**
> THE THREE TRAITS of persuasive leadership: virtue, practical wisdom, disinterest

Virtue—the audience believes you share their values

Practical wisdom, or street smarts—you appear to know the right thing to do on every occasion

Selflessness, or **disinterest**—the audience's interest seems to be your sole concern

Assuming that you think I'm a good person who knows what he talks about and whose only desire is to make you more persuasive, let's take a closer look at those three traits. We begin with that strange, highly subjective quality called virtue. As you shall see, persuasive virtue strays from the virtue of Mom and Dad—or Moses and Abraham, for that matter.

Janet Jackson's Impeccable Virtue

What defines a virtuous woman (assuming anyone still uses "virtuous" and "woman" in the same sentence)? Self-sacrificing loyalty to husband and children? Inviolate chastity? No wonder you rarely hear "virtue" mentioned in daily conversation. Now, a virtuous man, on the other hand, is . . .

Hey, pal, who are you calling virtuous? The word connotes weakness and dependency—a sexist's idea of femininity. In rhetorical terms, though, virtue means anything but. It continues to play a big role in argument; we just avoid using the term. Instead, we talk about "values." That's because a person who upholds the values of a group is rhetorically virtuous. This kind of persuasive virtue does not require purity of soul and universal goodness. You don't even have to do what your heart knows is right; you simply must *be seen* to have the "right" values—your audience's values, that is. Jesus Christ had the pure kind of virtue, while Julius Caesar's was decidedly rhetorical. The audience for each man considered him virtuous.

This is where values come in to deliberative argument—not as a subject of debate but as a tool of *ethos*. Values change from audience to audience; pop culture, for example, favors youth, money, good looks, and a body enhanced by gym and surgeon—which makes Janet Jackson a paragon of virtue to her fans. She lost virtue only when her audience expanded to include people who didn't appreciate exposed nipples on network television.

Members of the same family can have different ideas of virtue. Dorothy Junior proved that on a family hike

TRY THIS WITH YOUR RÉSUMÉ
Edit your résumé by *ethos* instead of chronology. Think of the company you would most want to work for, and list the values you share (virtue), your relevant knowledge and experience (practical wisdom), and how your ambitions match the company's goals (disinterest). Now redo it chronologically. It should be ethically persuasive now.

▸ **Persuasion Alert**
Interrupting yourself ("Hey, pal. . . .") to address a different audience, even a virtual one, keeps your original audience on its toes. It's an old trick; the Greeks played many variations on this theme.

▸ **Useful Figure**
The *litotes* ("didn't appreciate") understates a point ironically. It has fallen out of favor in our hyperbolic times, but makes for a more sophisticated kind of speech.

some years ago. The forest road on the way to the trailhead had washed out in a recent storm, lengthening an already long hike by two miles. My daughter values comfort and sense above all else; George and I believe that meeting a pointless challenge outweighs her values. (Dorothy Senior puts herself on Dorothy Junior's side, but she hikes nonetheless because she likes it.) We voted on whether to turn around at the washout, and Dorothy Junior lost. She went along as gracefully as an independent twelve-year-old can, until we were a mile from our car, when she suddenly ran ahead and disappeared around a turn.

> **Meanings**
> "Virtue" may sound schoolmarmish to our ears. But the Roman *virtus* meant "manliness"—good sportsmanship, respect for values, and all-around nobility.

ME: She knows she's not supposed to do that.

DOROTHY SENIOR: It's only a mile, and she has the best sense of direction in the family. Now, if *you* were to run ahead, I'd be worried.

ME: Very funny. But my pack has her raingear, and it's already starting to drizzle. She'll just have to stand there freezing in the parking lot until we come. Serves her right.

DOROTHY SENIOR: Not really.

ME: Why?

DOROTHY SENIOR: She has the car keys.

When we arrived at the car half an hour later, Dorothy Junior was happily locked inside with the stereo blasting. I knocked on the window.

ME: Fun's over. Unlock the car.

DOROTHY JUNIOR (*mouthing over the music*): Say you're sorry.

ME: *I'm* sorry?! You're the one who . . .

She unlocked the car, because she saw me say, "I'm sorry." It was probably for the best; an apology was the only way I could get her to let us in, other than a credible threat—the rhetorical "argument by the stick." There was no persuading her any other way; lacking her idea of virtue, I wasn't persuasive. In her eyes, I was just wrong.

Families are bad enough. When values differ, another group's behavior can seem downright bizarre. The House of Representatives mystified Europeans when it impeached Bill Clinton simply because he dallied with an intern and lied about it. Shortly before the impeachment hearings, both the wife and the mistress of François Mitterrand had attended the former French president's funeral. The French didn't understand Americans' insistence on sexual loyalty in a leader; to the French, an affair *adds* to a powerful man's *ethos*. And lying about your mistress is an *affaire d'honneur.*

> ▸ **Persuasion Alert**
> If attaching values to audiences sounds like relativism, you're in good philosophical company; Plato certainly thought it did. But the point of rhetoric isn't to transform you into a better person—or a worse one, for that matter—but to make you argue more effectively.

What seems ethical to you, in other words, can hurt a person's ethos. Atticus Finch, the Southern lawyer in *To Kill a Mockingbird,* seems utterly virtuous when we watch him on DVD. The townsfolk in the movie think he is, too, until he strays from the values of 1930s white Southern culture by defending a black man charged with raping a white woman. While we consider Finch even more virtuous for that selfless act of pro bono lawyering (my wife almost swoons when Gregory Peck leans in toward the jury), the more Finch does the right thing, the more his rhetorical virtue declines. Without the respect of many townsfolk, he loses persuasive power, along with the case.

What could he have done differently? Maybe nothing. But a clue lies in the informal language Lincoln used before he won the presidency. Friends said he loved darkie jokes and even saw fit to use the N-word now and then. That sounds terrible now, but keep in mind the culture at the time. Only the most extreme liberal whites took offense at racist jokes, and Lincoln's opposition to slavery put him in a small minority. To stop its expansion and eventually end it altogether, he needed to win over more than a few racists. He did that with rhetorical virtue—he talked the audience's talk. Many disliked his party's antislavery platform, but they liked him. Whether Lincoln actually was a racist or not

> ▸ **Try This with a Bigot**
> You can't talk a prejudiced person directly out of a prejudice. But you can dissuade him from its harmful results. If he says, "All foreign Arabs in the U.S. should have their green cards taken away," talk about a specific person who would be affected, and describe values that you all have in common.

doesn't matter rhetorically; his outward attitude was an effective *ethos* gambit.

Here we find ourselves back in the realm of decorum, but of a special kind; this decorum has nothing to do with clothing or table manners. It has to do with the ability to match the audience's beliefs. Lincoln made his audience *well disposed* toward him; emancipation was easier to accept coming from a racist than from one of those insufferable abolitionists up in liberal

Massachusetts. If he had sermonized about racial equality the way they did, he never would have become president.

Clearly, if you want to pack your own *ethos* with persuasive virtue, you need to determine your audience's values and then appear to live up to them—even if your audience comprises a single sullen teenager. Suppose you want the living room music turned down, only this time your adversary is a sixteen-year-old instead of a spouse. A kid that age values independence more than anything; if you simply issued an order, your *ethos* would do nothing for you, because you would simply prove to the kid that you never let him make his own choices. To dodge that rap, you could give him a choice:

> YOU: Would you mind turning that down? Or would you rather switch to headphones?

Otherwise, you could appeal directly to a different value, the passion that most kids have for fairness:

> YOU: How about giving me a chance to play my own music? Do you like Lynyrd Skynyrd?

In the workplace, values tend toward money and growth. Show a single-minded dedication to profit, and you gain business virtue. If the boss is a law-abiding type who values playing by the rules, then a straitlaced ethical approach to profit makes you even more rhetorically virtuous. But if you worked for Enron during the nineties, obeying the law would have made you *un*-virtuous. The top brass considered cutting ethical corners to be perfectly kosher. Not that you should have broken the law yourself, of course. But an atmosphere like that requires a Lincolnesque kind of virtue right at the start of the wrongdoing—talking the talk while tripping up the bad guys.

> ▸ **Classical Hits**
> AYE CANDY: In Rome, political candidates symbolized their pure virtue by wearing white togas; *candidus* means "white" in Latin, which is why "candidates" and "candy" (made of white sugar) share the same "candid" root. "Candid," in fact, used to mean "openminded." *The Federalist* often addresses the "candid reader."

> YOU: Let's not wait for the regulators to screw us up. They'll come in sooner or later. We should get the accountants in here right away and straighten this thing out. Do it ourselves.

Admittedly, it would take thousands of Lincolnesque arguments like that to stop an Enron. But what little persuasive virtue you display within the company has to start with the company's idea of virtue. At Enron, following your conscience or the laws would have lost you your audience. It is indecorous to stand in judgment of the very people you want to persuade. You don't want to stand apart from them. You want the audience to consider you the epitome of the company "Us." So you turn the *regulators* into "Them"—the judgmental types who'll screw everything up.

This isn't so easy. Virtue is complicated. You may find yourself trying to persuade two audiences at the same time, each with different values. Many years ago, I took over a college alumni magazine and turned a deficit into a profit by increasing advertising revenue. I never received a raise beyond cost-of-living increases. I couldn't understand what I was doing wrong until I saw the situation rhetorically: what was virtuous in a private company didn't help in academia. I was acting businesslike, while academics valued scholarship. My magazine, with its class notes and stories about life on campus, definitely wasn't scholarly. The values clashed when a faculty dean asked me to publish a professor's article in German.

ME: Why German?
DEAN: To send a message.
ME: But what if hardly anyone can *read* the message?
DEAN: You don't get it, do you?

Now I think I get it. While I valued profit and service to the readers, he valued scholarship and flattering the faculty. If I had treated my job more rhetorically and published an occasional research paper, on-campus scholars would have found me more virtuous. My pay probably would have improved. And the magazine would have been read by tens and tens of alumni.

▸ **Persuasion Alert**
A common if ham-handed *ethos* enhancer: Overwhelm the audience with examples of your erudition. An easily cowed audience will take your word for it rather than challenge your individual points. But I have a different motive for tossing you all these tools. Rhetoric is as much about awareness and attitude as it is about technique. Don't worry about knowing each tool. (At any rate, you'll find a list at the end of each chapter and in the back of the book.) Just read on, and you'll gain an instinct for persuasion that will take you further than any set of tools.

TRY THIS WITH YOUR EMPLOYER
Write down a personal mission statement. Why are you working? What are your motives, both selfish and noble? Now compare your mission statement with your employer's (or write your employer's yourself if his is meaningless). Is it a reasonably close match? Otherwise, follow the directions on p. 57 for redoing your résumé.

The Eddie Haskell Ploy

It's not hard to pump up your rhetorical virtue for a particular audience. I will give you a few ideas, but the essential point is to fashion yourself into an exemplar of their values. You want to look like a good person—"good," that is, in their eyes.

The most red-blooded American technique is simply to brag about all the good things you have done. Or you can get someone to brag for you. You can arouse sympathy by revealing an appealing flaw (we'll get to that). Or, when you find yourself on the wrong side, you can switch.

While **bragging** is the easiest way to show how great you are, it doesn't always work. God, for his part, bragged to great effect in the book of Job. Satan bets Jehovah that the most worshipful man on earth would curse God's name if his life were miserable. You're on, says God, who wipes out Job's cow and she-asses, kills his ten children, and, when Job continues to praise his name, allows Satan to give him loathsome sores from head to foot. Job finally yells to heaven.

> ▸ **Argument Tool**
> BRAGGING: Use it only if your audience appreciates boastful hyperbole in the mode of Muhammad Ali.

> JOB: Why are you punishing me? At least let me argue my case. If you do, you'll have to stop with the killing and the boils.

It may have been the bravest thing ever said by a man with raging dermatitis. But then a whirlwind appears out of nowhere and speaks in God's voice.

> GOD: Answer me this. Where were you when I laid the foundations of the earth? Can you rule the heavens? And the whale: who do you think made *it*? What makes you think you even *know* enough to argue with me?

Job backs right down. You don't mess with God's *ethos*. He has virtue to spare; in fact, he *constitutes* virtue. Unless you happen to be a god, though—or at least someone with enough power to give a State of the Union address—reciting your résumé is not the most effective way to enhance your ethos.

Aristotle said that **character references** beat your own bragging. John

McCain rarely talks about his heroism as a prisoner in Vietnam. But there are plenty of others who will. Similarly, a couple who make a pact to tag-team their teenager gain a mutually enhanced *ethos*. Have one talk up the other's virtue.

> ▸ **Argument Tool**
> CHARACTER REFERENCE: Get others to do your bragging for you.

> FATHER: Mind turning that down?
> KID: You never let me play my music!
> MOTHER: Your father *gave* you that stereo.

Then there is the **tactical flaw**: reveal some defect that shows your dedication to the audience's values. George Washington was the unequaled master of this device. Late in the Revolutionary War, his officers grew frustrated by the Continental Congress's delays in paying them, and they threatened mutiny. Washington requested a meeting and showed up with a congressional resolution that assured immediate pay. He pulled the document from his pocket and then fumbled with his spectacles.

> **TRY THIS IN A MEETING**
> Suppose your group decided to revamp its Web site and give it powerful new features. You worked at a dot-com briefly and would love to take over the Web content. Instead of bragging about your experience, use a shill. Get an ally to ask you in the meeting, "Didn't you work with the Internet?"

> ▸ **Argument Tool**
> TACTICAL FLAW: Reveal a weakness that wins sympathy or shows the sacrifice you have made for the audience.

> WASHINGTON: Forgive me, gentlemen, for my eyes have grown
> dim in the service of my country.

The men burst into tears and swore their fealty to the chief. It was a sentimental time. And it was George Washington, for crying out loud. His officers considered him to be God and Caesar rolled up in one.

Though you probably don't happen to be the father of your country, you can use the same technique to recover from a mistake. Turn it into a tactical flaw by attributing your error to something noble. Imagine you sent a memo to everyone in your office, only to find that you screwed up your figures by a decimal point or two.

> **TRY THIS IF YOU'RE SHORT**
> When a microphone is too high for you, don't lower it yourself. Get someone else to do it, then say, "The great thing about being short is you get good at making people do things for you."

> YOU: Sorry, my bad. I wrote it late last night and didn't want
> to wake the others to check the facts.

Of course, this strategy risks the loathing of the rest of your staff, but it might work on an impressionable boss.

You can also polish your virtue by heartily supporting what the audience is for, even when that means **changing your position.** This technique can be tricky, so you had better use it sparingly. To avoid looking like a waffler, show how your opponent—or, better, the audience itself—gave you new information or compelling logic that made the switch inevitable to anyone with an unbiased mind. Those who stick to your former opinion in the face of such overwhelming reasons aren't, well, reasonable.

▶ Argument Tool
OPINION SWITCH: When an argument is doomed to go against you, heartily support the other side.

Otherwise, if you can get away with it, simply pretend you were for your new stand all along. George W. Bush made a smooth switch in opposing the Department of Homeland Security and then fighting for it when its creation seemed inevitable. He never apologized, never looked back, and few people called him a waffler.

My own daughter used a more subtle variation of the switching-sides technique when she was in high school. Friends invited her to an unsupervised party. Aware that we would try to call the parents and then forbid her to go, Dorothy Junior decided to use the occasion to bolster her standing with us—a sort of rhetorical sacrifice fly.

DOROTHY JR.: I've been invited to a big party this weekend.

ME: Where?

DOROTHY JR.: Just some kid's house. But I've decided not to go. His parents won't be there and *(looking dramatically serious)* there'll probably be *alcohol.*

▶ Argument Tool
THE EDDIE HASKELL PLOY: Make an inevitable decision against you look like a willing sacrifice on your part.

TRY THIS AT HOME
The Eddie Haskell Ploy can work in reverse. Your sister, a ballroom dance instructor, offers to teach your son for free. You turn her down; you couldn't pay him to dance the rumba. You tell your son, "Aunt Sally said she'd give you free lessons, and I told her you weren't the type."

The kid had never seen *Leave It to Beaver,* yet she could do a dead-on Eddie Haskell. Even though I saw through the ruse, I admired it. Her virtue went way up in my eyes.

The Tools

Julius Caesar's *ethos* was so great, Shakespeare said, that he could say something normally offensive, and

.

"his countenance, like richest alchemy," would change his rhetoric "to virtue and to worthiness." The tools in this chapter are an alchemist's tools; use them to change your basest words into gold.

Virtue. Rhetorical virtue is the appearance of virtue. It can spring from a truly noble person or be faked by the skillful rhetorician. Rhetoric is an agnostic art; it requires more adaptation than righteousness. You adapt to the values of your audience. "Values" take on a different meaning in rhetoric as well. Rhetorical values do not necessarily represent "rightness" or "truth"; they merely constitute what people value—honor, faith, steadfastness, money, toys. Support your audience's values, and you earn the temporary trustworthiness that rhetoric calls virtue.

Among the ways to pump up your rhetorical virtue, we covered four:

Brag.
Get a witness to brag for you.
Reveal a tactical flaw.
Switch sides when the powers that be do. A variation is the Eddie Haskell Ploy, which throws your support behind the inevitable. When you know you will lose, preempt your opponent by taking his side.

7. Show Leadership

▲

They should rule who are able to rule best. —ARISTOTLE

Now that we have mastered virtue and its main tool, decorum, we can move on to the second major element of *ethos:* **practical wisdom.** I can think of no better way to illustrate this streetwise rhetorical knowledge than *Animal House.* After Dean Wormer expels the fraternity, John Belushi's Bluto addresses his brothers with a passionate oration.

> BLUTO: Was it over when the Germans bombed Pearl Harbor?
> Hell no! And it ain't over now. 'Cause when the goin' gets tough . . . the tough get goin'! Who's with me? Let's go!

He runs from the room, and nobody moves. How come? While it could use some fact checking, the speech is not so bad. Bluto uses several time-tested logical and emotional devices: the good old rhetorical question, the popular if well-worn *chiasmus* ("When the going gets tough . . ."), and a rousing call to action. So why does it fail?

The three traits of *ethos*—virtue, practical wisdom, and goodwill—show why the speech bombs. Bluto is the classic likable knucklehead; he lacks practical wisdom, the appearance of knowing what to do. He offers no idea about what should happen after he runs out. So why follow him? (He leaves a wiser character, Otter, to propose "a really futile and stupid gesture.")

Bluto's ethos is not all bad, however. His interest is their interest, particularly their interest for revenge.

> BLUTO: I'm not gonna take this. Wormer, he's a dead man!
> Marmalard, dead!

He wants what they want, and once Otter gives them a plan, they all pull together to sabotage the homecoming parade—a successful consensus. (According to the credits, Bluto eventually becomes a U.S. senator, understandably.) In short, he has plenty of selfless goodwill; Otter makes up for Bluto's lack of practical wisdom; and as for virtue, well, as you saw with decorum, almost anything can seem good and proper, depending on the occasion.

You have seen how much depends on the audience. The persuader must recognize what they believe, sympathize with their feelings, and fit in with their expectations—characteristics of *logos, pathos,* and *ethos.* All right, so Bluto clearly believes in what his brothers believe: nothing. Well, anarchy at any rate. He has the same feeling of wounded pride and injustice. He not only fits in, he personally bestowed names on each of the freshmen. He has the whole package of *logos, pathos,* and *ethos,* right?

Not exactly. He suffers a major *ethos* malfunction here. It's not enough simply to blend in with the brothers. Before they follow Bluto, they have to consider him worth following.

When you seem to share your audience's values, they believe you will apply them to whatever choice you help them make. If evangelical Protestants think you want to do what Jesus would do, they probably will find you trustworthy. If an environmentalist considers you earth-centric, she will respect your thinking about the proposed new power plant. But sharing your audience's values is not sufficient. They also have to believe that you know the right thing to do at that particular moment. While an evangelical Christian will respect you for trying to do what Jesus would do, he still won't let you remove his appendix.

This kind of trust is where **practical wisdom** comes in. The audience should consider you a sensible person, as well as sufficiently knowledgeable to deal with the problem at hand. When you remove an appendix, a medical degree proves your practical wisdom more than your knowledge of the Bible.

> ▸ **Argument Tool**
> PRACTICAL WISDOM:
> The audience thinks
> you know how to
> solve the problem
> at hand. Aristotle's
> word for this kind of
> wisdom is *phronesis.*

Practical wisdom entails the sort of common sense that can get things done. A persuader who shows it tends to be more Edison than Einstein, more Han Solo than Yoda. Look at past presidents, and you can see what Aristotle meant. John Adams, Herbert Hoover, and Jimmy Carter were among our most intellectually endowed presidents.

They were also among the least effective, being gifted with more IQ than street smarts.

Practical wisdom does not entail looking up decisions in books, or sticking to universal truths. It's an instinct for making the right decision on every occasion. Pure eggheads lack it. When we think of the *Apollo* space program, we rarely picture the rocket scientists. We remember a failed mission—*Apollo 13*—when three guys jury-rigged their spaceship and got back to earth alive. They were among the most highly trained people ever to leave the ground, but they had little training in the repair of carbon dioxide scrubbers. Still, they were able to combine instructions from the ground with their skill as first-class tinkerers. That's practical wisdom: flexibly wise leadership. All great heroes have it.

Strict rule followers lack it. Straitlaced Captain William Bligh's command of the *Bounty* was mediocre, to put it mildly; but after mutineers left him and eighteen men in a twenty-three-foot launch, he pulled off one of the greatest feats of navigation in history, steering an open boat more than thirty-six hundred nautical miles to safety. When he led by following rules, he failed; when he applied his navigational skills to solve a practical problem, he became a hero. He finally showed practical wisdom.

To get an audience to trust your decision, you can use three tools.

Show off your experience. If you debate a war and you're a veteran yourself, bring it up. "I've been in battle," you say. "I know what it's like." In an argument, experience usually trumps book learning. And it is fine to brag about experiences, rather than yourself. Even God did that with Job. Rather than call himself a great guy, God mentioned all the feats he carried out, like inventing the whale.

Bend the rules. Be Captain Bligh the navigator, not Captain Bligh the martinet. If the rules don't apply, don't apply them—unless ignoring the rules violates the audience's values. Indiana Jones showed some practical wisdom when a master swordsman attacked him with a scimitar. The man advanced with all the complex skill of a fencer, and Jones wearily shot him with his pistol. The rules didn't apply.

How does that work in real life?

TRY THIS WITH SOMEONE IN AUTHORITY
Chances are, when you ask the person in charge for something special, she'll recite the rules and tell you she can't make exceptions. Instead, start the conversation by praising her practical wisdom. "I've heard wonderful things about you. They say you treat everyone as an individual, not as some dough in a cookie cutter." Even if she sees right through your flattery, she'll be reluctant to contradict it.

SPOUSE: This book says that after three months we shouldn't
    let the baby sleep in our bed.

YOU: Too bad. The kid wants it. We want it.

SPOUSE: Yeah, but the writer says the separation will just get
    more difficult later.

YOU: So we should kick the kid out to make things easier?

SPOUSE: When do you think she should sleep in her own crib?

YOU: When she's old enough to reason with.

SPOUSE: You're *still* not old enough to reason with.

Nonetheless, you're the one showing the street smarts. Of course, if the decision proves a disaster, then you may want to check your practical wisdom.

Seem to take the middle course. The ancient Greeks had far more respect for moderation than our culture does. But humans in every era instinctively prefer a decision that lies midway between extremes. In an argument, it helps to make the audience think your adversary's position is an extreme one. (I once heard a congressional candidate call his opponent an "extreme moderate," whatever that means.) If the school board wants to increase the education budget by 8 percent, and opponents say taxes are already too high, you can gain credibility by proposing a 3 percent increase.

Presidents use the middle-course tactic when they choose a running mate with more extreme opinions than their own—Nixon with Agnew, Clinton with Gore, Bush with Cheney. Their vice presidents allowed them to look moderate even when their own politics strayed from the center of American opinion. Cheney's aggressive stance on cruel and inhumane treatment of suspected terrorists, for example, gave Bush some breathing room on the Iraq war.

TRY THIS WITH A PROPOSAL
Every proposal should have three parts (not necessarily in this order): *payoffs, doability, superiority.* Describe the benefits of your choice; make it seem easy to do; and show how it beats the other options. You might even keep your audience in suspense, not telling them your choice until you have dealt with the alternatives. Rhetoric is most effective when it leads an audience to make up their own minds.

If you have children, you can use the middle-course technique by playing good parent–bad parent. Suppose bedtime has slid later and later on weekends, and you want to get the kid to bed a half hour earlier.

BAD PARENT: Okay, time for bed. Chop-chop!

KID: But it's nine o'clock! I usually stay up till ten on Fridays.

GOOD PARENT: Custom's a pretty weak reason. Got a better argument?

KID: I wake up later on Saturdays. I'll get just as much sleep.

GOOD PARENT: All right, that's legitimate. We'll let you stay up a half hour later.

The kid may not like it, but she may well put up with the decision.

All three techniques—touting your experience, bending the rules, and taking the middle course—can help if you have more than one child. My wife and I made a pact with each other when our kids were little: we would not try to treat them equally. We would *love* them equally but avoid applying the rules consistently. We'd deal with each situation separately. At least the kids might learn practical wisdom on their own.

DOROTHY JR.: May I sit by my friends at the football game?

DOROTHY SR.: I guess so. Let's meet up at halftime, though.

GEORGE: Can I sit with my friends?

ME: May I . . .

GEORGE: *May* I sit with my friends?

ME: No.

GEORGE: But you let Dorothy . . .

ME: She's older.

GEORGE: You let her sit with her friends when she was my age. It's unfair!

ME: It certainly is. But consistency is the hobgoblin of little minds.

DOROTHY JR.: Then you should be consistent.

She knows I love a smart aleck. Nonetheless, Machiavelli said that inconsistency is a useful leadership tool—it keeps the ruler's subjects off guard. I had my reasons; girls mature more quickly than boys do, and I doubted that George was ready to sit without adults. But Machiavelli was not just being cynical. My children knew they could count on me to make decisions, not just enforce rules. That made them listen more closely, if only because they had no idea what would come out of my mouth. While I lacked much virtue in their eyes, they saw me as practically wise in anything that didn't involve moving parts.

The Tools

We're still talking about the ways to use the appearance of wisdom to persuade. The practically wise rhetorician seems to have the right combination of book learning and practical experience, both knowledge and know-how.

Tools for enhancing your practical wisdom:

Show off your experience.
Bend the rules.
Appear to take the middle course.

8. Win Their Trust

▲

To be not as eloquent would be more eloquent. —CHRISTOPH MARTIN WIELAND

The third *ethos* asset, which Aristotle called "disinterested goodwill," combines selflessness and likability. Think of a friend picking up the dinner tab. The benevolent persuader shares everything with his audience: riches, effort, values, and mood. He feels their pain and makes them believe he has nothing personal at stake. In other words, he shows himself to be "disinterested"—free of any special interest.

Most people use "disinterest" and "uninterest" interchangeably today. But in earlier times, a reputation for selflessness determined whether a politician got elected. In *The Federalist*, Alexander Hamilton, James Madison, and John Jay not only wrote anonymous letters in favor of the proposed new Constitution; they were so eager to disguise their "interest" that they pretended they had never attended the Convention in the first place. Hamilton and colleagues would have wondered at our preference for billionaires; the founders considered rich people the most "interested" of all. Eighteenth-century leaders were extremely anxious to show their disinterest; a number of them even gave away their fortunes and bankrupted themselves. This passion for disinterest continued through the early nineteenth century, when politicians clamored to claim an impoverished childhood in a log cabin. The up-by-the-bootstraps story showed a man's ability to make it on his own, beholden to no one.

> ▸ **Meanings**
> *Libertas* originally meant both freedom and frankness. Free people—those who weren't beholden to a source of income—could speak freely because they were "disinterested."

Although our society has mostly forgotten the original meaning of the word, disinterest can still work for you. I'll show some tricks, but the main point is make your audience believe in your selflessness—by seeming either wholly objective or nobly self-sacrificing.

Cicero mentioned an excellent tactic to hype your objectivity.

Seem to deal reluctantly with something you are really eager to prove.

▸ Argument Tool
THE RELUCTANT
CONCLUSION:
Act as though
you felt com-
pelled to reach
your conclusion,
despite your
own desires.

Make it sound as if you reached your opinion only after confronting overwhelming evidence. This is what Hamilton and Madison did in *The Federalist*. It also works for a teenager who wants to borrow his father's car.

> KID: You know, I'd just as soon walk my date to the movie. The theater is only three miles from her house, and there are sidewalks at least a third of the way. But her dad says no.
>
> FATHER: So you want to borrow my car.
>
> KID: No, I want you to call her father. Tell him I can protect her against gangs of rapists, and I'll have a cell phone in case she's hit by a truck.

Excellent goodwill, kid. Your interest lies in walking, not driving; you make it your dad's interest to loan you his car. If Dad isn't a complete fool, he'll laugh at this ruse—and lend you the car. Either way, you move the issue away from interest to the girl's safety.

You can apply the same method yourself. Simply claim you used to hold your opponent's position.

> HE: I'm against capital punishment. The government shouldn't be in the death business.
>
> YOU: Yeah, I was against capital punishment, too, because of the chance of executing an innocent person. But now that DNA testing has become almost universal, I'm convinced that we could avoid that problem.

What a fair-minded person you are! You once believed what your opponent believed, but found yourself overwhelmed by sheer logic. This approach helps you disguise changing the issue from a values question to a practical one—from government-sponsored killing to avoiding mistakes.

Another disinterest technique:

Act as if the choice you advocate hurts you personally.

> YOU: The company probably won't give me credit for this idea, boss, but I'm still willing to put in the hours to make it work. It's just too good to ignore.

Or:

> YOU: Look, kid, I hate brussels sprouts, too. But I've learned to eat them because they make me smart.

How Bluto Became a U.S. Senator

Look at leadership breakdowns in real life and you see the same *ethos* principles, or lack of them.

Jimmy Carter: In speaking of a "national malaise," he failed in rhetorical virtue. Carter went against his nation's values. This is America. The French have malaises, not us. We don't even have problems—they're opportunities!

▸ **Persuasion Alert**
Can I really place Carter and Nixon in the same unvirtuous boat? Sure. In rhetorical terms, both men lacked virtue.

Richard Nixon: Another virtue failure. Watergate violated the American notion of fair play.

Herbert Hoover: Failure of practical wisdom. He followed the rules of traditional economics and tried to balance the budget during a depression. Roosevelt showed practical wisdom when he broke the old rules, promoted deficit spending, and became a hero.

▸ **Persuasion Alert**
I'm making a double point here. Marie Antoinette didn't actually say, "Let them eat cake"; her enemies planted the quote. But her lousy *ethos* made it believable. An argument rests on what the audience believes, not on what is true.

Marie Antoinette: Major goodwill breakdown. Instead of making her constituents believe that their interest was her sole concern, she let her *ethos* suffer with that quote about cake.

Hamlet: No practical wisdom whatever. He follows a *ghost's* directions. No wonder his girlfriend cops it.

Your *ethos* counts more than any other aspect of

rhetoric because it puts your audience in the ideal state of persuadability. Cicero said you want them to be **attentive, trusting,** and **willing to be persuaded.** They're more likely to be interested if they find you worth their attention. The trusting part goes with the ethical territory of virtue, practical wisdom, and goodwill. As for their willingness to be persuaded, you want them to consider you a role model—the essence of leadership. And where does this attitude come from? The same perceived traits: virtue, practical wisdom, and goodwill.

Honest Abe's Shameless Trick

While your audience must *think* you have these noble attributes, that does not mean you must have them in reality. Even if you are chock-full of virtue, street smarts, and selflessness, if your audience doesn't believe that you are, then you have a character problem. Your soul may rise to heaven but your *ethos* sucks. On the other hand, every character has its flaws, which is where the rhetorical trickery comes in. The best trick of all:

Make it seem you have no tricks.

One of the chief rhetoricians of the early Roman Empire, a Spaniard named Quintilian, explained.

> *A speaker might choose to feign helplessness by pretending to be uncertain how to begin or proceed with his speech. This makes him appear, not so much as a skilled master of rhetoric, but as an honest man.*

The Romans called the technique *dubitatio,* as in "dubious." Abraham Lincoln was a wizard at *dubitatio.* He used it to help him get elected president. A lawyer and two-term former congressman who had lost a race for a Senate seat, Lincoln was a political nobody in the winter of 1860, when he traveled east to explore a bid for the presidency. What he lacked in background, he made worse in appearance: freakishly big hands, aerodynamic cheeks, a Western rube's accent; and when he

▸ **Argument Tool**
DUBITATIO: Don't look tricky. Seem to be in doubt about what to say.

addressed New York's elite in its premier athenaeum, the Cooper Union, he did nothing to raise expectations. Speaking in his characteristic harsh whine, he warned the crowd that they weren't about to hear anything new. Absolutely brilliant.

What was brilliant? The speech, for one thing. It segued into a first-class summary of the nation's problems and how to fix them. It was rational and lawyerly. His dubious opening set his highbrow audience up, not just by lowering expectations but also by conveying absolute sincerity. The speech was a smash. Without it, Lincoln likely "would never have been nominated, much less elected, to the presidency that November," according to Lincoln scholar Harold Holzer.

Modern persuasion research confirms Quintilian's dubious theory: a knowledgeable audience tends to sympathize with a clumsy speaker and even mentally argue his case for him. *Dubitatio* also lowers expectations and causes opponents to "misunderestimate" you, as Bush (a master of *dubitatio*) puts it. Lincoln's country-bumpkin image disguised a brilliant political analyst who could speak lucidly about the issues. His *ethos* made the audience trust his sincerity while doubting his intellect—until he showed them his intellect.

You can use the same technique without being a Lincoln. When you give a talk to a group, begin hesitantly, and gradually get smoother as you go. Speakers often think they have to grab the audience's attention right off the bat. Not necessarily; most people start with an attention span of at least five minutes. Just make sure your pauses don't stretch too far; legend has it that a Dartmouth president known for his thoughtful silences gave a speech at MIT with such a long hiatus that the host finally felt compelled to nudge him. He promptly fell to the floor; the podium apparently had been propping him up. He wasn't thoughtful, he was dead. Still, as long as you and your audience have a heartbeat, a slow beginning works better than the classic opening joke.

You can use a subtler form of *dubitatio* in a one-on-one argument. It works like this: When your partner finishes talking, look down. Speak softly and slowly until you're ready to make your main point. Then stare intensely into the eyes of the other person. Get the technique right, and it can convey passionate sincerity. My son will testify to this form of personal *dubitatio*. I had described it to him a year or so back when I was researching Quintilian, and forgot I ever mentioned it; then, several weeks ago, he came home from school looking pleased with himself.

> GEORGE: I tried that thing you told me about.
>
> ME: What thing?
>
> GEORGE: That—I forget what you called it. The thing where you look down until you make your point and, blam! Stare into her eyes.
>
> ME: *Her* eyes? What were you telling her?
>
> GEORGE: None of your business.
>
> ME: None of my . . . ?
>
> GEORGE: We were just talking politics, Dad. You have a dirty mind.

Ethos works best when it disguises its own trickery, even to the point of deliberate ineptness. Blue-staters laugh at Bush's Bushisms, and that makes red-staters love him all the more. (In fact, a lot more goes on with the president than mere syntactical clumsiness, as you shall see in a few chapters.) For your own *ethos* to be credible, your audience must not notice your rhetoric's inner workings. This does not mean just "being yourself." It may require the opposite. In argument, you don't rest on your personality and reputation, you *perform* them. *Ethos* is not karma; you can start afresh with your virtue, practical wisdom, and selflessness in every argument.

Does this seem unethical? Not in the original sense of *ethos*. Paying attention to the attitude of your audience, sharing its trials and values, makes you agreeable—both literally and figuratively. You're not manipulating . . . well, all right, you are manipulating them. But you're also *sharing*. In the next chapter, where we deal with *pathos*, we're into big-time *caring*.

Rhetorical caring, that is—like real caring, only better.

▸ **Classic Hits**
BUSH TALKS LIKE A GREEK: Literati of every generation have bemoaned the decline of fine language. But even in ancient Greece, audiences trusted plain-spoken leaders more than skilled ones. They said that fancy talk made a speaker sound "Asian," and preferred the "pure" Greek of Athens.

The Tools

The single best word for Aristotle's selfless goodwill is "disinterest," the appearance of having only the best interest of your audience at heart—even to the point of sacrificing for the good of the others. Its tools:

> ***The reluctant conclusion:*** Act as if you reached your conclusion only because of its overwhelming rightness.
>
> ***The personal sacrifice:*** Claim that the choice will help your audience more than it will help you; even better, maintain that you'll actually suffer from the decision.
>
> **Dubitatio:** Show doubt in your own rhetorical skill. The plain-spoken, seemingly ingenuous speaker is the trickiest of them all, being the most believable.

9. Control the Mood

▲

THE AQUINAS MANEUVER
The most persuasive emotions, at your service

The Oratour may lead his hearers which way he list, and draw them to what affection he will: he may make them to be angry, to be pleased, to laugh, to weepe, and lament: to loue, to abhorre, and loath.
— HENRY PEACHAM

I f you know an imperfect child, you may find this familiar: just as I was withdrawing money in the lobby of a Hanover, New Hampshire, bank, my three-year-old daughter chose to throw a temper tantrum, screaming and writhing on the floor while a couple of matrons looked on in disgust. (Their children *had* been perfect, apparently.) I forget what triggered the outburst by Dorothy Junior—now a self-directed college junior who aspires to med school—but I gave her a disappointed look and said, "That argument won't work, sweetheart. It isn't pathetic enough."

> ▸ Meanings
> *Pathos* means more than just "feelings" in the emotional sense. It also has to do with physical sensations—what a person feels or, more precisely, suffers. (The Greeks were into suffering.) Hence the medical term *pathology*, the study of diseases.

She blinked a couple of times and picked herself off the floor.

"*What* did you say to her?" one of the ladies asked.

I explained that I was a passionate devotee of classical rhetoric. Dorothy had learned almost from birth that a good persuader doesn't merely express her own emotions; she manipulates the feelings of her audience. Me, in other words.

> LADY: But did you say she wasn't *pathetic* enough?
> ME *(lamely):* That's a technical term. It worked, didn't it?

Back when people knew their rhetoric, "pathetic" was a compliment; my daughter knew that the persuader bears the burden not just of proof but of emotion as well. As long as she tried to persuade me, her feelings didn't count. Only mine did. An argument can't be rhetorically pathetic unless it's *sym*pathetic.

Matt Damon's Pathetic Joke

Done properly, the ancient Sophists said, *pathos* affects an audience's judgment. Recent neurological research has confirmed their theory; the seat of the emotions, the limbic system, tends to overpower the more rational parts of the brain. As Aristotle observed, reality looks different under different emotions; a change for the better, for example, can look bad to a depressed man. Protagoras, a famous Sophist, said that food tastes bitter to an invalid and the opposite to a healthy person. "While the doctor makes changes with drugs," he said, "the Sophist does it with words."

Words can indeed act like a drug, though to paraphrase Homer Simpson, what works even more like a drug is drugs. Aristotle, that rational old soul, preferred to modify people's emotions through their *beliefs*. Emotions actually come from belief, he said—about what we value, what we think we know, and what we expect. Aristotle didn't separate *pathos* entirely from rhetorical logic. It may sound strange to combine the emotional with the rational, but rhetoric does precisely that.

▸ Classic Hits
IT'LL FEEL GREAT WHEN I STOP HITTING YOU: We don't count physical hurt as an emotion these days, but many Greeks thought that pain was the secret to all emotions. The good passions, like joy, were the absence of pain. This fun bunch called themselves the Stoics.

Take fear. Suppose I made you believe that your heart might stop right now, even while you read this. It could happen; in the susceptible victim, the slightest fear could trigger an arrhythmia that sets off an electrochemical storm within your heart muscle. It could start to beat wildly out of sync, destroying critical tissue and causing you to clutch your chest and die.

That didn't scare you, did it? Your disbelief kept you from fear. Emotion comes from **experience** and **expectation**—what your audience believes has happened, or will take place in the future. The more vividly you give the audience the sensations of an experience, the greater the emotion you can arouse.

Suppose you wanted to make me angry at your next-door neighbor. You could tell me what a jerk she is—that she flirts in front of her husband and watches bad TV. None of this would make me angry at her. You describe her personality, not an experience. To make me angry, give me a vivid description of a specific outrage.

> YOU: She called the Boy Scouts a fascist organization.
> ME: Well, she's entitled to her—
> YOU: On Halloween? When my little boy comes to her stoop wearing his older brother's uniform?
> ME: How do you—
> YOU: I was there. When he started to cry, she said, "If you turn out to be gay, you'll be glad you met me." Then she looked straight at me and slammed the door.

That would make me angry at the neighbor. You re-created a dramatic scene, making me see it through your eyes. This works much better than name-calling. You made me believe the woman did something mean to an innocent little boy.

When you want to change someone's mood, tell a story.

Don't call names. Don't rant. Aristotle said that one of the most effective mood changers is a detailed narrative. The more vivid you make the story, the more it seems like a real experience, and the more your audience will think it could happen again. You give them a vicarious experience, and an expectation that it could happen to them.

> ▸ **Argument Tool**
> STORYTELLING:
> The best way to change an audience's mood. Make it directly involve you or your audience.

Storytelling works for every kind of emotion, including humor. A joke sounds funnier if you pretend you were there. Matt Damon's character in *Good Will Hunting* uses the technique when he talks to his therapist, played by Robin Williams.

> WILL: You know, I was on this plane once. And I'm sittin' there and the captain comes on and is like, "We'll be cruising at thirty-five thousand feet," and does his thing, then he puts

the mike down but forgets to turn it off. Then he says, "Man, all I want right now is [insert unmentionable sex act here] and a cup of coffee." So the stewardess goes runnin' up towards the cockpit to tell him the mike's still on, and this guy in the back of the plane goes, "Don't forget the coffee!"

SEAN: You've never been on a plane.

WILL: I know, but the joke's better if I tell it in the first person.

TRY THIS IN FRONT OF AN AUDIENCE
You already know that audiences love anecdotes. But if you want to put them in a particular mood, don't just tell a personal story; tell one that gives them a thrill of recognition. Suppose you advocate a new senior center. Invoke guilt by talking about a lonely elderly relative who lost her husband; she begs you to visit more often, but you have a full-time job and home responsibilities. Say, "This may sound familiar." Comedians use this technique all the time, because emotions are linked to the familiar.

The same technique works for seduction. To get someone in the mood, describe in detail what you plan—champagne, soft music, unmentionable stuff, and the evening's activities. Your story takes place in the future. Provide enough details, and your mate will be yours. The anecdote is a powerful tool. Use it responsibly. In the movie *Ruthless People,* the nasty "spandex miniskirt king" played by Danny DeVito calls his mistress after she sends him a sex tape.

SAM: I know why you sent me this tape, honey. And you know what I'm gonna do? I'm gonna do the same damn thing with you. And you, too, could scream your brains out, because no one's gonna hear.

Sam succeeds in changing the mood of his mistress, though not the way he wants. She thinks the tape shows a murder. Still, the more imminent your audience thinks an event will be, the more that belief will affect their mood.

How Webster Made the Chief Justice Cry

Besides storytelling, pathos depends on **self-control.** A persuader who apparently struggles to hold back her emotions will get better results than one who displays her emotions all over the floor of a bank. My daughter's temper tantrum showed the danger of pouring it on too much; she already knew Cicero's dictum that good pathetic argument is understated. **When you argue emotionally, speak simply.** People in the middle of a strong emotion rarely use elaborate speech. The most emotional words of all have just four letters. Less is more, and in pathetic terms, less *evokes* more.

> ► **Argument Tool**
> EMOTIONAL VOLUME CONTROL: Don't visibly exaggerate your emotions. Let your audience do that for you.

The conservative talk show host in *The Simpsons* commits a rhetorical error when he forgets his pathetic volume control at a town meeting:

> B. T. BARLOW: Mr. Mayor, I have a question for you. . . . what if YOU came home one night to find your family tied up and gagged, with SOCKS in their mouths? They're screaming. You're trying to get in but there's too much BLOOD on the knob!!!!!
>
> MAYOR QUIMBY: What is your question about?
>
> B. T. BARLOW: It's about the budget, sir.

You might prefer to follow a skilled rhetorician like Daniel Webster. We remember him as a blowhard, but his contemporaries considered him the most persuasive person in the country. He prosecuted a case in Massachusetts where a well-known ship captain—a Captain White, no less—had been murdered in his sleep. It was the O. J. Simpson case of its day. The suspect was a farm boy with no prior record, and people wondered how such a nice young man could commit something so heinous. Webster stood before the jury and, looking as though he could barely contain his outrage, narrated the murder in ordinary, everyday terms, making the crime sound like a farm chore to this twisted soul and anticipating *In Cold Blood* by more than a century. The jury hanged the boy.

> **TRY THIS WITH A BAD EMPLOYEE**
> If you're angry at an underling—say, you caught him bad-mouthing you to higher-ups—call him into your office and keep your heat inside. Speak more softly than usual, don't gesture with your hands, and let your eyes betray your cold fury. The overall effect can terrify the most blasé employee.

Holding your emotions in check also means taking your time to use them. Pathos tends to work poorly in the beginning of an argument, when you need to make the audience understand what you want and trust your character; that's the bailiwick of *logos* and *ethos*. Let emotion build gradually. Aristotle said that you can turn it up loudest in a speech before a large crowd; *logos* and *ethos* are your main strengths in a one-on-one argument, he

> ► **Argument Tool**
> THE PATHETIC ENDING: Emotion works best at the end.

said. But even when you harangue a political convention, your emotions will work best in gradually increasing doses.

When you speak before a small group—say, the Supreme Court—*pathos* can work, but only if you use it subtly. Some years after the Captain White affair, Webster argued a case before the Supremes on behalf of Dartmouth College, his alma mater. The state of New Hampshire was trying to take it over and turn it into a university. At the end of two days of rational argument, Webster came to his peroration—an apt time for *pathos*. Fighting tears, he turned to Chief Justice John Marshall. "It is, sir, as I have said, a small college." His voice cracked a little. "And yet, there are those who love her." A witness at the hearing said Justice Marshall's own eyes misted over. It was the most pathetic thing.

▶ **Persuasion Alert**
We live in a much more ironic time. I'm compelled to use an ironic comment to distance myself from Webster's pathetic appeal, lest you think the "small college" shtick makes me cry, too. That works only on the more zealous Dartmouth alums.

Webster won the case, and Dartmouth—an Ivy League university with engineering, business, and medical schools—remains Dartmouth College.

How does this work in real life? Suppose the reason for my daughter's bank fit was a sudden yen for ice cream. Instead of prostrating herself, she could have begun quietly:

> DOROTHY JR.: Daddy, can I have an ice cream cone?
> ME: *May* I have an ice cream cone.
> DOROTHY JR.: May I have an ice cream cone?
> ME: No.

Even at that age she knew me well enough to expect that answer. So, if she was well prepared, she'd be ready with her peroration—a *silent* peroration. She could simply have looked up at me and let the tears well up; not a tough feat for a kid denied a cone. Both Aristotle and Cicero listed compassion as a useful emotion, and it works for a besotted father at least as well as for a Supreme Court justice. If tears failed her, she could have resorted to humor, giving me the long-lashed open stare that my kids called "Bambi eyes." It cracked me up every time. The odds in favor of ice cream would have soared.

TRY THIS IN A PRESENTATION
While rhetoricians encourage you to start quietly and turn up the volume gradually, a veteran adman told me he did the opposite, lowering his voice more and more so that people would have to lean in to hear what he was saying. Then he ended with an emotional crescendo. The soft voice made the peroration that much more dramatic, he said.

Now grown up, Dorothy Junior tells me that losing my temper never worked on her.

DOROTHY JR.: When you got really mad, you sort of got funny.

ME: What do you mean, funny?

DOROTHY JR.: You did this, you know, Yosemite Sam thing.

ME: Well, if you just treated your father with a little—

DOROTHY JR. *(laughing)*: Yeah, like that! It was when you talked quietly and let your eyes get all scary—that was frightening.

ME *(making scary eyes):* Like this?

DOROTHY JR.: No, Dad. That's just pathetic.

I believe she meant "pathetic" in the modern, unrhetorical sense.

Other Passion Plays

Humor ranks above all the other emotions in persuasiveness, in part because it works the best at improving your *ethos*. A sense of humor not only calms people down, it makes you appear to stand above petty squabbles. The problem with humor, though, is that it is perfectly awful at motivating anyone into any sort of action. When people laugh, they rarely want to do anything else. Humor can change their emotions and their minds, but the persuasion stops there.

Aristotle, who was as close to a psychologist as an ancient Greek could get, said that some emotions—such as sorrow, shame, and humility—can prevent action altogether. These feelings make people introspective. They draw a bath, listen to Billie Holiday, and feel sorry for themselves.

Other emotions—such as joy, love, esteem, and compassion—work better, Aristotle said. Some people tend to revel in them, while others start fund drives. Hurricane Katrina showed the power of compassion, but a disaster carries more force than an argument. When you want action to come out of argument, your most useful emotions arouse people's tribal instincts—exploiting their insecurities about where they

▸ **Persuasion Alert**
We talked about fear earlier, but Aristotle called its use a fallacy—argument by the stick—even if the speaker isn't the one doing the threatening. Fear compels people to act, and compulsion precludes a choice. No argument there, only naked instinct.

stand in a group, and how much they belong to it. I mentioned in an earlier chapter that you want the audience to identify with you and, through you, the action you promote. We will delve further into identification in a later chapter. But it's enough to know that action requires identification. This is why Aristotle listed **anger, patriotism,** and **emulation** among emotions that can get an audience out of its seats and make it do what you want.

A person who desires something is especially susceptible to **anger.** Frustrate her ability to assuage that desire, Aristotle said, and you have an angry person. (Try withholding ice cream from a feisty daughter.) Young people have more desires than old people, so they rouse to anger more easily. Ditto the poor and the sick.

The easiest way to stimulate anger, Aristotle went on, is to belittle that desire. Keep in mind that he lived in a culture that resembles the modern street gang—macho, violent, and sensitive to any slight. Disrespect an ancient Greek or an ancient Greek's woman, and you should be prepared to hop the next trireme. But for the purposes of persuasion, the kind of anger that comes from belittlement is especially useful. If you want a hospital patient to sue a doctor, convince the patient that the doc neglected to take her problem seriously. Most personal lawsuits arise out of this sense of belittlement. It's an identification thing: people who feel themselves being cast out by the elite will go to great lengths to restore their status.

> **Argument Tool**
> THE BELITTLEMENT
> CHARGE: Show
> your opponent
> dissing your audi-
> ence's desires.

TRY THIS IN A PROTEST
If you want to stir up the masses, don't just promote your cause or attack its opponents; portray the enemy as belittling your cause. "The president calls you and me soft-headed on global warming. Our glaciers are melting! Coral reefs are dying! And what does the president do? He calls for more research! He's laughing all the way to the lab!"

A few weeks after writing this, I am scheduled to testify before the New Hampshire legislature on broadband Internet access in rural areas. I like to tell people that my dial-up connection here is so slow, a stamped envelope gets delivered faster than e-mail. (That literally happened once.) The problem is the phone company, which holds a monopoly in this state. Its lobbyists oppose any plan that would create competition; on the other hand, the company does nothing to bring broadband to my area. Which of these two statements has the best chance of getting a law that forces the company to provide statewide broadband?

ME: The company shows it couldn't care less about rural customers like me.

ME: The company has mocked this legislature for years, saying,
"Sure, we'll provide broadband, leave it to us," and then
forgetting you the moment it leaves this hearing room.

Actually, both might work, and I might use them.
But which argument will make the representatives an-
griest at the phone company? I vote for number two;
as Aristotle would say, the state reps will feel personally belittled.

On the other hand, I may play down the *pathos* in
my testimony. Anger gets the fastest action, which is a
reason why most political advertising tries to make you
mad. The problem is, while angry people are quick on
the trigger, they tend not to think far ahead; hence the
crime of passion. So anger isn't the best emotion for
deliberative argument, where we make decisions about
the future. The Greeks reserved it for courtroom rhetoric, when they wanted someone to hang.

Patriotism does a much better job of looking into
the future. This rhetorical group loyalty doesn't have
to be all about country. You can be patriotic for a high
school, a British soccer team, or—rarely these days—a
company. Do not confuse it with idealism, which is not
an emotion. Soldiers have died for democracy and freedom, indeed, but their patriotism burns for a country,
not an idea—the stars and bars, not the Constitution. An effective argument against flag burning is bound to be emotional, because it's all about
zeal for country. An argument to *allow* flag burning must use *logos* more
than *pathos,* because it emphasizes ideals more than patriotism.

Few colonists supported the founders' democratic notions when the
Revolution started, which is understandable from a rhetorical perspective.
Not until the British began stomping over the countryside did Americans'
patriotism rouse them to join the cause of independence. In the same light,

TRY THIS WITH
RECRUITING
To show you how well
Aristotle knew his
stuff, look at the tech-
nique that managers
use to pry a star
employee away from
a rival company:
"You're doing all this,
and you're still mak-
ing that crummy
salary?" "If you'd
been working for us,
you'd have had your
own parking space
ages ago." The man-
ager gets the recruit
angry by making him
believe his company
belittles him.

▶ Argument Tool
PATRIOTISM: Rouse
your audience's
group feelings by
showing a rival
group's success.

the Patriot Act has little to do with defending American ideals; it's about defending America. This is patriotism—*pathos,* not *logos.*

On a somewhat less profound level, Dartmouth College showed its patriotism when it built its own expensive ski area. The impetus was provided by Middlebury College, a school in next-door Vermont that had opened a "snow bowl." Middlebury was smaller than Dartmouth and, unlike Dartmouth, did not belong to the Ivy League; of *course* Dartmouth had to build a ski area. It was an act of patriotism—not so much a rational decision as an emotional one.

> **TRY THIS WITH ANY INSTITUTION**
> When managers talk about "pride," they really mean patriotism, an essentially competitive emotion. If you want that win-one-for-the-Gipper attitude, focus on a single rival. "Their church raised twenty percent more for disaster relief than our church, and they don't even kneel during Communion!"

You can use patriotism to your own advantage: show how a rival is besting your own group. The old suburban phenomenon of keeping up with the Joneses is a matter of patriotism; they have a statusmobile, and we're at least as good as they are. Patriotism has its personal side, as a form of competitive jealousy.

> PARENT: I hear that Mary got into Harvard early decision.
> KID: Yeah.
> PARENT: You don't like her much, do you?
> KID: She thinks too much of herself.
> PARENT: Smart kid, though. Works hard.
> KID: Not as smart as me.
> PARENT: Mmm, maybe not. Hard worker, though.

Where patriotism often gets triggered by something negative—you get patriotic when your group is under threat—**emulation** works the opposite way. We find it hard to see emulation as an emotion; the ancients were much bigger on imitation than we were. But emulation makes sense in modern times when we view it as an emotional response to a role model. A kid sees the Three Stooges on cable and gives his younger brother a noogie: that's emulation. It also comes out of our atavistic need to belong.

> ▸ **Argument Tool**
> EMULATION: Provide only the kind of role model your audience already admires.

Unfortunately, parents and children tend to choose different role models. For emulation to work, you need to start with a model the audience already looks up to, which is not always easy. A mother wants her daughter to emulate the head of the honor society, while the daughter dreams of wearing a leather jacket and riding a Suzuki motorcycle like her older cousin. Imagine a nineteen-year-old who wants to see the world, views a documentary about the World Trade Center attack, and watches his high school quarterback enlist—that kid will be especially susceptible to an army recruiter.

All of the most persuasive emotions—humor, anger, patriotism, and emulation—work best in a group setting. TV sitcoms invented that marvel of rhetorical humor, the laugh track, for this very reason. Aristotle noted that a big crowd expects big drama in a speech. When your audience is only one person, though, you had better know your *logos*. And you don't want to overplay your emotions.

That goes for announcing them as well as projecting them. Emotions should sneak up on people, especially if your audience doesn't already feel them. For that reason, never announce the mood you foster. Anyone who has ever told a joke knows not to proclaim its humor in advance. As they say in writing classes, show, don't tell. Yet people still hype emotions before they introduce them. My son was guilty of this just the other day, when he came home in a bad mood and found me in a perverse one.

> **TRY THIS WITH PUBLICATIONS**
> If you publish a newsletter or run a Web site that has reader participation, edit brutally. People will imitate what they see, and soon you won't have to edit much at all. I learned this in magazines: when readers see short, witty letters to the editor, they write short, witty letters.

> ▶ **Argument Tool**
> THE UNANNOUNCED EMOTION: Don't advertise a mood. Invoke it.

> GEORGE: I heard something today that's going to make you really mad.
>
> ME: No it won't.
>
> GEORGE: How do you know?
>
> ME: It won't make me mad if I'm prepared for it.
>
> GEORGE: Will you let me talk?
>
> ME: Sure. I just won't get mad.
>
> GEORGE: Dad, just shut up!
>
> DOROTHY SR.: Don't speak to your father that way.

By giving me advance warning of an emotion, George inoculated me from it. But he was unprepared to get mad himself. It's amazing how much fun it is to manipulate emotions.

The Tools

Rhetorical tradition has it that when Cicero spoke, people said, "What a great speech." When the fiery Athenian orator Demosthenes spoke, people said, "Let's march!" The Greek spoke more pathetically than the Roman; emotion makes the difference between agreement and commitment. Use the tools of *pathos* to rouse your audience to action.

Belief: To stir an emotion, use what your audience has **experienced** and what it **expects** to happen.

Storytelling: A well-told narrative gives the audience a virtual experience—especially if it calls on their own past experiences, and if you tell it in the first person.

Volume control: You can often portray an emotion most effectively by underplaying it, in an apparent struggle to contain yourself. Even screaming demagogues like Hitler almost invariably began a speech quietly and then turned up the volume.

Simple speech: Don't use fancy language when you get emotional. Ornate speech belongs to *ethos* and *logos;* plain speaking is more pathetic.

Anger often arises from a sense of belittlement. You can direct an audience's fury at someone by portraying his lack of concern over their problems.

Patriotism attaches a choice or action to the audience's sense of group identity. You can stir it by comparing the audience with a successful rival.

Emulation responds emotionally to a role model. The greater your *ethos,* the more the audience will imitate you.

Unannounced emotion lets you sneak up on your audience's mood. Don't tip them off in advance. They'll resist the emotion.

10. Turn the Volume Down

▲

THE SCIENTIST'S LIE
Transforming anger into receptiveness

Even if you persuade me, you won't persuade me. —ARISTOPHANES

This talk of pathetic manipulation will make the argument-squeamish uncomfortable. If only the world could follow formulas and conduct its affairs scientifically. But in actuality, even scientists regularly employ a pathetic trick. Their writing uses a thousands-year-old rhetorical device to calm the passions, the **passive voice.** "The experiment was conducted upon thirty domestic rhesus monkeys," says the researcher who did the experiment on monkeys. When you think about it, scientists seem almost childish pretending their work somehow just happened. They behave like the golfer who looks away innocently as he nudges his ball toward the hole. The technique works to calm the emotions because it disembodies the speaker and removes the actors, as if whatever happened was what insurers piously call an "act of God." Of course, it also can serve as a political subterfuge.

Creationists use the passive voice as a sneaky weapon *against* science. Lehigh University biologist Michael Behe, a leading proponent of intelligent design, argues that some biological phenomena are too complex for Darwinism to explain.

Perhaps molecular machines appear to look designed because they really are *designed.*

▸ **Argument Tool**
THE PASSIVE VOICE:
Pretend that things happened on their own. You didn't track mud across the living room floor. Mud was tracked across the living room floor.

TRY THIS WITH AN ANGRY BOARD
The passive voice can help you describe wrongdoing by a friend or coworker while calming the audience: "The account got fouled up," not, "Marcia fouled up the account." Just don't use the passive voice when you are the culprit. If your audience sees through your ruse, you want them thinking you're just defending a coworker, not weaseling out of something yourself. Elected officials who say, "Mistakes were made," don't win votes.

By whom? Steve Jobs? The intelligent design crowd presents a difficult target. They don't have to defend their Designer in Chief, because they have taken care not to drag him into the argument. With God out of the picture, molecular machines "were created." (It would be uncharacteristic for the Old Testament Jehovah to use the passive voice himself.)

The passive voice encourages passivity. It calms the audience, which makes it a great *pathos* trick. That hardly argues for its users' objectivity. Still, you have to applaud scientists for at least trying to be objective. Science determines facts, and emotions would only get in the way. But as we have seen, deliberative argument has a touchier relationship with the facts.

Kick My Ass or I'll Tell a Joke

Suppose your audience has already worked itself into an emotional state, and that state happens to be raging anger—against you. The passive voice may not be enough here. A dose of mild humor could reduce the tension, as you will see in a bit. Anything that neutralizes an acidic mood with a little basic calm can't hurt.

But a riskier, sneakier, and far more enjoyable technique does just the opposite: **set a backfire.** Artie Fufkin, the publicist in *This Is Spinal Tap*, does a superb backfire defense when no one shows up for a record signing.

> ARTIE: Do me a favor. Just kick my ass, okay? Kick this ass for a man, that's all. Kick my ass. Enjoy. Come on. I'm not asking, I'm telling with this. Kick my ass.

A backfire inspires sympathy through a *mea culpa* routine that exaggerates the emotions the audience feels. It works in just about any setting except politics. (Bids for sympathy won't help you get elected unless you're the widow of a popular, and recently dead, incumbent.)

Early in my publishing career, I worked for a small magazine that had no fact checkers. When Mount Saint Helens erupted for the first time, I wrote a short news piece in which I cluelessly

TRY THIS WITH A CLIENT
A caveat: the backfire works best one-on-one, with someone you know and like. Strangers may take your dramatic statement at face value. If you have a good client, use a screwup to strengthen the relationship. Say you wanted to be the one to tell her, detail what you have done to fix the problem, and mention how angry you are at yourself for not living up to your usual standards. If you have the right kind of client, she'll defend you, and think the better of you.

placed the volcano in Oregon. I didn't realize my mistake until after the magazine was published and a reader pointed it out to me. I walked into the editor's office and closed the door.

> ME (*looking stricken*): I've got bad news, Bill. Really bad news.
> BILL: What?
> ME: It was sloppy and stupid and I swear, boss, it'll never happen again.
> BILL: *What* will?
> ME: I put Mount Saint Helens in the wrong state.
> BILL: It's in Washington, right?
> ME: I put it in Oregon. I'm dying over this one.
> BILL: Hey, don't be so hard on yourself. These things happen. Just write a correction for the next issue.
> ME (*handing him the correction*): Done.
> BILL: Well, great. Lesson learned. Let's put this behind us.

Only later did I tell him that the first reader to point out the mistake was Dixy Lee Ray, the governor of Washington. She said her state wanted its volcano back.

My wife uses the backfire constantly; she loves to oversympathize with my mood.

> ME (*wincing*): This firewood is heavier than I thought.
> DOROTHY SR.: Is your back okay?
> ME: It hurts a little. (*Thinking fast*) I could use a backrub.
> DOROTHY SR.: Sure. Let's get you some ibuprofen first, and I'll heat up a compress in the microwave. Lie on the bed.
> ME: I was about to go swimming.
> DOROTHY SR.: You're not going anywhere with your back in that condition!
> ME: I'm fine.
> DOROTHY SR.: I thought you said your back hurt.
> ME: It doesn't hurt anymore.

If she weren't such a good person, I'd say she talked her way out of giving me a backrub.

Use the backfire only if you're willing to risk a blaze that gets out of hand. This is one instance where agreement may not serve you; tell someone to kick your ass, and the danger is that they might comply.

Humor is much safer—provided that you use the right kind. Sigmund Freud said that making people laugh "relieves anxiety" by releasing impulses in a disciplined manner. The wisest rhetoricians knew that you can't teach it; Cicero noted that the Greeks put out several manuals on humor, all unintentionally funny. Freud should have learned that lesson.

▶ **Argument Tool**
HUMOR: the best calming device for most emotions—except anger.

If you ever get a chance, take a look at his book *Jokes (Der Witz)*. It's hilariously full of unfunny jokes. (Prisoner on his way to the gallows: "Well, this is a good beginning to the week.")

Although the rhetoricians found it hard to teach, they had a good time codifying it. One type of humor may work better for you than the others.

Urbane humor depends on an educated audience; it relies on word play. When British general Charles Napier captured the Indian province of Sind in 1843, he alerted his superiors with a one-word telegram: PECCAVI. Every educated Brit knew that *peccavi* is Latin for "I have sinned." Damned droll, that Napier chap.

▶ **Persuasion Alert**
I devote more space to humor than to any other emotion, because that's what Cicero did. I try to practice what he preached; this book is full of my attempts at wit. Humor relaxes the more fearful emotions and, I hope, makes you less wary of my argument for argument.

Urbanity has fallen out of favor. A good pun gets a groan these days; but wordplay, like a mind, is a terrible thing to waste. You don't force this kind of humor. Just be ready for any opportunity. The other day, as my family sat around the dinner table discussing *Transamerica*, a movie about a transsexual, the conversation turned to the actors we would most want to see playing transsexual roles, and whether the actors would ever agree to playing them.

DOROTHY SR.: Would John Wayne?
ME: No, he would wax.

Get it? "To wax" is the opposite of "to wane," and men have to wax their legs in order to play women. A double pun! That's urbane humor, though my family failed to appreciate it. It is the only kind of humor that

TRY THIS AT A PROFESSIONAL MEETING
One way to inject urbane humor into a talk is to invent a neologism that only your audience would understand. I did this once while lecturing on political rhetoric. Having explained the difference between deliberative rhetoric and the verbal fighting called *eristic,* I suggested calling talk show hosts "eristicrats." I'm sure I saw at least two people smile.

you can teach yourself. If you lack a sense of humor otherwise, the urbane version makes a reasonable substitute.

Wit isn't ha-ha funny either, just mildly amusing. Its humor is drier than urbanity, and instead of wordplay, it plays off the situation. When Chief Justice John Roberts worked for Ronald Reagan, the White House asked his advice on whether the president should send the Irish ambassador a Saint Patrick's Day greeting on stationery printed with *An Teach Ban* (Gaelic for "The White House"). Roberts said he saw no legal problem, but he encouraged the staff to fact-check the Gaelic. "For all I know it means 'Free the I.R.A.,' " he wrote. Not ha-ha-funny. But rather witty.

Facetious humor, which covers most jokes, is *supposed* to make you laugh. That is its sole purpose. Rhetoricians through the ages have frowned on this kind of funny. If your *ethos* is on par with Calvin Coolidge's, joke telling could win you the sympathy of your audience—but only if you have a staff of professional yuck scribes, as Laura Bush did before her famous send-up of her husband at the White House Correspondents Dinner in 2005. The former school librarian told what ABC News claimed to be "the first public joke ever by a First Lady about the president of the United States engaged in intimate contact with a randy male horse." The crowd went wild, and the president's own ratings got a boost.

A joke can defuse a touchy argument, if only through sheer distraction. If it's funny enough, people will forget what they were talking about.

Banter is a form of attack and defense consisting of clever insults and snappy comebacks. The traditional African-American game of snaps offers the most competitive banter today. The object is to out-insult your opponent.

▶ **Classic Hits**
CICERO KILLED 'EM, AND THEY RETURNED THE FAVOR: Banter was Cicero's favorite kind of humor. While he was famously quick with a comeback, though, not everyone appreciated his talent. One of the many victims of his ridicule put a hit on him. Cicero literally bantered himself to death.

> Your mama's so fat, when she hauls ass she has to make two trips.
> Man, that snap was staler than your breath.
> Your mama's so ugly, her birth certificate was an apology letter from the condom company.
> Well, *your* mama's idea of safe sex is locking the car doors.
> Hey, I don't have a mama. Me and my dad just use yours.

But that's demonstrative rhetoric. When you use deliberative argument, you might prefer to banter with **concession,** agreeing with a point only to use it against your opponent. Cicero cited an example during a trial in the Forum, when a brash young man used concession to rebut an elder:

> ELDER: What you are barking at, pup?
> YOUNG MAN: I see a thief.

The young man accepted the elder's point: maybe I *am* a dog. Then he used it right back at his opponent. There is a technique to this. First, accept your adversary's statement at face value, then follow its logic to a ridiculous conclusion; or simply throw it back with a twist. Kids often use a crude version of this concession: *Yeah? Well, if I'm a [insert insult], then that makes you a [insert worse insult].* In deliberative argument, though, banter works best in defense, conceding a point to your advantage. No one did this better than Winston Churchill; witness his famous reply.

TRY THIS WITH YOUR CHILDREN
Admittedly, it's not easy to perform a bantering concession well. My children have made themselves alarmingly good at it by practicing with the television. They banter with the ads and talking heads.

Talking Head: America is a faith-based culture.
Dorothy Jr.: Right. It takes faith to believe an ape like you has a culture.

> LADY ASTOR: Winston, if you were my husband I'd flavor your
>   coffee with poison.
> CHURCHILL: Madam, if I were your husband, I should drink it.

You have seen the advantages of rhetorical jujitsu already. Combine concession with wit, and you get banter. If you find an opportunity to follow up with a great retort, go for it. You might disarm your opponent. But make sure you're capable of this rapid-response humor. Frankly, I'm hit-or-miss, which is why I try to entertain my unappreciative family with puns.

▸ Tips from the Ancients
TWO CORPSES WALK INTO A BAR: Cicero helpfully advised Romans not to make jokes about a shocking crime or a pitiful victim. Apparently, they needed to be told that.

Otherwise you can limit your banter to slower forms of communication, such as snail mail, to allow more time for cleverness. In an old Cold War joke, the Soviet Union places an order for 20 million sixteen-inch-long condoms from the United States, just to mess with our minds. We Americans comply, sending 20 million condoms in packages marked "small." That's banter—not live banter, but postal.

The Tools

Passive voice: If you want to direct an audience's anger away from someone, imply that the action happened on its own. *The chair got broken,* not *Pablo broke the chair.*

Backfire: You can calm an individual's emotion in advance by overplaying it yourself. This works especially well when you screw up and want to prevent the wrath of an authority.

Humor: Laughter is a wonderful calming device, and it can enhance your ethos if you use it properly. **Urbane humor** plays off a word or part of speech. **Wit** is situational humor. **Facetious humor** is joke telling, a relatively ineffective form of persuasion. **Banter,** the humor of snappy answers, works best in rhetorical defense. It uses concession to throw the opponent's argument back at him.

11. Gain the High Ground

▲

ARISTOTLE'S FAVORITE TOPIC

How to use your audience's point of view

Speech is the leader of all thoughts and actions. — ISOCRATES

A man feels sick, so he goes to a clinic.

DOC: I have good news and bad news.

MAN: Give me the bad news first.

DOC: You have a rare and incurable illness, with less than twenty-four hours to live.

MAN: My God! What's the good news?

DOC: You know that nurse who took your blood pressure, the one with the huge . . .

MAN: Yeah, so?

DOC: We're having an affair.

Nice bedside manner, dude. It sums up the prevailing enough-about-you-let's-talk-about-me mind-set. People often pitch an argument that sounds persuasive to themselves, not to their listeners. This rhetorical mistake can be fatal, because messages that appeal only to the speaker have a tendency to boomerang. You saw how important sympathy is in argument by emotion; the same thing goes with argument by logic. In deliberative argument, you need to convince your audience that the choice you offer is the most "advantageous"—to the advantage of the audience, that is, not you. This brings us back to values. The advantageous is an outcome that gives the audience what it values.

> ▶ **Argument Tool**
> THE ADVANTAGEOUS:
> Base your argument
> on what's good for the
> audience, not for you.

If you can persuade a two-year-old that eating her oatmeal is to her advantage, for example, then she may actually comply. Suppose the toddler holds the value that older brothers should be taken down a peg.

> YOU: Eat half your oatmeal and you can fling the bowl at your
> brother's head.

While your argument may seem morally dubious—and from the brother's point of view, personally objectionable—at least it does what an argument is supposed to do. Aristotle maintained that the person most affected by a decision makes the best judge of it. The diner is more qualified to judge a dish than the chef, he said, meaning that the girl outweighs you rhetorically. While the decision is up to the audience, the burden of proof is on you. To prove your point, start with something your audience believes or wants.

> ▸ Classic Hits
> HE WOULD HAVE LOVED GITMO: In reality, Aristotle would have caned the kid. He was a great believer in corporal punishment; he said a slave's testimony was invalid except under torture.

Unfortunately, most parents base their arguments on what *they* want—such as strong bones and healthy bodies. That sounds like Esperanto to two-year-old ears. You want strong bones. She doesn't. What does the kid want? What is to her advantage? And is it worth the trouble of choking down a bowl of oatmeal? That's the stuff of *logos*.

My friend Annie had a *logos* problem during the 2004 presidential campaign. Annie grew up in Ohio and now lives on the East Coast. A passionate Democrat, she called all the Ohioans she knew to try and tilt the state to Kerry. Her former college roommate turned out to be her toughest customer. After chatting about the weather and their families (weather is Topic One in the Midwest), Annie segued into politics.

> TRY THIS IN A POLITICAL ARGUMENT
> Many debates divide between morals and the advantageous. In politics, the advantageous usually wins in the long run (statecraft is a selfish art). If you believe in military action to depose violent dictators, for example, argue the morals of your side; but spend more time showing how your country would benefit. You're more likely to win your point.

> ANNIE: So, Kath, who are you going to vote for
> in November?
> KATHY: Oh, I'll vote for Bush, I guess.
> ANNIE: Kathy, you need to know some reasons
> why I think that would be a mistake.

She ran through a list of problems with Bush. Annie was well-prepared for this call: logical, concise . . .

> KATHY: I don't want my taxes to go up.
>
> ANNIE: But those tax cuts are causing the deficit to spin out of control!
>
> KATHY: I just don't want my taxes to go up.
>
> ANNIE: But they *won't* go up. All the Democrats want is to let the tax cuts on the rich expire. Let's face it, Kathy, you're married to a lawyer who makes a godawful amount of money.
>
> KATHY *(doing perfect stone wall impression):* If Kerry gets elected, my taxes will go up. And I just don't want them to.

> ▸ **Argument Tool**
> BABBLING: "Babbling" is what Aristotle calls an arguer's tendency to repeat himself over and over. This reveals the bedrock of your audience's opinion.

An unpersuadable audience tends to repeat the same rationale over and over. Is it a good rationale? Doesn't matter. Kathy has made her mind up. She can't be persuaded.

Or *can* she?

Cracking Good Clichés

Before you begin an argument, first determine what your audience is thinking. You need to know its beliefs and values, the views it holds in common. The common sense of your audience is square one—the beginning point of your argument. To shift people's point of view, start from their position, not yours. In rhetoric, we call this spot a **commonplace**— a viewpoint your audience holds in common. You can use it as your argument's jumping-off point.

> ▸ **Argument Tool**
> THE COMMONPLACE: Use it as the jumping-off point of your argument.

We equate a commonplace with a cliché, but the term once had a broader connotation. The rhetorical commonplace is a short-form expression of common sense or public opinion. It can range from a political belief (all people are created equal) to a practical matter (it's cheaper to buy in bulk). Commonplaces represent beliefs or rules of thumb, not facts; people are created equal only if you agree on the definitions for "created" and "equal," and it's not always cheaper to buy in bulk. A commonplace is not just anything that pops into a person's head, however. "I'm hungry" does not represent a commonplace. But "When I'm hungry, I eat right away" *is* a commonplace, as is "When I'm hungry, that's good; it means I'm burning fat." Different groups (such as dieters and healthy eaters) have different commonplaces. In fact, people identify with their groups through the groups' commonplaces. These attitudes, beliefs, and values also determine a person's self-identity—the assumptions and outlook on the world that define an

> **Meanings**
> Rhetoric loves geographical metaphors. Besides the commonplace, there's the *topic.* The word comes from the Greek word *topos,* meaning "place." "Topic" and "topography" share this same root; both offer points of view.

individual. We will delve into identity later; right now, let's look at the commonplace as the starting point of rhetorical logic.

A commonplace takes advantage of the way humans process information. When you spot your friend Bob, your nervous system fires up common networks of synapses. This neural shortcut saves your brain from having to identify Bob's hair, then his eyes, then his nose, then his mouth. When the signals come in for Bob's face, the set of neurons associated with that face all light up at once. Bob! A commonplace works the same way. I say, "The early bird catches the worm," and you instantly know that I refer to the habit of waking up before most people. It's an argument shortcut that skips what prevailing wisdom already agrees with:

> **TRY THIS IN A COMMENCEMENT ADDRESS**
> Suppose you want to encourage students graduating from an elite private liberal arts college to enlist in the military. Use the audience's commonplaces, not the military's. Instead of "A strong nation is a peaceful nation," say, "Our armed forces can use independent, critical thinkers."

> *People who get out of bed earlier than the average Joe tend to have more success in life blah blah blah.*

You probably would avoid a cliché like the early bird except to annoy your children. Fine. A commonplace doesn't need a cliché. The concept—rising early holds moral and practical superiority over rising late—constitutes a commonplace on its own. When most CEOs discuss their schedule, they brag about getting up early more than they do about working late. American public opinion strongly favors early rising, making it a commonplace.

Filmmakers use commonplaces, clichéd and otherwise, as a shorthand to express character without unnecessary dialogue or explication. A two-day

TRY THIS WITH A
PUBLIC ISSUE
Rhetorical labeling
is all about com-
monplaces. If you
can define an issue
in language that's
familiar and com-
fortable to your
audience, you will
capture the higher
ground. What does
your audience hold
most dear: Safety,
or risk? Lifestyle,
or savings? Educa-
tion, or instinct?

beard and a glass of whiskey connote an alcoholic. A movie hero will take a beating stoically and then wince when a woman dabs him with antiseptic—an efficient way of showing the big lug's sensitive side. We make fun of devices like these, and they can betray lazy directing; but by playing to shared assumptions about people and things, the director can establish a movie's characters and themes without taxing our attention span.

Conversational commonplaces offer the same efficiency; they let us cut to the topical chase and bring us closer as a group. In my family, for instance, we value an occasional obscenity, so long as one utters it skillfully. Instead of saying, "Yes," or, "Well, all right," to my children, I say sweetly, "You do whatever the hell you want, sweetheart." My children picked it up at an early age. That was our commonplace, and—bizarre as it would seem to a family with more conventional verbal taboos—it raised a smile whenever one of us said it. Of course, there are those outside our family who object to that sort of thing; one of them was Dorothy Junior's nursery school teacher, who informed me that my daughter had answered a request to share a toy, "You do whatever the hell you want, sweetheart." It was a Heinrichs commonplace, not one shared by the nursery school.

Not every commonplace is all that benign (assuming you think teaching vulgarities to small children is benign). An evil twin lies in the stereotype. "Three black guys came up to me last night" will spark a different image in most Americans' minds from "Three Frenchwomen came up to me last night." We should also recognize commonplaces that corporations and campaigns use on us. Ancient rhetoricians would applaud most of the labels the Bush White House attached to policies and legislation: No Child Left Behind. Operation Iraqi Freedom. Clear Skies. Healthy Forests Initiative. Culture of Life. Marriage Protection. Each of these phrases represented a prefab consensus. Our culture loves the idea of an even playing field where every kid gets a shot at a future, for instance, and anyone opposing a bill titled No Child Left Behind

▸ Argument Tool
THE COMMONPLACE
LABEL: When politi-
cians speak of labeling,
they really mean the
application of com-
monplaces to legisla-
tion, bumper stickers,
and talk radio.

would seem to oppose that basic American value. Similarly, who would argue against freedom, clear skies, healthy forests, life, or marriage? All these are commonplaces: our shared notions of what's advantageous for our society. They help define our peculiar culture and our identity as enlightened twenty-first-century citizens.

The same phrases may not have worked in a different setting. The ancient Spartans, who practiced infanticide, may have objected to "No Child Left Behind." Politicians would have had to rewrite it as something like "No Healthy Male Spartan Child Left Behind." Britons might not have endorsed "Iraqi Freedom" when the empire was at its height. Iraq was part of that empire. And the French would wonder what we were "protecting marriage" against. Those are American commonplaces. They help define Americans as Americans. And any politician who fails to get on board risks looking un-American.

The right seems better at this game than the left. The antiabortion movement's Pro Life, for example, trumped Pro Choice; conservatives knew instinctively that "life" has more pathetic value than the murkier "choice." But commonplaces represent opinion, not truth, and every one has a potential counter-commonplace. Liberals would have done better if they had countered the Republicans' labels. Match Culture of Life with Culture of Freedom. Marriage Protection with Family Protection ("Because Gays Have Families Too"). Propose replacing the Patriot Act with the Courage Act ("Take Courage Not Cover"). Instead, liberals came up with the "Safe Act," implying they would rather be safe than patriotic. Commonplaces are powerful weapons. Do not aim them at your foot.

We Got Commonplaces in River City

To persuade an audience, it helps to know the commonplaces it already uses. Suppose you want a group of conservatives to support low-cost housing in your city. "Marriage needs protection" would be an excellent commonplace to start. Keep the family together and foster the culture of ownership. (Another commonplace!)

Listen for the commonplaces. If your audience refers to her volunteer work as a "journey," then you know she views the ordinary activities of life in terms of adventure and growth (and that she will not shrink from a cliché).

If she refers to "kids these days," it is extremely unlikely that your audience enjoys rap music.

If she says, "It's not PC to say this, but . . . ," then she probably holds cultural nuance in low regard.

Do you share these opinions? If not, no rhetorical rule says you have to pretend to. But every commonplace offers a potential jumping-off point. Professor Harold Hill stood on the "kids these days" platform to sell band instruments in *The Music Man*. Playing off parents' concern about wayward youth, Hill coined a slogan:

We got trouble in River City.

An audience's commonplaces are easy to find, because you hear them frequently. When someone rejects your argument, she usually does it with a commonplace. Take Kathy, for instance. Hers is hard to miss: Democrats raise taxes. Taxes taxes taxes. She favors Bush because she believes his promise to keep taxes down. Indeed, Democrats tend to be more pro-tax than Republicans—a commonplace in politics. If you're a Democrat, you doubtless have a great rebuttal, but that doesn't matter. The audience, Kathy, *believes* Bush will keep taxes down, while Kerry will raise them. She will stand her ground, and that ground is her commonplace. Annie made a mistake when she argued against it.

> **Argument Tool**
> THE REJECTION: An audience will often say no in the form of a commonplace. You now have your new starting ground—provided you can continue the argument.

ANNIE: The Republicans will increase the deficit! The Democrats won't raise taxes!

What if she chose to agree with it instead?

ANNIE: Oh, I know what you mean. The taxes I pay are unbelievable!

Here she jumps onto the commonplace instead of running away from it. Next, she expands her argumentative territory by adding the politicians-are-all-alike truism.

ANNIE: You know what, though? Mine are high *and* we have a Republican governor and legislature. They're all alike, aren't they, Kath?

> **Useful Figure**
> The *anadiplosis* ("She will stand her ground, and that ground . . .") builds one thought on top of another by taking the last word of a clause and using it to begin the next clause. Ben Franklin uses it famously: "For want of a shoe the horse was lost, for want of a rider the battle was lost . . ." It turns your argument into an unstoppable juggernaut of logic.

Having established her proof, Annie can now push a little bit.

> ANNIE: I'll tell you what, Kathy. Both Bush and Kerry promise they won't raise taxes. I want you to do something for me. I'll e-mail you a link to a Web site that talks about what the deficit will do to your taxes. Will you look at it for me?

Would that work? Maybe. Pitching it in terms of a personal favor can't hurt. A phone call out of the blue may not be the right occasion to launch a political discussion, but at least it would *be* a discussion, instead of the yes-it-is, no-it-isn't kind of squabble they actually had. With a little deft rhetoric, when they hang up, they remain friends.

Commonplaces are the sort of things everybody knows. What makes them clichés is that they get repeated until we're sick of them. Nonetheless, commonplaces are useful to track. When you stop hearing one, you know that the common ground of public opinion is beginning to shift. If you want to keep close track of maxims that serve politics, just follow the opinion polls. After 9/11, you heard a lot of political language with "safety" and "security" in it, and the election turned on a cautious maxim.

> *Don't switch horses in midstream.*

After four years without a major terrorist attack on the homeland, however, we increasingly heard a maxim about putting limits on security.

> *Americans have a right to privacy in their own home.*

Not everyone subscribes to the prevailing maxims. Almost half of Americans would have been happy to switch presidents in midstream, and

---

TRY THIS BEFORE A JOB INTERVIEW
When you do your Web research on a prospective employer, don't just delve into facts and history. Google the CEO and write down the catchwords he uses. Now try to think up a few bumper stickers using these catchwords as commonplaces. ("Hire Mary for Value-Driven Management"). You'll get a feel for the company's lingo and tone, even if you don't blatantly repeat the phrases themselves.

▸ **Tips from the Ancients**
WHY JEFFERSON DIDN'T BLOG: Starting with the Renaissance, students kept commonplace books—collections of practical wisdom that they could use in arguments. Rhetoricians taught how to organize the material, which could be original or copied from someone else's wisdom. Thomas Jefferson kept commonplace books all his life, and they nicely reveal the public attitudes of his day.

supporters of a ramped-up Patriot Act counter the right-to-privacy commonplace with

> We're at war.

Still, maxims help you follow trends in values, such as puritanism versus libertarianism. You can almost set your epochal clock by this particular values pendulum. Who but aging hippies say, "It's your thing" anymore?
Remember the song?

> It's your thing. Do what you want to do.
> I can't tell you who to sock it to.

That was a solid-gold maxim a few decades ago, an
age that saw soaring crime, abortion, and divorce
rates. By the early nineties (1990s, that is), understandably, it wasn't your thing anymore. Doing what
you wanted to do was not accepted wisdom. Instead,
people began to use an opposing maxim—

> It's about values.

—meaning, I sure as heck can tell you who to sock it
to, and I'm lobbying Congress to criminalize socking
it to the wrong people. Libertarian stock went down,
and puritan stock went up. And so it will go forever—
with any luck.

When commonplaces clash, arguments begin.

**TRY THIS WITH A
NEW BOSS**
Again, Google the boss
to get a sense of her
commonplaces. Now
place them side by
side with her predeces-
sor's commonplaces.
Put "value-driven
management" next to
"employee-empowered
management," for ex-
ample. The comparison
will tell you a lot about
the changes the new
boss will bring in values
and style—and give you
logical ammunition in
future meetings.

The Tools

Public opinion "is held in reverence," said Mark Twain. "It settles everything. Some think it is the Voice of God." The original definition of "audience" had the same pious tone. It meant a "hearing" before a king or
nobleman. The first audience, in the other words, was a judge. According

to Aristotle, it still is. Your audience judges whether your opinion is the right one.

But we're talking deliberative argument, not a court of law. So the statute books don't determine the outcome; the audience's own beliefs, values, and naked self-interest do. To persuade them, you offer a prize: the advantageous, which is the promise that your choice will give the judges what they value.

In order to convince them, you have to start with what they believe, value, or desire. You begin, in other words, with the commonplace.

The Advantageous: This is the über-topic of deliberative argument, persuasion that deals with choices and the future. The other forms of rhetoric cover right and wrong, good and bad. Deliberative argument talks about what is best for the audience. That is where persuasion comes in; you make the audience believe your own choice to be the advantageous one.

The Commonplace: Any cliché, belief, or value can serve as your audience's boiled-down public opinion. This is the starting point of your argument, the ground the audience currently stands on. *Logos* makes it think that your own opinion is a very small step from their commonplace.

Babbling: When your audience repeats the same thing over and over, it is probably mouthing a commonplace.

The Commonplace Label: Apply a commonplace to an idea, a proposal, or a piece of legislation; anyone who opposes it will risk seeming like an outsider.

The Rejection: Another good commonplace spotter. When your audience turns you down, listen to the language it uses; chances are, you will hear a commonplace. Use it when the argument resumes.

12. Persuade on Your Terms

▲

How to define the issue in your favor

....

MR. BURNS: *Oh, meltdown. It's one of those annoying buzzwords. We prefer to call it an unrequested fission surplus.*

—THE SIMPSONS

....

I've stopped arm-wrestling my son. He no longer finds me much of a challenge, and I get tired of feeling my arm bend the wrong way and slam against the table. Up until a year or so ago, however, we were closely matched—even though he got stronger than I long before that. I was better because I knew the right kind of grip: subtle enough that he didn't feel me squirm for advantage, while enclosing enough of his hand to allow full use of my arm muscles. The moment he learned the same technique, I didn't stand a chance.

This is exactly how the persuasive strategy of **definition** works: as a rhetorical method for getting a favorable grip on an argument. In this chapter you will learn the technique of top lawyers and political strategists: the ability to define the terms and the issue in a way that stacks an argument in your favor.

The ancients listed "definition" as the tool to fall back on when the facts are against you, or when you lack a good grasp of them. If you want, you can harness definition to win an argument without using any facts at all. Facts and definitions are part of a larger overall strategy called **stance.** It was originally designed for defense, but it works offensively as well. Before you begin to argue, or when you find yourself under attack, take your stance:

▸ **Argument Tool**
STANCE: The technical name is "status theory." *Status* is Latin for "stance." It comes from the stance wrestlers would take at the beginning of a match. The technique is a fallback strategy: fact, definition, quality, relevance. If the first won't work, fall back on the second, and so on.

If **facts** work in your favor, use them. If they don't (or you don't know them), then . . .

Redefine the terms instead. If that won't work, accept your opponent's facts and terms but . . .

Argue that your opponent's argument is **less important** than it seems. And if even that isn't to your advantage . . .

Claim **the discussion is irrelevant.**

Use fact, definition, quality, and relevance in descending order. The facts work best; fall back through definition, quality, and relevance until one works for you.

Suppose a father catches his kid smuggling a candy bar into her room before dinner. The kid takes me on as counsel for the defense. What do I advise her?

The facts don't work for her. She was caught red-handed.

She could try to redefine the issue by saying she was not *smuggling* candy, exactly, but *hiding* it from her brother before he grabbed it for dessert. Suppose she doesn't have a brother, though. Plus, any lame excuse risks an angry parent. So she has to fall back again.

The quality defense would have her admit she smuggled the candy. But she would argue that it wasn't as big an offense as you might think. Maybe she hadn't had time to eat lunch, and was faint with hunger. With luck, the father lectures her on proper nutrition and lets her off without punishment. The quality defense just might work.

If it doesn't, relevance remains as her last fallback. In a real trial, the relevance tactic entails arguing that the court has no jurisdiction in the matter. In the girl's case, it would mean claiming that Dad has no right to judge her. Didn't she see him pop a cookie into his mouth when he came home from work? And is his customary predinner whiskey *good* for him?

You can see why relevance is the last position you want to take. It carries big risks. But you normally won't have to fall back that far. Most of the time, defining the issue wins the day. Definition is such a great tool, actually, that you may want to use it even when the facts are on your side.

Tax-and-Spend Labelers

Let's start with the terms. You can accept the words your opponent uses.

> SPOUSE: That kid of ours is plenty smart. He's just lazy.
> YOU: Yes, he's lazy. So how do we motivate him?

Or you can change the terms.

> YOU: No, I don't think he's lazy. He's bored.

Or you can redefine them.

> YOU: If "lazy" means frantically shooting aliens on a computer, then he's lazy.

One of the best ways to define the terms is to redefine them.

▸ **Argument Tool**
REDEFINITION:
Don't automatically accept the meaning your opponent attaches to a word. Redefine it in your favor.

Don't accept your opponent's definition. Come up with your own instead. That way you sound as though you agree with your opponent's argument even while you cut the legs out from under it. For most lawyers, redefining is a matter of instinct. When President Clinton told the special prosecutor, "That depends on what your definition of 'is' is," he was redefining a term—in the slickest, most lawyerly way, unfortunately. Wayne in the movie *Wayne's World* does better.

> WAYNE: Garth, marriage is punishment for shoplifting in some countries.

Now, when I talk about defining the terms, I don't necessarily mean choosing which of *The Oxford English Dictionary*'s eight definitions of "marriage" to use. The dictionary simply offers the literal meaning of the word, its denotation. Wayne does something different. He redefines the *connotation* of the word—the unconscious thoughts that the term sparks in people's minds. Garth has teased Wayne by asking whether he plans to marry his girlfriend; to Garth, marriage connotes something adult and mushy. Wayne's reply erases whatever marital image Garth has in his mind and replaces it with criminal justice.

Redefinition works well in politics, where candidates try to stick labels on each other.

> CONSERVATIVE: My opponent is another tax-and-spend liberal.
>
> LIBERAL: "Liberal" doesn't mean tax-and-spend. That's just a nasty label. "Liberal" means caring about working-class families. My opponent is a conservative, which means robbing from the working class and giving to the rich.

Definition tactics can serve you just as well at home and in the office. They can help you fend off labeling—the rhetorical practice of attaching a pejorative term to a person or concept. The definition tactic gives you an effective instant retort. Do you accept your opponent's definition, or not?

You may find that your opponent's insult actually favors you, presenting an opportunity for argument jujitsu.

▸ **Argument Tool**
DEFINITION JUJITSU: Accept your opponent's term and its connotation, then defend it as a positive thing.

> SIBLING: You're just talking like an egghead.
>
> YOU: Yes, I'm talking like an egghead. I *am* an egghead.

If that definition fails to suit your argument perfectly, change it, or redefine it.

> YOU: If talking like an egghead means knowing what I'm talking about, then I'm talking like an egghead.

When you're on your best definition game, you can spike any label that comes your way, slamming it back at your opponent with double the power. In fact, this is one instance where the best offense is a good defense. (That is not the case when you define whole issues instead of people and individual concepts.)

Obviously, you want to avoid giving your opponent

TRY THIS IN THE OFFICE
Arguments don't just attach labels to people; they also label everything you do at home or work. If a coworker labels your idea "unoriginal," say, "Sure, in the sense that it's been used successfully." Better to employ your opponent's language than to deny it. "Sure" trumps "No, it's not."

an easy label to spike. Make sure the definitions you start with work in your favor. Suppose you're the one who accuses a sibling of talking like an egghead. Make sure you include an airtight definition.

> YOU: You're just talking like an egghead—using fancy jargon
> to show everybody how educated you are.
> SIBLING: So I'm educated. If you're insecure about your own
> lack of knowledge, don't go attacking me.

Whoa, what went wrong? You defined "egghead" neatly—as showing off with fancy jargon—but then you dropped another term, "educated," without defining it. Better just to stick with:

> YOU: You're just talking like an egghead—showing off with
> fancy jargon.
> SIBLING: I'm not showing off! I'm using words that any edu-
> cated person would know.

Now you have your opponent on the defensive, and you can bear down.

> YOU: Using obscure words doesn't show you're educated.

At this point you can feel free to switch the argument to the future tense and win the day.

> YOU: So let's talk in simple terms how we're going to pay for
> Mom's insurance.

My Word Versus Theirs

Now we're ready to begin defining entire issues. It works like the definition tactics we just talked about, except on a grander scale. Defining an issue means attaching words to it—making those words stick to the issue whenever it pops up in the audience's heads. The politicians' glue of choice is repetition. In the 1980s, conservatives called up the image of the "welfare cheat" who claims nonexistent children and lives high on the government dole. They repeated this message in speeches and ads until it was difficult for many Americans to see welfare as anything but a rip-off. More recently,

President Bush promoted tort reform by referring over and over to "frivolous lawsuits." Opponents of tort reform—particularly the Democratic Party, which receives a big chunk of money from trial lawyers— have had a hard time redefining the issue as a citizen's right to a day in court. That's a less vivid label than "frivolous." They might do better with "the right to sue bad doctors and corporate crooks." A personalized definition usually beats an impersonal one.

▸ **Useful Figure**
The *periphrasis* swaps a description for a name—good for labeling a person or an issue. A more general word for this is "circumlocution."

You don't have to repeat yourself to attach a label to an issue. Just define your side with a term that contrasts with your opponent's. Let me give you a personal example. I'm currently consulting with a publishing company that is bidding for the privilege of doing a major airline's in-flight magazine. Several other publishers are competing with my client; one of them puts out a highly respected general interest magazine that sells on newsstands. Its editors are some of the brightest in the business—well educated, imaginative, with a thorough knowledge of magazines. My client, on the other hand, has only one editor dedicated to the project, besides me. I'll help hire a staff only if my client wins the bid.

I can picture walking into a conference room after the well-dressed, articulate rival team has finished its brilliant presentation. Gulp. What rhetorical device could I use to beat it?

Make your opponent's most positive words look like negatives.

I don't mean trashing them to the airline executives, calling them sissy intellectuals and making fun of their (terrific) shoes. Nor am I going to maintain that professionalism and editorial talent are bad. Instead, our team will pitch a magazine around one simple-sounding word:

▸ **Argument Tool**
DEFINITION JUDO: Use contrasting terms that make your opponents look bad.

"*fun*." The airline uses that word frequently in its materials. It likes to convey a spirit of egalitarian informality. So my clients and I will pitch a fun magazine—one filled with humor and pleasant surprises. Because the airline doesn't offer movies, we'll provide an "in-flight cinema" right in the magazine: tiny flip-book images that animate when you flip the pages' lower right corner.

TRY THIS AT A PUBLIC MEETING
If you want to attack a person's reputation without appearing to, say, "I'm not here to make personal attacks; I just want to . . . ," then name the opposite of your opponent's weakness. For instance, if you're debating a college professor who has a tendency to overtheorize, say, "I'm not got going to get personal; I just want to talk about the practicalities."

See what I'm doing? The competition defines a good magazine as "professional"—an approach that favors them. But I redefine the issue as "fun," using the corporation's commonplace and moving the argument to an arena where I have a fighting chance—while making the competition's professionalism actually work against them.

Imagine the discussion in the following days, when the airline's execs try to decide who should get the bid. They sit around the table with mock-ups of each bidder's proposed magazine. "I really liked the professionalism of that team that does that great magazine," says one exec. Everyone nods. Meanwhile, several of them thumb through our mock-up and watch the little flip-book flower spit out the bee. They fill in the space for "competitive doodling." (We'll give prizes for the best doodles sent in.) And they quietly show one another our funny plot summaries of current (real) movies. With any luck, "professionalism" will sound like a bad thing. And pop will go our rival's beautifully made balloon.

Will the technique win us the bid? Well, more goes into a pitch than that. But look how well defining the terms worked for Antony in Shakespeare's *Julius Caesar*. In his "I've come to bury Caesar, not to praise him" speech, Antony calls Brutus "an honorable man" so many times in the context of Caesar's assassination that "honorable" begins to sound like an accusation. The crowd is ready to tear Brutus from limb to limb for his honorableness.

Nuclear Commonplaces

You want to choose terms that favor you while putting your opponent in a bad light. That means using words that already carry a big emotional throw weight with your audience. Let's call them **commonplace words**—the key words that form commonplaces.

Look at the quotation at the beginning of this chapter. Mr. Burns is the owner of a nuclear power plant that has had an accident. He tries to define the issue by replacing "meltdown" with "unrequested fission surplus." "Meltdown" is a commonplace word, heavily laden with emotion; he swaps it for jargonistic terms that don't show up in any commonplace. They have almost no emotional effect. While we might object to his new terms, his dislike of "meltdown" is understandable. The term is burdened with so much connotative baggage that Burns feels compelled to swap it out. The words "chemicals" and "logging" have a similar negative connotation—unfairly in many cases. Where would we be without chemicals and wood? Yet you would have a hard time redefining either of these words for just about any audience except chemists and loggers.

> **Persuasion Alert**
> I'm trying to make my own issue, rhetoric, appeal to as broad an audience as possible. So when I talk about "defining" and "labeling"— terms that carry negative emotional baggage for many readers—I emphasize defense over offense. Notice how I use spare, oh-by-the-way language when I refer to attacking with commonplace words. The technical name for this technique of skipping over an awkward subject is *metastasis*. It's one of the more manipulative figures.

Your job as a persuader is to find the commonplace words that appeal most to your audience—or if you're on the attack, repel them. Politicians use focus groups to test terms like "reform" and "protection," which resonate with American voters—for now. Attach "reform" to enough pork legislation, though, and politicians may find themselves stuck with a negative commonplace word. You don't need focus groups to deal with smaller audiences. Just listen to the expressions people use, and spot the key persuasive words.

> We need to be more *aggressive*.
> Welcome to the *team*.
> If we *work smarter*, we'll *win*.
> I like him. He has a good *heart*.
> We need to change the *paradigm*.
> I can't *relate* to her way of working.
> Chalk it up to a *learning* experience.
> He was *traumatized* in his last job.

All of the italicized words reflect certain attitudes and come with varying emotional charges—all positive except for the last one. Don't call your new plan *innovative* if you hear the word "aggressive" repeatedly. Call it *aggressive*. Refer to your plan as a *team effort* that *changes the paradigm*. Of course, you don't have to speak like a cliché-programmed humanoid. I exaggerate for effect. Just remember to spot the key words and use them to define the issue.

Get Out of a Tough Scrape

An issue doesn't have to entail big, overarching political fights or global concerns. An issue is simply what your argument is about. The words people use to sum up an argument constitute the issue's definition: "It's about values." "It's about getting things done." "This is really about wanting to go out Saturday night." The rhetorical tenet that there are two sides to everything applies to issues as well: there are two descriptions to every issue.

Suppose you returned your rental car with big scrapes down each side. (I actually did this in Nice, France.) What's the issue? The agency will obviously call it an "operator error." The driver (me) can try to redefine the issue to one of "wrong equipment." What did the company mean by renting me a car too big for the Riviera's narrow, walled streets? That issue favored me. (Fortunately, I didn't have to use it. The worker in the return lot took one look at the car, gave a Gallic shrug, and sent me on my way.)

Look at other issues and their two-sided descriptions.

> *Abortion:* A baby's right to live, or a woman's right to her own body.
> *Gun control:* Our increasingly violent society, or a citizen's right to protect himself.
> *Borrowing the car:* A privilege, or a matter of fairness (big sister got to borrow it last week).

Political consultants—and just about everybody else these days—call this kind of issue definition "framing." A framing consultant lurks behind almost every candidate, and universities offer courses in the subject. But framing essentially follows the same rhetorical principles we have been talking about.

First, look for the most popular commonplaces among the persuadable audience—the undecideds and moderates. You might call this the bumper sticker phase of an argument. As always, the most persuadable audience is the one in the middle. If you happen to debate abortion, your most persuadable audience is the one that wants neither to ban all abortions nor to allow them without restriction. A good pro choice

> ▸ **Argument Tool**
> FRAMING: The same thing as defining an issue. Find the persuadable audience's commonplaces. Define the issue in the broadest context. Then deal with the specific problem at hand, using the future tense.

slogan might be "An Egg Is Not a Chicken" or "Make Abortions Safe and Rare." (Hillary Clinton and her husband, Bill, have been fond of the second one.) While "An Egg Is Not a Chicken" isn't exactly a household rule of thumb, it still counts as a commonplace in Aristotle's book, because it appeals to the commonsense notion that you can't make an omelet out of a chicken. The slogan also works to convey the image of an embryo as an egg and not something that moves and responds to you.

Once you have your commonplaces nailed down, you want to make sure that the issue covers as broad a context as possible—appealing to the maximum number of people with the widest ideological and institutional diversity.

To continue with the abortion example: the pro life movement did a wonderful job of attaching "culture of life" to the issue. This definition welcomed into the pro-lifers' big ideological tent everyone who happened to be alive. (Of course, the commonplace may cause some political discomfort among pro-lifers who also support the death penalty. Executing criminals has its political merits, but fostering a culture of life isn't one of them.)

The pro choice side likes to define the issue as one of government intrusion. That's fairly broad—many Americans are concerned about government intrusion—but still not as broad as "culture of life." Besides, the antiabortion movement managed to define the issue in positive terms (pro choice; pro culture of life), while the pro-abortion-rights crowd got stuck with a negative issue (antigovernment intrusion). In politics, "pro" usually beats "con." What's a poor advocate to do?

TRY THIS AT WORK
A broad context trumps a narrow one in a political situation; this includes office politics. Suppose the company wants to merge your department with one headed by an idiot. How should you define the issue? In terms of fairness? The manager's competence? Or your department's ability to produce more as an independent entity? Productivity is the broadest of the three issues, because it appeals to the widest array of company managers.

A wise one would separate the "rights" part of the equation from the "abortion" part. Rights are a positive thing, and a substantial majority of voters are indeed for abortion rights. Abortion, though, is a negative; and the same polls show that most voters are uncomfortable with it. So the most effective way to keep abortions legal is, paradoxically, to oppose them. The Clintons did just that with their slogan "Abortions Should Be Safe, Legal, and Rare." (Personally, I would leave out the "legal" part, since "safe" already implies it. But that's quibbling.) The issue turns from government interference to making abortions theoretically unnecessary. And when your audience thinks your stand will make abortions unnecessary, you have not just broadened the issue, you've solved it.

Am I just saying that activists appeal to a larger number when they moderate their stands? No, I'm saying that they expand their appeal when people *see* them as moderate. In the late 1990s, the pro-life movement abandoned most of its overt efforts to outlaw abortion altogether; instead, it worked around the edges, fighting late-term abortion and requiring parental permission for minors. The pro-lifers appealed to the commonplace that abortion is a bad thing, while avoiding the pitfall of rights. Meanwhile, some of the most prominent pro-choicers insisted on portraying abortion as another form of contraception. While neither side actually moderated its views—the pro choice people continued to oppose any restrictions on abortion, while most pro life organizations opposed any form of abortion—the choice crowd portrayed itself as extreme while the pro-lifers looked relatively moderate.

TRY THIS AT HOME
You can frame a family issue broadly by appealing to the values you know everyone shares. If your kids accuse you of working late too often, don't say, "That's what puts the meat on the table." The alternative, starvation, is probably unimaginable to well-fed children. Say instead, "I'm working late so we can go to Disney World."

You can understand why the decade from 1995 to 2005 saw a steady erosion of abortion rights, with clinics shutting down across the country.

But then it was the pro life movement's turn to look extreme. South Dakota passed a draconian law banning all abortions regardless of the mother's health or circumstances. A twelve-year-old girl raped by her father would have no choice under state law but to bear the child. Big rhetorical—and political—mistake.

Now Switch Tenses

After you choose your commonplaces and define the issue in a way that directly concerns the largest audience, switch the tense. Commonplaces deal with values, and values get expressed in the present tense. To make a decision, your audience needs to turn to the future. This isn't hard; just deal with the specific issue. Say you want abortions to be safe and rare. Now what? If you are a politician, you might want to support a ban on thirdtrimester abortions while allowing the "morning after" pill. On the other hand, a pro-life politician might advocate abstinence. Both positions deal with specifics of the issue, with concrete steps, and they take place in the future.

Advocates who give rhetoric its due—working the commonplaces, defining the issue in the broadest context, and switching from values to the future—increase their batting average. The country benefits as well. Out of sheer political self-interest, the advocates find themselves on the middle ground. Suddenly, an intractable, emotional, values-laden issue like abortion begins to look politically arguable. Making abortions rare is to the nation's advantage, as Aristotle would say. Now, what are the most effective (and politically popular) ways to make abortions rare? The answers might give the extremes of both sides a lot to swallow; on the left, pro-choicers would have to agree that abortion is a distasteful form of contraception. On the right, pro-lifers would have to allow some abortions.

Of course, they don't have to. They can stick to their guns. And remain unpersuasive.

The Tools

Defining an argument's *terms* and *issues* is like doing the reverse of a psychologist's word association test. You want to attach favorable words and connotations to people and concepts—a practice politicians call "labeling." When you define a whole issue, then you're "framing"—placing the whole argument within the bounds of your own rhetorical turf.

Here are the specific **techniques for labeling:**

> **Term changing:** Don't accept the terms your opponent uses. Insert your own.
>
> **Redefinition:** Accept your opponent's terms while changing their connotation.
>
> **Definition jujitsu:** If your opponent's terms actually favor you, use them to attack.
>
> **Definition judo:** Use terms that contrast with your opponent's, creating a context that makes them look bad.

Here are the **framing techniques**:

> First, find audience **commonplace words** that favor you.
>
> Next, define the issue in the **broadest context**—one that appeals to the values of the widest audience.
>
> Then, **deal with the specific problem** or choice, making sure you speak in the **future tense**.

The definition tools fall under the strategy of **stance,** the position you take at the beginning of an argument. If the facts don't work for you, define (or redefine) the issue. If that won't work, belittle the importance of what's being debated. If that fails, claim the whole argument is irrelevant. In sum, stance comes down (in descending order) to

> **Facts**
> **Definition**
> **Quality**
> **Relevance**.

13. Control the Argument

▲

HOMER SIMPSON'S CANONS OF LOGIC
Logos, inside out

A fool may talk, but a wise man speaks. — BEN JONSON

....

Enough with the care and feeding of your audience. You made it think you're a Boy Scout, insinuated yourself into its mood, put it in an ingenuous state, offered it the rich rewards of its own advantage, and plucked the beliefs and desires from its mind. Now let's use that audience to your own advantage. It's time to apply some *logos* and win our own goals.

The commonplace gives us our starting point. Homer Simpson employs a pair of them—the value of safe streets and his audience's presumed affection for the weak and nerdy—in a speech he gives to a group of Australians.

> *In America we stopped using corporal punishment and things have never been better. The streets are safe. Old people strut confidently through the darkest alleys. And the weak and nerdy are admired for their computer programming abilities. So, like us, let your children run wild and free, because as the saying goes, "Let your children run wild and free."*

▸ **Persuasion Alert**
I bring in Homer Simpson so often because *The Simpsons* satirizes America's social fallacies; its humor relies on twists of logic. You couldn't find a better set of examples in Plato.

The passage is doubly notable, for its logical use of commonplaces and its bold unconcern for the facts. If you want your streets to be safe and your nerds to be cherished, Homer says, don't hit your kids. (Whether Australians actually want their nerds to be cherished, and whether safe streets are an outcome of unhit kids, lie beyond our discussion at the moment.) Homer dangles before them the Advantageous Prize that every rational persuader should offer, and he struts confidently through the dark alley of his own ignorance.

For many of us, the most frustrating thing about an argument is the feeling that we don't know enough about an issue. That happens to be where *logos* shines, because it allows us to skip the facts when we have to, focusing instead on rational strategy, definition, and subtle tactics of manipulation.

Logos also works well in defense, since you don't have time to fact-check every argument. What do you say to a kid who swears she has finished her homework? How should you respond to a television commercial that attacks a candidate's war record? Is there any way to listen to talk radio and separate fact from fiction? The nastiest political ads, the most underhanded sales pitches, and the stupidest human mistakes all rely on our ignorance of logic.

Bad logic wastes time, and it ruins our health and our budgets. Children use it to torture their parents ("All the other kids get to"). Parents respond with bad logic ("If your friends told you to go jump in a lake . . ."). Doctors kill patients with it ("There's nothing wrong with you; the tests came back negative"). It can make you fat ("Eat all of it—children are starving in Africa"). Candidates base their campaigns on it (John Kerry: "Every American family has to live within their means. Their government should, too"). We even wage wars over bad logic ("If we pull out now, our soldiers will have died in vain"). Push polls—fake surveys with loaded questions—*are* bad logic ("Do you support government-financed abortions and a woman's right to choose?"). These are no mere logical punctilios. We're talking credit lines and waistlines, life and death, the future of human existence!

> ▶ **Persuasion Alert**
> *Hyperbole* is an incredibly useful figure (to coin a hyperbole); to make it easier to swallow, start small and work your way up—budget and diet, life and death, and the future of humanity. One Ivy League slogan—"God, man, and Yale"—got it backward. But perhaps they thought otherwise.

Excuse the hyperbole—which, by the way, is not necessarily illogical, despite what you learned in school or on *Star Trek*. My own logical education before college consisted entirely of Mr. Spock, who led me to believe that anything tainted by emotion or values was "illogical" and that my status as an Earthling got me off the hook. Vulcans could be logical; the rest of us were hopeless. This was fine with me, because his kind of logic was a one-man date repellant. But in rhetoric—and among some branches of formal logic—emotions do not a fallacy make. Mr. Spock, it turns out, was no philosopher. He was just a stiff.

The elementary logic taught in school is a step up from *Star Trek*, but it fails to apply to many real-life situations. One reason is that, while rhetoric helps us understand how humans communicate, formal logic has little use on this planet. Strictly logical argument, called *dialectic,* is mathematical and formulaic. While it trains the mind and can help you learn to spot fallacies, dialectic is too rule-bound to help you in daily conversation. In fact, some arguments that count as fallacies in formal logic are perfectly kosher in rhetoric.

In this chapter, we'll deal with formal logic—not formulaically, but in a way you can actually use. In the next two chapters, we'll get into specific fallacies and rhetorical fouls that bollix up our arguments.

Socrates and Sports Cars

You can already see that *logos* means more than just logic. Bible translators interpret it as "word." But the Greeks also applied *logos* to logic, conversation, delivering a speech, and all the words and strategy that go into an argument. The tools of *logos* let you apply facts (if you have them), values, and attitudes to a particular problem.

Rhetorical logic works differently than the logic taught in philosophy classes, thank God. Rhetoric is much less boring, for one thing, and far, far more persuasive. While philosophy scorns public opinion, in rhetoric, the audience's beliefs are at least as important as the facts. For persuasive purposes, the opinion of your audience is as good as what it knows; and what it *thinks* is true counts the same as the truth.

To show you how rhetorical logic works, I have to give you a brief—very brief—summary of the philosophical kind of logic, starting with that torturous device, the *syllogism.* You may have suffered from syllogisms sometime during your education. They're a widely used introduction to logic, and almost entirely useless in day-to-day conversation. Aristotle himself seemed committed to make the syllogism as boring as possible. Here's an example he himself used to illustrate it:

▶ **Meanings**
The gospel of John, written in Greek, begins, "In the beginning was *logos*"— in the beginning was the *word.* You could also translate the sentence as, "In the beginning was the *plan.*" The early Renaissance philosopher and rhetorician Desiderius Erasmus chose, "In the beginning was the *speech.*" Erasmus, who uncovered many of Cicero's writings in old libraries and monasteries, thought it perfectly natural for the Creator to talk, or even persuade, the world into being.

All men are mortal.
Socrates is a man.
Therefore, Socrates is mortal.

Many syllogisms have this "Well, duh" quality to them, but they make more sense if you see them thrown up on a screen. Marketers use a kind of syllogism all the time in Venn diagrams—those interlocking circles in PowerPoint presentations. Suppose the automotive designers at Ford came out with a new muscle car called the Priapic, designed to appeal to testosterone-challenged men aged twenty-five to forty. What's the size of the potential market? The Priapic marketing team pulls the stats and projects them as circles at the next managers' meeting. The biggest circle contains the annual number of car buyers; the second circle contains all twenty-five- to forty-year-old men; and the third shows the number of households with incomes that can afford a Priapic. The target is the overlap between youngish men and affluent households. The three circles form a syllogism: things slotted into categories to reach a conclusion.

Similarly, you could convert Aristotle's syllogism about Socrates into a Venn diagram. Make a big circle representing all mortals, place the circle for men inside it, and then a dot for Socrates within the men's circle. The market size of male mortals named Socrates totals one. Logicians call this sort of reasoning "categorical" thinking. Most political labeling falls under this kind of logic, with candidates trying to shove one another like sumo wrestlers into unflattering Venn circles. All Democrats are tax-and-spend liberals; my opponent is a Democrat; therefore, my opponent is a tax-and-spend liberal.

A second kind of syllogism comes from "if-then" thinking:

If most men aged twenty-five to forty read "lad" magazines, and
If ads in these magazines sell lots of cars,
Then we should advertise the Priapic in lad mags.

That's formal logic. Start with something true, follow it with another truth, and you reach a conclusion that also must be true. The rhetorical version works a little differently, since it concerns decisions instead of "the truth." Assumptions or beliefs—commonplaces—work just as well as facts. Our Priapic marketers could use the commonplace "Babes go for guys with the newest sports cars."

If babes go for Priapic drivers, and
If you go for babes,
Then you should buy a Priapic.

But that ad copy would appeal only to philosophy majors. Even the Greeks found syllogisms boring, because the middle line tends to be painfully obvious. One already assumes that the Priapic market is babe-prone.

Aristotle made rhetorical logic zippier by streamlining the syllogism, ditching the middle line and leaving out the "if-then" part. The result is a neat little argument packet called the **enthymeme**. It takes a commonplace—a belief, value, or attitude—and uses it as a first step in convincing the audience.

Let's apply Aristotle's enthymeme to the Priapic.

Babes go for Priapic owners.
You should buy a Priapic.

> ▸ **Argument Tool**
> THE *ENTHYMEME*
> (EN-THIH-MEEM):
> A logic sandwich that
> slaps a commonplace
> and a conclusion to-
> gether. "Enthymeme"
> means "something in
> the mind." It uses
> a commonplace—
> something in the
> audience's mind—to
> support a choice.

When a car ad portrays a pouty young woman, in other words, it simply employs Aristotle's enthymeme. The car ad, the enthymeme, and the tired old syllogism all fall under **deductive logic.** It starts with a **premise**—a fact or commonplace—and applies it to a specific case to reach a conclusion. "All men are mortal" is a general concept. "Socrates is mortal"—that's the specific case. Conclusion: "Socrates is mortal."

Inductive logic works the opposite way, taking specific cases and using them to prove a premise or conclusion:

> **TRY THIS WITH A**
> **PAPER OR MEMO**
> Use an enthymeme to
> nail down your central
> argument. Choose a
> commonplace or
> commonly accepted
> axiom and link it to
> your conclusion. "To
> gain more point-of-
> purchase awareness,
> we should simplify
> our logo." Now use
> that as an abstract on
> your title page.

Socrates, Aristotle, Cicero, and anyone else
    born more than a century and a half ago
    are dead.
[The enthymeme would skip the obvious line "All of them were
    human."]
Therefore, all humans are mortal.

Sherlock Holmes made deduction a household word when he applied commonsense principles—commonplaces—to his detective-story observations. In "A Scandal in Bohemia," Holmes guesses that poor, ingenuous

Dr. Watson had been out in the rain (in London? No way!) and that he had
an incompetent servant girl:

> SHERLOCK HOLMES: It is simplicity itself . . . my eyes tell me
> that on the inside of your left shoe, just where the firelight
> strikes it, the leather is scored by six almost parallel cuts.
> Obviously they have been caused by someone who has very
> carelessly scraped round the edges of the sole in order to
> remove crusted mud from it. Hence, you see, my double
> deduction that you had been out in vile weather, and that
> you had a particularly malignant boot-slitting specimen of
> the London slavey.

Leaving aside that passage's fetishistic tone, you
can see Sherlockian deduction working the way the
Aristotelian enthymeme does:

> If a shoe sole with scoring marks means
>   careless scraping,
> And if such careless scraping must be done
>   by an incompetent serving girl,
> Then a gentleman with a carelessly scraped
>   shoe has an incompetent serving girl.

▶ **Useful Figure**
The *paralipsis* ("leaving aside") mentions something by saying you're not going to mention it. It's the not-to-mention figure, as in, "Not to mention the fact that you snore like a buzz saw in bed." It makes you sound fairer than you are—denying you'll kick a man when he's down while digging a boot into his ribs.

Like Aristotle, Holmes skips the middle line—careless scraping equals
incompetent servant—because his snooty Victorian audience already knows
that.

Similarly, Annie could have used an enthymeme's deductive logic to talk
Kathy into voting for a Democrat.

> ANNIE: All politicians are alike when it comes to taxes; the
> only difference is that the Republicans won't admit it.
> Given two politicians, I'd vote for the more honest one.

Put it in a pair of syllogisms, and the logic works like this:

> If all politicians are alike on taxes, and
> If taxes are bad,
> Then all politicians are equally bad.

But:

> If the Republicans lie about raising taxes, and
> If lying is bad,
> Then the Republicans are worse than the Democrats.

Since Kathy presumably hates both taxes and lying, Annie can skip the middle line in each syllogism. Deduction is really quite elementary, as our smug detective would say. Take something the audience believes—a fact or commonplace—and apply that premise to a choice or conclusion that you want the audience to accept. Skip the part that goes without saying—taxes are bad, lying is bad—and voilà! An enthymeme.

Deductive logic starts with a general premise and works toward the specific, applying a fact or commonplace (all politicians are alike) to a situation (the election). The premise is the **proof.** The choice you want your audience to make is the **conclusion.** Every logical argument has a proof and a conclusion.

In deliberative argument, the conclusion is a *choice*—you can take your umbrella, or you can take your chances. The persuader bears the burden of proof; it's up to her to back up the choice she wants you to make. She can prove her point in two ways:

> **Examples** In this kind of argument, the evidence leads to either a
> premise or a conclusion. This is *inductive logic.* "Nine out of ten
> dentists recommend Dazzle toothpaste." The dentists are the
> examples. They comprise the proof. If they think it works, you
> probably will, too. On the other hand, if the ad said, "Nine out
> of ten toothless convicts recommend Dazzle toothpaste," you
> probably wouldn't buy it. The proof wouldn't stand up.
>
> **Premise** This is part of *deductive logic.* A premise is something the
> audience knows or believes.

So much for the proof. The conclusion in deliberative argument is a choice—what you want the audience to decide. Sometimes, though, you may find it hard to distinguish an argument's proof from its conclusion. Here are two ways to spot the proof.

If you already accept part of the argument, it probably constitutes the proof.

Eat your peas because they're good for you.

You already know that peas are good for you, so that's the proof. The choice is between eating your peas and not eating them. If you already planned to eat them, then you don't have an argument in the first place.

Another way to spot the proof is to look for the word "because." It usually heads up the reason: eat your peas "because they're good for you." Arguments often imply "because" without actually stating it.

Vote Republican and keep taxes down.

If you have trouble finding the reason in this argument, restate it with "because" in the middle. If the sentence makes no sense with "because" in it, then someone may be pitching you a fallacy. In this case, though, it works fine: "Vote Republican, because Republicans will keep taxes down."

▸ **Argument Tool**
PROOF SPOTTER:
A proof consists
of examples or a
premise. A prem-
ise usually begins
with "because,"
or implies it.

I think I'll use the "because" technique to abuse a pollster.

POLLSTER: Do you plan to vote Democratic and protect the middle class?

This is a classic example of a push poll, that sleazy argument disguised as a survey.

ME: You mean I should vote Democratic *because* that'll help the middle class?
POLLSTER: I'm not supposed to answer questions.
ME: I *only* answer questions. You didn't ask one.
POLLSTER: Yes, sir, I did. I said . . .
ME: You're right. Actually, you asked two questions. Do I plan to vote Democratic, and do I want to help the middle class? Now, which would you like me to answer?
POLLSTER: *[Click.]*

I had a deductive exchange recently with a subscriber to my blog. The woman, named Martha, objected to my accusing intelligent design advocates of "kidnapping God and forcing him to teach biology."

MARTHA: What issue do you have exactly with teaching *both* approaches, intelligent design *and* evolution, in school? Isn't this hijacking Darwin and forcing him to teach biology? Since when does being balanced mean believing in only ONE approach, belief, theory, etc.?

ME: Oh, I'm certainly for teaching both sides, whenever there are two of them. But in this case—creationism and biology—we're dealing with a logical fallacy: if intelligent design people refuse to name the designer, then they have an effect without a cause, a disconnect that Aristotle, pagan as he was, abhorred. If they *can* name the designer, then they're in the realm of faith, not science.

TRY THIS IN YOUR OWN ARGUMENTS Your opponent will often begin her argument with a commonplace, as Martha did. Try using concession, as I did. See if you can agree with her commonplace, then show how it fails to suit her conclusion. Teaching both sides is good, agreed. But creationism and biology are not two sides. They're the side of an apple and the side of an orange.

Martha had offered a good enthymeme: her premise—there are two sides to every issue—is a commonplace that she and I both hold. Her conclusion is that classes in evolution should teach the other side. I replied agreeably, conceding her point that students should learn two sides. But then I used deduction to prove that there *aren't* two sides—just two separate arguments, about science and faith. I gave her a pair of enthymemes—syllogisms with the goes-without-saying middle line left out.

If intelligent design people won't name the designer,
[And if every effect in a logical argument must have a cause,]
Then intelligent design isn't a logical argument.
If intelligent design people do name the designer,
[And if such a metaphysical designer must be outside the realm of science,]
Then intelligent design isn't science.

Did Martha see the error of her ways and become an ardent foe of intelligent design? I doubt it. She is way too smart for that. But I wasn't trying to convince her; my audience was the readership of my blog, a proudly geeky crowd that gets ecstatic at the sight of an exposed fallacy. The strange thing is, though, I *did* convince her—not about intelligent design, but about my blog. She had originally asked to unsubscribe, but changed her mind after reading my reply.

> MARTHA: That's a good argument. I do like to hear both sides . . . Please reinstate my membership.

Then she seduced me—rhetorically, I mean—through a little flattery.

> MARTHA: I laugh more than I am irritated when I receive your daily figure actually . . . Come to think of it I laugh very hard, and then my boss thinks I am really loving my job.

You could almost say that Martha beat me. While I won her back as a subscriber, she won me over, making me think twice before I trash the intelligent design people's intelligence again. See what a little agreeability can get you? And I think to myself, what a wonderful rhetorical world—at least until I read the next comment on my blog, which calls me a "Godless bastard."

I am *not* godless.

Mozart Induces Hell

Rhetorical deduction goes like this: *premise, therefore conclusion.* You believe this, so you should do that. That is an enthymeme. In Annie's case, I'm afraid that her enthymeme about all politicians being alike may not work. It has a problem with its commonplace: Kathy probably does not believe that all politicians are alike. She thinks that Democrats and Republicans are very different species. Annie will have to come up with some serious proof before she can sew doubts in Kathy's mind.

Once again, Aristotle comes to the rescue, with deduction's fraternal twin, induction. In rhetoric, inductive logic uses examples for its proof instead of commonplaces. Induction is great for when the audience's commonplaces don't work for you.

Induction would look like this in Annie's argument:

ANNIE: I live in a Republican state, and my taxes keep going up. Your own mayor is Republican, and look how much taxes have increased in your city. Plus, Congress keeps borrowing money. How do you think they'll pay for the deficit? It just shows that both parties raise taxes. The Democrats are simply honest about it. And given two politicians, I'll vote for the honest one.

> **Meanings**
> If you have trouble remembering the difference between inductive and deductive logic, consider their roots. Induction comes from Latin for "to induce" or "to lead." *Inductive* logic follows a trail, picking up clues that lead to the end of an argument. *Deduction* (both in rhetoric and expense accounts) means "to take away." Deduction uses a commonplace to pull you away from your current opinion. If that still doesn't work, skip the terms altogether and just use the argument tools you like.

That's inductive logic. Annie's examples prove that Republicans raise taxes. Therefore you should vote for the party that will not lie about it. Of course, Annie doesn't prove that the Republicans raise taxes as much as Democrats do. But that's for Kathy to argue.

You can combine deduction and induction to make an especially strong argument. In this case, your proof has two parts: examples and premise. Once again, we can observe Homer Simpson's logical pyrotechnics for illustration.

> **Meanings**
> The point you prove with examples is technically called a *paradigm*— a rule that you apply to the choice you want your audience to make.

HOMER: I'm not a bad guy! I work hard, and I love my kids. So why should I spend half my Sunday hearing about how I'm going to hell?

A splendid instance of logical induction as argument. Homer's examples—works hard, loves his kids—show he is not such a bad guy. Having established his nice-guy premise, he heads straight to his conclusion: church wastes his time. Whether the examples actually do prove his case is up to the audience. And God. But the logic works.

Homer recites **facts,** sort of. That's one kind of example.

But his examples are really more **comparison** than fact. Comparisons are the second kind of example. He works harder and loves his kids more than the average churchgoer.

> ▸ **Argument Tool**
> THE RHETORICAL EXAMPLE: Fact, comparison, or story.

Then there's a third kind of example, the **story**—jokes, fiction, fables, and pop culture. Most of the examples I use in this book fall in the story category.

Let's use all the logic we gained in this chapter. Suppose I want to persuade you to go to a poker game instead of the Mozart concert you had planned to attend. I start with an enthymeme:

> ME: You want to relax, right? Then there's no choice. You're going to play poker.

That's deductive logic. You want to relax. Therefore, let's play poker. I skip what would have been the middle line of a syllogism: poker is more relaxing than Mozart. You already knew that. But then again, maybe you didn't. Maybe I should use inductive logic—facts, comparisons, and stories—to shore up our premise that poker relaxes more than Mozart.

Fact:

> ME: You yourself said nothing's more soothing than a good cigar and a full house.

Comparison:

> ME: Do they let you drink beer during a Mozart concert? Huh? Do they?

Story:

> ME: I knew a guy who went to see *Don Giovanni* a few years ago. He suffers through the whole thing until right at the end, when he clutches his heart and slumps over dead. The last thing he sees before he dies is Don Giovanni getting sucked into Hell.

I suggest you try a similar argument on your significant other before

TRY THIS IN A PRESENTATION
Work up a logical outline. First, construct an enthymeme that uses something your audience believes in. It sums up your entire talk. The rest of the outline rests on inductive logic. List the facts, compare your argument with an opposing one, and include at least one anecdote that illustrates your point on the micro level. Go back and read Reagan's speeches, and you'll find that most of them use exactly this logical method. Or skip ahead to Chapter 23, where Cicero shows you how to outline a speech.

your next night out. Scope out your partner's commonplaces: do you hear the word "relax" a lot when you plan a date, or does the word "boring" repeat itself?

Now apply the commonplace to an argument packet: "Since *[commonplace]*, then we should *[your choice]*."

Throw in a few examples: fact, comparison, story, or all three.

Now button your lip, baby. Button your coat.

The Tools

The historian Colyer Meriwether says the American founders were masters at rhetorical *logos:* "They knew how to build an argument, to construct a logical fortress; that had been their pastime since youth. They could marshal words, they could explore the past . . . they had been doing that for years."

You now have the foundation to build your own logical fortress. Actually, it should be more like a logical mansion; the best persuaders are comfortable within their logic, and not afraid to let people in. Don't worry; we'll cover many more tools to make you feel more at home with logic.

We started with the basic tools of *logos.*

> **Deduction:** Deductive logic applies a general principle to a particular matter. Rhetorical deduction uses a commonplace to reach a conclusion, interpreting the circumstances through a lens of beliefs and values.
>
> **Enthymeme:** The logical sandwich that contains deductive logic. "We should *[choice]*, because *[commonplace]*." Aristotle took formal logic's syllogism, stripped it down, and based it on a commonplace instead of a universal truth.
>
> **Induction:** In rhetoric, induction is argument by example. This kind of logic starts with the specific and moves to the general. Whereas deductive logic interprets the circumstances through an existing belief—a commonplace—inductive logic uses the circumstances to *form* a belief. It works best when you're not sure your audience shares a commonplace.
>
> **Fact, Comparison, Story:** These are the three kinds of example to use in inductive logic.

DEFENSE

14. Spot Fallacies

▲

THE SEVEN DEADLY LOGICAL SINS

Ways to use logic as a shield

. . . who ever knew Truth put to the worse, in a free and open encounter?

—JOHN MILTON

....

HOMER: *Lisa, would you like a doughnut?*
LISA: *No, thanks. Do you have any fruit?*
HOMER: *This has purple in it. Purple is a fruit.* —*THE SIMPSONS*

....

Not all fallacies are hard to spot. Homer's is obvious—he mistakes a fruity color for the thing itself. It's the same fallacy as this one:

> *Elephants are animals. You're an animal. That makes you an elephant.*

Actually, this is just stupid, and no one would fall for it. The most insidious fallacies, on the other hand, seem valid until you take them apart.

There are dozens of logical fallacies; I collected the ones most common to daily life and organized them around seven logical sins. But while the sins will help you understand what we're talking about, you don't have to remember them—let alone the fallacies' formal names—unless you want to impress (and annoy) your friends.

All logical fallacies come down to . . . bad logic. In the logic of deliberative argument, you have the proof and a choice. We saw in the last chapter how deductive logic works; it starts with what the audience knows or believes—the commonplace—and applies it to a particular situation to prove your conclusion. In deduction, the commonplace serves as your proof. The proof in induction is a set of examples.

▶ **Persuasion Alert**
I committed a fallacy with "All logical fallacies come down to bad logic." As you'll see, that constitutes a *tautology*—repeating the same thing as if I'm proving something. Politicians love this trick.

So, to see whether a fallacy lies hidden in an argument, ask yourself three questions:

1. Does the proof hold up?
2. Am I given the right number of choices?
3. Does the proof lead to the conclusion?

I suppose I should add a fourth question:

4. Who cares?

Honestly, there's no need to care, provided you never fall for fallacies yourself. In fact, one big difference between formal logic and the art of persuasion is their attitudes toward the rules. Logical fallacies are verboten in logic, period. Commit one, and logic sounds the gong and you're booted off the stage. (Never mind that there is no stage for formal logic, which exists only in theory.)

In rhetoric, on the other hand, there really are no rules. You can commit fallacies to your heart's content, as long as you get away with them. Your audience bears the responsibility to spot them; but if it does, there goes your *ethos*. Your audience will consider you either a crook or a fool. So before you commit a fallacy, you will want to know your fallacies.

Besides, assuming that you have fallen for logical tricks like the rest of us, this chapter will come in handy as a defensive tool. An ability to detect a fallacy helps you protect yourself—against politicians, salespeople, diet books, doctors, and your own children. All you have to do is look for a bad proof, the wrong number of choices, or a disconnect between the proof and the conclusion.

Bad proofs include three sins: false comparison (lumping examples into the wrong categories), bad example, and ignorance as proof (asserting that the *lack* of examples proves something).

Wrong number of choices covers one essential sin, the false choice: offering just two choices when more are actually available, or merging two or three issues into one.

Disconnect between proof and conclusion results in the tautology (in which the proof and the conclusion are identical), the red herring (a sneaky distraction), or the wrong ending (in which the proof fails to lead to the conclusion).

I'll throw some fallacies in along the way, if only to show you I know what I'm talking about. The seven sins show the beautiful variety of ways that people cheat, lie, and steal. Just keep in mind that they all boil down to bad proofs, wrong number of choices, or a disconnect between the proof and the conclusion.

First Deadly Sin: The False Comparison

Plums and grapes are purple, but they don't make purple a fruit. You need not be an Aristotle to figure that one out. But how many consumers have fallen for the same kind of fallacy?

Made with all natural ingredients.

It may not seem like it, but the "all natural" pitch commits the "purple is a fruit" error: because an ingredient belongs to the same group as things that are good for you (natural substances, purple fruit), the ingredient also must be good for you. But botulism is natural, too, and not at all good for you. (Not to mention the sneaky syntax that implies a hyphen between "all" and "natural." Add a gram of grape pulp and a gram of wheat germ to a doughnut's chemical blend and voilà! All-natural ingredients. *Two* all-natural ingredients, to be exact.)

You can spot the **all natural fallacy** by breaking it in half. "This doughnut has purple, and purple is a fruit, so you should eat this doughnut." Purple's fruitiness constitutes the "reason."

But purple isn't a fruit, which means the proof doesn't hold up, and the argument is spoiled. If I said, "This doughnut has a grape jelly filling, grapes are fruit, so this doughnut is a fruit," the proof (grape jelly, grapes) would have been legit. But the argument would still be a fallacy. The proof, even a correct one, has to lead to the conclusion. Just because the doughnut

> **What Makes This a Sin**
> The examples don't hold up. Why? Because they were slotted into the wrong category. Imagine those Venn circles in the previous chapter. Purple is a big circle. Fruit is another big circle. Grapes fall in the overlap. But purple still won't fit entirely within the fruit circle. All the fallacies I listed under this sin have the same wrong-circle problem.

> **Meanings**
> One category of fallacy that I don't deal with is *ambiguity*, logic's version of "Eats shoots and leaves." The hyphen in "all-natural ingredients" commits this fallacy.

> **Common Fallacy**
> THE ALL NATURAL FALLACY: It assumes that members of the same family share all the same traits.

has fruit doesn't make the doughnut fruit. It's a false comparison.

Small children seem to have a passion for proofs, judging by their love of "Why."

> PARENT: Don't go into the living room.
> KID: Why?
> PARENT: Because the dog was sick.
> KID: Why?
> PARENT: Because your father fed it hot dogs from the table.
> KID: Why?
> PARENT: Go ask him.

That may explain their equal love of fallacious reasoning.

> KID: Why won't you drive me to school? All the *other* parents drive their kids to school.

Other parents drive their children; therefore you should drive me. The kid falsely compares her parents with all the others. What makes it false? For one thing, not all parents are chauffeurs; surely some make their kids take the bus. For another, her parents happen not to be the parents of the kid's schoolmates; what is good for those others may not be good for her. How does one respond? First, you might raise the child's self-esteem.

> PARENT: That was an Aristotelian enthymeme, dear!

Now squash her.

> PARENT: But I see Wen Ho at the bus stop every morning. And even if all the other parents drove their kids, your proof doesn't support your choice.

The kid may not understand a word you say, but she will eventually; and when she does, look out. You may

TRY THIS IN ACADEMIA
College administrators like to say each school is unique, but then they do all they can to imitate one another. In the eighties, Ivy League schools began favoring candidates interested in one thing rather than the well-rounded students of tradition, and the fad spread. An alumnus who objects to the policy could ask officials what other schools use that policy, and if the administrator offers his list with a smug tone, retort, "When my kids said, 'Everyone else does it,' I'd tell them, 'Don't you want to rise above the crowd?'"

▸ **Common Fallacy**
THE APPEAL TO POPULARITY: Because all the other kids get to, I should, too. The premise fails to prove the conclusion.

never win another argument. Meantime, if you feel especially obnoxious, name the fallacy: the **appeal to popularity,** which legitimizes your choice by claiming that others have chosen it. My children would rather suffer an old-fashioned caning than hear me label their fallacies.

If you simply used a parental cliché instead of logic, you yourself would be guilty of a similar fallacy.

> PARENT: What if all the other children's parents told them to jump off a cliff? Would you follow?

> ▸ **Persuasion Alert**
> What about persuasion by character? Isn't any appeal to *ethos* an appeal to popularity? Indeed it is. This is one of the logical fallacies allowed in rhetoric, as you'll see in the next chapter.

John Locke, the philosopher (and rhetoric professor!) who described many logical fallacies in the early 1700s, would call this shot a foul. The collective parents of an entire school are extremely unlikely to propose mass suicide, which makes your fallacy a **reductio ad absurdum,** reducing an argument to absurdity. You falsely compared being driven to school with jumping off a cliff. The proof crumbles and the conclusion collapses.

Logic can do more than save you from driving your kid to school. It can also save your life.

> ▸ **Common Fallacy**
> *REDUCTIO AD ABSURDUM:*
> Reducing an argument to absurdity. The premise is unbelievable.

> DRIVER: I don't have to slow down. I haven't had an accident yet.

Since there are no examples here—just one adrenaline-challenged driver—you know to look for a reason. He thinks he can speed safely because he has a good driving record. Does his proof lead to his conclusion?

Does the man's perfect record keep you safe? It may increase the likelihood of an accident-free trip, but weigh that against the guy's lead foot and, personally, I would take the bus. His claim is a form of false comparison; because what he did in the past is perfect, what he does in the future must be perfect, too. The official name for this logical error is **fallacy of antecedent,** but you probably won't have the presence of mind to trot it out at eighty miles an hour. Instead, try conceding.

> ▸ **Common Fallacy**
> THE FALLACY OF ANTECEDENT: It never happened before, so it never will. Or it happened once, so it will happen again. Another reply to the antecedent fallacy: "That's a long time to tease fate." Or for a certain audience: "Your karma must be terrible."

YOU: I'm sure you're a great driver, but going this fast scares me. So it's irrational. Humor me.

Or if you don't mind risking road rage on top of unsafe driving, give a snappy answer.

PROPER RHETORICAL REPLY: No one is DOA a *second* time!

> ▸ **What's Wrong with This Argument?**
> "My dog doesn't bite." That's a classic fallacy of antecedent.

Another sham comparison, the **false analogy,** bollixes up government across this great land of ours.

> ▸ **Common Fallacy**
> THE FALSE ANALOGY: I can do this well, so I can do that unrelated thing just as well.

CANDIDATE: I'm a successful businessman. Elect me mayor and I'll run a successful city.

So the guy made a lot of money in business. The problem is that City Hall is not a business. Many entrepreneurs have successful political careers, but at least as many do not. Entrepreneurs have learned the hard way that in public service, political skills count for more than business skills.

> ▸ **What's Wrong with This Argument?**
> When told I cut my own trees for firewood, a New Yorker gasped, "How can you make yourself do it? Someone told me they shriek when they fall." They do sometimes, but sounding human doesn't make them human. She committed a type of false analogy called *anthropomorphism.* You see this fallacy in reverse when people refer to sex offenders as "predators" and other criminals as "animals." It's a false analogy: because they act inhumanely, they must be another species.

PROPER RHETORICAL REPLY: I'll vote for you if you give me dividends and let me sell off my shares of the city.

False comparisons also cause very bad math.

YOU: Our profits rose by 20 percent this fiscal year.
PAL: What was your margin at the beginning of the year?
YOU: Twelve percent before taxes.
PAL: Wow, so your profit's 32 percent!

The proof is that your profits started at 12 percent and grew by 20 percent. So what's the problem? Twelve plus 20 equals 32, right?

The problem is called a **unit fallacy,** mistaking one kind of unit for another. People commit this error all the time in business. To avoid it, try to keep track of the difference between a piece of the pie and the whole pie.

I give you a piece that amounts to one-eighth of a pie.
Not big enough, you say. So I give you an additional tiny
sliver that measures just one-fifth the size of the first
piece I gave you. I'm not giving you a fifth of the pie,
am I? A percentage is a piece of the pie. A percentage

▸ **Common Fallacy**
THE UNIT FALLACY:
One apple plus
one orange equals
two apples.

of a percentage (20 percent of 12 percent profit) is not a fraction of the
whole. If this still confuses you, just stick to this rule: never add up percent-
ages without a calculator.

> PROPER RHETORICAL REPLY: That 20 percent was on top of
> 100 percent of our profit. So we actually made 120 percent!

A simpler version of the unit fallacy helps pad the profits on consumer
goods. This laundry detergent sells for less than that laundry detergent in
the same size box, which mysteriously weighs less. The unit cost—the
amount you pay per ounce of detergent—is actually more on the "cheaper"
box. The manufacturer hopes you don't notice, and that you fail to pay attention to the unit prices on the store shelves. My wife figured she was onto
that trick. One day she asked me to lug a huge box of detergent out of the
car trunk. The box was so large, you had to decant some of the stuff into a
smaller container so you could lift it up to the washing machine.

> ME: Why did you buy this?
> DOROTHY SR.: It's the super economy size. It's cheaper.
> ME: Than what?
> DOROTHY SR.: Than the smaller sizes. If you did more of the
> shopping, you'd know about these things.

That stung. I found a receipt from the previous month with a smaller
box of detergent on it. I went to the basement and read the box to see how
much it held. And then I found a calculator, which produced a very satisfying result.

> ME: Unless prices jumped dramatically this month, the super
> economy size costs 7 percent more per ounce than the
> regular size.
> DOROTHY SR.: Yes, but it's a larger box, so it works out as less
> expensive.

ME: No, dear, a larger box doesn't *make* something cheaper.
You would save money buying the smaller box.

DOROTHY SR.: Oh.

ME: So do you think maybe you're sorry for saying I don't
know these things?

DOROTHY SR.: Yes, I'm sorry. I'm very, very sorry. It's clear that
I don't have the math skills to do the shopping. From now
on, you'd probably better do it.

Oh.

Second Deadly Sin: The Bad Example

Not all proofs depend on a reason or a commonplace. Many use examples—facts, comparisons, or
anecdotes. You find numerous fallacies among bad
examples, or examples that fail to prove the conclusion. For instance, fallacies that misuse examples
keep security companies in business.

> **What Makes This a Sin**
> There's a disconnect
> between the examples
> and the choice. While
> the examples them-
> selves might be true
> and relevant, they
> don't actually support
> the choice.

PARENT: Seeing all those crimes on TV makes me want to
lock up my kids and never let them out.

The examples don't support the conclusion, because local television news—which depends on crime
for ratings—misrepresents the crime rate. The actual rates of most crimes have been dropping for
years, but perceptions of crime continue to rise. In
other words, the parent uses unrepresentative examples to reach her para-
noid conclusion. This is a fallacy called **misinterpreting the evidence.**

> **Common Fallacy**
> MISINTERPRETING
> THE EVIDENCE: The
> examples don't sup-
> port the conclusion.

PROPER RHETORICAL REPLY: Good! That'll keep a couple
more potential criminals off the streets.

An offspring of misinterpreting the evidence is
the **hasty generalization,** which reaches vast con-
clusions with scanty data.

> **Common Fallacy**
> HASTY GENERALIZATION:
> The argument offers too
> few examples to prove
> the point.

COWORKER: That intern from Yale was great. Let's get another Yalie.

The proof won't hold up. One example won't suffice to prove that the next kid from Yale will make a good intern. There are fifty-three hundred undergraduates at Yale, which makes the sample size of the company's intern experiment 0.019 percent of the study population.

PROPER RHETORICAL REPLY: Didn't that jerk in Legal go to Yale?

> **What's Wrong with This Argument?**
> "You don't have many black people in New Hampshire," a bigot said to me. "You'd think differently about them if you had to live with them." It's a standard-issue hasty generalization. Similarly, an argument that begins, "You have no right to argue . . . ," will often precede the fallacy: "because you're not black." A legitimate answer: "No, I'm not. But we're talking about race relations, not one person's relations."

Third Deadly Sin: Ignorance as Proof

Scientists and doctors often screw up logic by assuming that their examples cover all *possible* examples—a mistake appropriately called the **fallacy of ignorance:** what we cannot prove, cannot exist.

> **Common Fallacy**
> THE FALLACY OF IGNORANCE: If we can't prove it, then it must not exist. Or if we can't disprove it, then it must exist.

DOCTOR: There's nothing wrong with you. The lab tests came back negative.

PROOF: The lab tests are all negative. So . . .
CONCLUSION: Nothing is wrong with you.

But a logical chasm lies between the negative tests and perfect health. The proof doesn't support the conclusion. Never mind that you happen to be doubled over in pain and seeing spots; the doctor has no data of illness, so you must be well. The only way to respond to this illogical argument, other than throwing up on his shoes, is to suggest more examples.

> **What Makes This a Sin**
> Again, there's a disconnect between the proof and the choice. The examples—or lack of them—don't support the choice.

YOU: Then you must have tested for everything.
DOC: Well, not everything . . .
YOU: Did you test for beriberi?

DOC: You don't have beriberi.

YOU: How do you know?

DOC: There hasn't been a case of beriberi in the United States since . . .

YOU: But you didn't test for it. So I could be the first.

DOC: It *is* possible, though unlikely, that you may have one of several other diseases.

YOU: So what should we do?

DOC: We'll run some more tests.

You often see the same fallacy in reverse among unscientific types.

BELIEVER: Dude, I believe in extrasensory perception and UFOs because scientists have never disproved them.

PROPER RHETORICAL REPLY: They never disproved that the moon can talk, either.

BELIEVER: You think it can?

YOU: Never mind.

Fourth Deadly Sin: The Tautology

One of the most boring fallacies, the **tautology,** basically just repeats the premise.

FAN: The Cowboys are favored to win since they're the better team.

The proof and the conclusion agree perfectly, and there lies the problem. They agree because they're the same thing. The result is a tautology, a favored fallacy for political campaigns.

CAMPAIGN WORKER: You can trust our candidate because he's an honest man.

PROPER RHETORICAL REPLY: I don't trust you, so that makes your guy seem twice as shady.

▸ Common Fallacy
TAUTOLOGY: The same thing gets repeated in different words. Logicians call this fallacy "begging the question," but "tautology" is a better term. To most people, "begging the question" means asserting a conclusion without stating the premise. "The Republicans will win the White House next election" begs the question: Who will get the nomination? "Whoever wins that election will become president"— that's a tautology.

The tautology may seem like a harmless if knuckle-headed sin, but it can be used deliberately to lead you astray. I once lived in a town with a road that a developer named "Vista View." It had a view of a vista: a rubble-strewn parking lot. Was the developer ignorant, or sneaky enough to conjure the vision of a vista (to coin another tautology) in your head? The comedian Alan King loved to tell how his lawyer used a tautology to talk him into doing a will. "If you die without a will," the lawyer warned, "you'll die intestate!" Only later did he realize that "intestate" means "without a will." "In other words," King said, "if I die without a will, then I'll die without a will. This legal pearl cost me five hundred dollars!"

> ▶ **What Makes This a Sin**
> Another disconnect. The proof doesn't support the choice, because the proof *is* the choice.

Fifth Deadly Sin: The False Choice

Fallacies come in a number of flavors, but all of them suffer from a breakdown between the proof and the conclusion, either because the proof itself doesn't hold up or because it fails to lead to the conclusion. Here's another push poll that tries to exploit that confusion.

> ▶ **Common Fallacy**
> MANY QUESTIONS: Two or more issues get squashed into one, so that a conclusion proves another conclusion.

POLLSTER: Do you support government-financed abortions and a woman's right to choose?

Here you have a conclusion being used to prove an-other conclusion. It's a "When did you stop beating your wife?" kind of fallacy called **many questions,** in which two or more issues get merged into one. If I want people to think you beat your wife, I imply it by asking "when." I skip the first question and ask the second one. Similarly, the pollster's abortion survey presumes a single answer to two questions—that opposing government financing of abor-tions necessarily makes you pro life.

> ▶ **What Makes This a Sin**
> There may be nothing wrong with the proof, and the proof may lead to a choice, but the problem is that you're being given the wrong number of choices.

PROPER RHETORICAL REPLY: I support a woman's right to choose government-free abortions.

A related fallacy arises from a false choice. Suppose your company plans to produce a new line of lingerie for cats.

> MARKETING DIRECTOR: We can appeal either to the cat fancier or to the general consumer. Since we want to target our market, we obviously should limit sales to cat shows.
>
> PROOF: What's the reason? "We want to target the cat fancier."
> CONCLUSION: What's the choice? "We should focus on cat shows."

The reason fails to prove the conclusion, because it doesn't tell you whether shows are the best place to target the cat fancier. This is the fallacy of the **false dilemma:** the marketing director gives you two choices when you really have a slew of them. You could also sell the cute little catnip-impregnated negligees and garter belts in department store lingerie sections, on eBay, or at house parties.

> PROPER RHETORICAL REPLY: Do cat fanciers do anything but go to shows?

Choices aren't the only things that get fallaciously limited. So do proofs.

> LAWYER: My client's motorcycle helmet failed, leaving him with a permanent, devastating headache. This jury should find the manufacturer grievously at fault.

The proof checks out: helmet failed, guy has a headache. But did the helmet's failure *cause* the headache? Was it the *only* cause? The name for this fallacy is **complex cause:** more than one cause is to blame, but only one gets the rap.

▸ **What's Wrong with This Argument?**
"What did the president know, and when did he know it?" That famous Watergate question committed the fallacy of many questions. "When did he know it" implied Nixon's guilt by assuming he knew something about Watergate in the first place. Two issues are at stake here: First, did the president know anything, and if so, what? Second, if he knew something, when did he know it?

▸ **Common Fallacy**
FALSE DILEMMA: You're given two choices when you actually have many choices.

▸ **What's Wrong with This Argument?**
"You Can Help This Child, or You Can Turn the Page." This ad raised a bundle for charity, but it was a false dilemma. You may have helped the child already by putting money in the church collection plate.

▸ **Common Fallacy**
COMPLEX CAUSE: Only one cause gets the blame (or credit) for something that has many causes.

PROPER RHETORICAL REPLY: Should the helmet have had a label warning against driving a hundred miles an hour while cracking open a beer and talking on a cell phone? Because that's what the litigant was doing.

> ▸ **What's Wrong with This Argument?**
> "If you're so smart, how come you ain't rich?" This commits any number of fallacies, including complex cause. Lots of things can make you rich, and being smart is not a sufficient cause—not in my experience.

Sixth Deadly Sin: The Red Herring

At some vague point in history, some bad guys theoretically used strong-smelling smoked herrings to throw dogs off their scent. Hence the name of this fallacy, in which the speaker deliberately brings up an irrelevant issue. But since no one even knows what a red herring is, a more common name is sneaking into the lexicon: the **Chewbacca defense,** named after a *South Park* episode. A record label sues one of the show's characters for harassment after the man requests credit for a song the label plagiarized. The company hires Johnnie Cochran, who launches into the same argument that, *South Park* claims, he used for O.J.

> ▸ **Common Fallacy**
> RED HERRING, A.K.A. THE CHEWBACCA DEFENSE: It switches issues in midargument to throw the audience off the scent.

COCHRAN: Why would a Wookie, an eight-foot-tall Wookie, want to live on Endor, with a bunch of two-foot-tall Ewoks? That does *not make sense!* But more important, you have to ask yourself: what does this have to do with this case? Nothing. Ladies and gentlemen, it has nothing to do with this case! . . . And so you have to remember, when you're in that jury room deliberatin' and conjugatin' the Emancipation Proclamation *[approaches and softens]* does it make sense? No! Ladies and gentlemen of this supposed jury, it does *not make sense!* If Chewbacca lives on Endor, you must acquit! The defense rests.

> ▸ **What Makes This a Sin**
> Here the problem may not be with the proof or the conclusion at all. The problem is that they're the wrong argument— a distraction from the real one.

The show satirizes the rhetorical red herring that Johnnie Cochran held in front of the jury's noses: the glove that the prosecution said O.J. wore to kill his wife and wife's lover. "If the glove doesn't fit, the jury must acquit!" Nice Chewbacca defense. He hijacked the murder trial and made it revolve around one piece in a very large and confusing body of evidence. (The *South Park* Cochran's defense—and the one the real-life Cochran actually used in the O.J. trial—also qualifies as a *complex cause*.)

You would think that lobbyists go to some secret red herring school, because they base whole careers on it. Take the TV industry. The number of sex scenes on television has doubled over the past seven years, according to a Kaiser Family Foundation study—now five per hour on 70 percent of all network shows. Instead of admitting that every network is turning into the Porn Channel, industry flack Jim Dyke, executive director of the misleadingly named TV Watch, argued against government interference.

> DYKE: Some activists will only see another opportunity to push government as parent, but parents make the best decisions about what [TV] is appropriate for their family to watch and have the tools to enforce those decisions.

Dyke uses the **straw man** tactic, which ignores the opponent's argument and sets up a rhetorical straw man—an easier argument to attack. The interview was about TV's disgusting stats; rather than hire lobbyists to fend off legislation, the industry might consider policing itself. Instead, the lobbyist switches topics to "government interference."

▶ **Sneaky Tactic**
THE STRAW MAN:
A version of the Red Herring fallacy, it switches topics to one that's easier to fight.

PROPER RHETORICAL REPLY: Can you say that naked?

Seventh Deadly Sin: The Wrong Ending

> LIBERAL: Affirmative action is needed because campuses are so white.

The proof is fine: college campuses remain predominantly Caucasian. But does it support the choice? No. The real argument is over whether affirmative action works. The premise only proves that a problem exists—

assuming you think that a Waspish campus and un-educated minorities are a problem.

> POSSIBLE REPLY: Affirmative action is mostly needed to assuage our guilt.

▶ **Common Fallacy**
THE SLIPPERY SLOPE: If we allow this reasonable thing, it'll inevitably lead to an extreme version of it.

One of the fallacies that result from the sin of the wrong ending is called **slippery slope**: if we do this reasonable thing, it'll lead to something horrible. You hear it a lot in politics. Allow a few students to pray after class, and one day gospel ministers will be running our public schools. If Congress bans machine guns, pretty soon cops will be shooting hunters out of tree stands. But politicians aren't the only slippery slope culprits.

▶ **What Makes This a Sin**
The proof may be okay, but it leads to the wrong conclusion.

> PARENT: If I let you skip dinner, then I'll have to let the other kids skip dinner.

This argument is so weird, you wonder why so many parents use it. Letting one kid skip will not *cause* you to dismiss the other kids. What law of parenting says that every rule has to apply equally to every child? Come on, Mom and Dad, show a little logical backbone.

But the most common kind of reason-conclusion confusion mixes up cause and effect. Suppose your town cut education funding dramatically and student test scores plummeted the following year.

▶ **Try This in Any Argument**
One of the best replies to the slippery slope is *concession.* Seem to take your opponent's premise seriously, and solemnly oppose it. "I am adamantly against shooting hunters out of tree stands." The slippery slope has a built-in reductio ad absurdum. It practically ridicules itself.

> EDUCATION ADVOCATES: Budget cuts are ruining our children!

Where's the reason, and what's the conclusion? Figure it out by inserting "because."

> Because the district cut the budget, our children are being ruined.

Now you know the reason: the district cut the budget. Does the reason prove the conclusion? Did the budget cuts *cause* the bad grades? You see no proof of that. In fact, I doubt that scores would fall so soon. The education advocates in this case commit the same fallacy as Chanticleer, the rooster in the French fable who thinks his crowing makes the sun come up. The fallacy's official name is *post hoc ergo propter hoc*—after this, therefore because of this—but I call it the **Chanticleer fallacy.** Another example:

▸ Common Fallacy
THE CHANTICLEER
FALLACY, a.k.a. *POST
HOC ERGO PROPTER
HOC:* After this,
therefore because
of this. The reason
("This *followed* that")
doesn't lead to the
conclusion ("This
caused that").

> COLLEGE ADMINISTRATOR: Our newsletter is a big success. After we started publishing it, alumni giving went up.

The boost in giving followed publication of the newsletter. Does that mean the letter *made* giving go up? Not necessarily. Nonetheless, this fallacy is rampant in academia, which explains why alumni get showered with stupid college mailings.

> PROPER RHETORICAL REPLY: Congratulations! But the percentage who gave declined. Did the newsletter cause that, too?

Babies instinctively commit the Chanticleer Fallacy.

> BABY *(internal babbled monologue):* I kicked and got milk! I'll kick again and get more!

So do governments, with potentially disastrous results.

TRY THIS BEFORE
YOU HIRE
SOMEONE
Scan a résumé's
list of accomplish-
ments for possible
Chanticleer crow-
ing, then probe for
them in the inter-
view: "It says here
that profits rose
by 48 percent the
year after you
were hired. So you
think your work as
a stock boy made
all the difference?"

> GOVERNMENT *(external babbled monologue):* We ran up the deficit and the economy improved! We'll increase the deficit more and the economy will get even better!

And so do superstitious types.

> JEREMIAH: That hurricane wiped out a whole city. See what happens when you allow gay marriage?

Crow on, Chanticleer, and fill your lungs to the glory of the sun. But don't let it go to your head.

The Tools

Samuel Butler, a seventeenth-century author, loved neither logic nor rhetoric. He wrote a poem abusing an imaginary philosopher who was good only at splitting hairs.

> *He was in logic a great critic,*
> *Profoundly skill'd in analytic;*
> *He could distinguish and divide*
> *A hair 'twixt south and south-west side.*

There are scores of hair-splitting logical fallacies; I focused on the ones that infest politics and your daily life, and grouped them into seven sins. My list of seven logical sins can be boiled down still further, to just three:

Bad proof
Bad conclusion
Disconnect between proof and conclusion

1. False Comparison: Two things are similar, so they must be the same. The *all natural fallacy* falls under this sin: some natural ingredients are good for you, so anything called "natural" is healthful. The *appeal to popularity* makes another false comparison: other kids get to do it, so why don't I? *Reductio ad absurdum* falsely compares a choice with another, ridiculous choice. The *fallacy of antecedent* makes a false comparison in time: this moment is identical to past moments. I've never had an accident, so I can't have one now. The closely related *false analogy* joins apples to oranges and calls them the same. Because gay men are sexually attracted to other men, we should keep them out of the classroom—they must be pederasts as well. Finally, the *unit fallacy* does weird math with apples and oranges, often confusing the part for the whole. Violent crime dropped by 5 percent last year, and by another 8 percent this year, so it dropped a total of 13 percent. A part of a part gets confused with a part of the whole.

2. Bad Example: The example that the persuader uses to prove the argument is false, unbelievable, irrelevant, or wrongly interpreted. The *hasty generalization* uses too few examples and interprets them too broadly. Michael Jordan uses these sneakers; buy them and you'll become a basketball star.

A close relative is the fallacy called *misinterpreting the evidence*. It takes the exception and claims it proves the rule. That guy lost weight eating Subway sandwiches. If you eat at Subway, you'll lose weight!

3. Ignorance as Proof: In this case the argument claims that the *lack* of examples proves that something doesn't exist. I can't find any deer, so these woods don't have any. The *fallacy of ignorance* has its flip side: because my theory has never been disproved, it must be true. Just about any superstition falls under this fallacy.

4. Tautology: A logical redundancy in which the proof and the conclusion are the same thing. (We're here because we're here because we're here because . . .) We won't have trouble selling this product because it's easily marketable.

5. False Choice: The number of choices you're given is not the number of choices that actually exist. The *many questions* fallacy is a false choice; it squashes two or more issues into a single one. (When did you stop beating your wife?) A related fallacy, the *false dilemma*, offers the audience two choices when more actually exist.

6. Red Herring: This sin distracts the audience to make it forget what the main issue is about. A variant is the *straw man fallacy*, which sets up a different issue that's easier to argue. ("Who drank up all the orange juice?" "Well, you tell me why the dishes aren't done.")

7. Wrong Ending: The proof fails to lead to the conclusion. Lots of fallacies fall under this sin; one of the most common is the *slippery slope*, which predicts a dire series of events stemming from a single choice. (Allow that newfangled rock music, and kids will start having orgies in the streets.) Another is *post hoc ergo propter hoc*, the *Chanticleer fallacy*. It assumes that if one thing follows another, the first thing caused the second one.

15. Call a Foul

▲

The pitfalls and nastiness that can bollix an argument

Rhetoric is an open palm, dialectic a closed fist. — ZENO

M y first experience in debating was in junior high school. We didn't have a debating team; this was more like a Lunch Period Repartee Society. My friends and I sat in the cafeteria and amused ourselves by arm-wrestling over half-melted slabs of ice cream; when we tired of that game, we turned to another, equally intellectual pursuit called "If You Do That." The object was to threaten each other with such elaborately disgusting harm that the loser wouldn't be able to finish his lunch. It was like snaps, the game of bantering insults, except that we didn't insult each other. We just grossed each other out.

▸ **Meanings**
Philosophers call the mannerly dialogue of formal logic *dialectic*. It's like the figures in figure skating: precise, self-contained, and boring. Zeno, the ancient Greek philosopher-mathematician, contrasted dialectic's "closed fist" with rhetoric's "open palm."

If you do that, I'll dig out your eyeballs and shove them . . .

I'm sorry, but it is impossible to describe this game without alienating the reader, and myself for that matter. The point is that we used our thirteen-year-old wit competitively in a classically useless and time-wasting fashion. Without knowing it, we mimicked some of the early Sophists, who included the sleaziest rhetoricians. They argued simply to win arguments, using logical and pathetic trickery to tie their opponents in knots. This is where the term "sophistry" comes from, and how rhetoric got its less than stellar reputation. These argumentative types were out to win, not deliberate. In rhetoric, that constitutes the biggest foul of all: to turn an argument into a fight.

Fighting also happens to be practically the only foul you *can* commit in rhetoric. In sports they say it's only a foul if the ref blows the whistle; the same is true in argument. When someone commits a logical fallacy, it rarely helps to point it out. The purpose of argument is to be persuasive, not "correct." Pure logic works like organized kids' soccer: it follows strict rules, and no one gets hurt. Argument allows tackling. You wouldn't want to put yourself in a game where the opposing team gets to tackle while your team plays hands-off. That's what happens when you stick to logic in day-to-day argument; you play by the rules, and your opponents get to tackle you. While it is important to know how to spot and answer a logical fallacy, if you limit yourself to simply pointing them out, your opponents will clobber you. Rhetoric allows logical fallacies, *unless* they distract a debate or turn it into a fight.

So long as you stick to argument, making a genuine attempt to persuade instead of win, rhetoric lets you get away with many fallacies that formal logic forbids. Take this old-time family argument.

> PARENT: Eat everything on your plate, because kids are starv-
> ing in *[insert impoverished nation]*.

The parent commits the logical sin of the wrong ending: the proof fails to lead to the choice. Eating everything is unlikely to end starvation in the Third World; in fact, a kid can point out that the opposite might be true.

> CLASSIC WISE-ASS REPLY: Well, hey, let's send them my vege-
> tables. I'll help pay postage.

My children love to talk back like that, which is my own fault. Proud as I am that they know how to handle a fallacy, I have been a lenient parent, rhetorically speaking. But you can do more than just recognize fallacies. In rhetoric, it's actually kosher to use many of them in your own arguments. Strangely enough, while logic forbids illogical thinking, rhetoric allows it.

▸ **Common Fallacy**
THE FALLACY OF POWER: The person on top wants it, so it must be good. This logical fallacy is fine to use in argument.

The kids-are-starving angle, for example, is rhetorically wrong only if it fails to persuade. That's because, nonsensical as the argument is logically, it makes *emotional* sense. The parent uses it not to end starvation but to make his child feel guilty. So while not a logical argument, it makes a decent pathetic one—provided the kid misses the fallacy.

Here's another logical mistake, which I deliberately excluded from the seven deadly logical sins: the **fallacy of power.** Because the guy in charge wants it, this fallacy says, it must be good.

> COWORKER: Hey, if the boss wants to do it, I say we should do it.

Does the boss's inclination make the choice a good one? Besides, what does she have underlings for? Surely not to think.

> PROPER RHETORICAL REPLY: Are you making a good decision or just being a suck-up?

But back up a second. Was that response really fair? What if the boss is smart and knows the business better than anyone else? Is it such a bad idea to trust her decision? The appeal to authority is a logical fallacy but an important *ethos* tool. If your boss thinks it wise to relocate the company to Anchorage, and you know her to be a savvy businesswoman, then you have a decent probability that Anchorage is a good idea.

This is where pure logic and rhetorical *logos* part ways. In most cases, there are no right or wrong decisions in argument; there's only likely and unlikely. We find ourselves back in the misty realm of deliberative argument, where black-and-white becomes the Technicolor of probability. If the boss's inclination makes the decision seem more legitimate, then your colleague has a good reason to try it on you. After all, he is not trying to persuade the boss; he's talking to *you*.

Logically inclined parents (no, that is not an oxymoron) usually call a fallacy when a kid uses a peer as an authority.

> KID: My friend Eric says Mr. LaBomba is a mean teacher.
> PARENT: Just because Eric says he's mean doesn't mean it's true.

But do we really deal with the truth here? The kid states an opinion, not a fact. Aristotle might actually back her up, since in deliberative argument the consumer makes the best judge. If she can convince her parent that Eric is a psychological prodigy, then the probability of Mr. LaBomba's meanness goes way up.

> KID: Oh, yeah? Well, remember when Eric said there was
> something sneaky about Miss Larson and the cops caught
> her stealing money from all the other teachers and she
> went to jail?

Eric is starting to look like a pretty good forensic psychologist. If I were the parent, I would keep an eye on Mr. LaBomba.

The essential difference between formal logic and rhetoric's deliberative argument is that, while logic has many rules, argument has but a few. Actually, it has just one rule, with a few ramifications.

Never argue the inarguable.

In other words, don't block the argument. Anything that keeps it from reaching a satisfactory conclusion counts as a foul.

Imagine a game of no-rules soccer, where the field has no bounds, you can body-check and tackle any way you want, and all you have to do is get the ball past the goalie. Even though things might get rough, as long as everybody has the right attitude, the game is playable. But what if players went beyond body-checking and started kicking one another in the groin? Or worse, stopped to take calls on their cell phones? Then the game would deteriorate. Alternatively, if there was only one ball and a player picked it up and took it home, that would end the game altogether. Even a "no-rules" game has a few minimal rules: you need a ball and goals, and the players have to play.

The same thing goes for argument, only without the ball. You need goals, and everyone has to remain intent on real persuasion. Things can get a little rough—you might have some logical horseplay, an ad hominem attack or two, some intense emotions, crude language, even—but the game continues. The argument can reach its conclusion so long as no one fights

▸ **Meanings**
Ramification is an eponym—a word named after a person. Petrus Ramus was a sixteenth-century French rhetorician who banished logic from rhetoric. A strict Calvinist who believed that only God and truth could rule us, he emasculated rhetoric by dividing it into dysfunctional academic departments. In short, Ramus *ramified.* French authorities had him burned at the stake as a heretic.

or distracts. In rhetoric, fighting and distracting constitute the same foul: in each case it means arguing the inarguable.

I love rhetoric's refreshing lack of rules. It forgives your logical sins. It says to humanity, Don't ever change, you're beautiful. Any sort of discourse that required reforming humans would make me hide in my cabin. Idealists who begin sentences with, "Can't we all just . . ." should have their guitars smashed and their flowers trampled. I don't want to buy the world a Coke and live in perfect harmony; harmony means unanimity, and history shows that unanimity is a scary thing. I'd prefer to play rhetoric's no-rules game with just a few rules.

> **Persuasion Alert**
> Who said anything about buying the world a Coke? I set up an idealistic straw man to make my no-rules argument sound more reasonable.

Fine Nixonian Rhetoric

In deliberative argument, the only real foul, arguing the inarguable, makes the conversation grind to a halt or turn into a fight. Take this next quote, which, like the last one, commits the sin of the wrong ending; the proof fails to lead to the choice.

> **Useful Figure**
> The *yogiism* ("no-rules game with just a few rules") is a figure of logical nonsense named after the immortal baseball manager Yogi Berra, the man who said, "No one goes there anymore. It's too crowded."

If we pull out now, our soldiers will have died in vain.

The proof is the supposed endgame—soldiers dying for nothing. (You can find it by planting "because" in the sentence: "We shouldn't pull out now, because that means our soldiers will have died in vain.") The choice is to pull out or not to pull out. But the proof fails to lead to the choice. We have a real cause-and-effect problem here. Will continuing the war add meaning to the soldiers' sacrifice? Yes, but only if continuing the war leads to victory, and the quote says nothing about the likelihood of success.

When corporate types commit this fallacy, they throw good money after bad. A corporation buys a rotten company and then pours money into the lousy merger for fear of wasting the money it already spent.

> **Common Fallacy**
> GOOD MONEY AFTER BAD: Trying to rectify a mistake by continuing it. A logical fallacy, but you can use it pathetically without breaking rhetorical rules.

Householders do it, too. A guy brings home a pricey flat-screen television and discovers he can't hang it on his wall. So he spends another thousand on a custom-made shelf. But the TV is a lemon, and he returns it, only to find that the company has discontinued that model and all the replacements are a different size. So he returns to the cabinetry store . . .

TRY THIS IN A MEETING
When someone says of a losing investment, "After all we put into it, we can't stop now," ask him: "If it were a double-or-nothing bet, do you think the odds would be good enough to take it?"

You can see why you want to recognize a logical fallacy when it hits you. But while fallacies will gum up formal logic, they can help you in an argument. As with the kids-are-starving chestnut, you can use it as a legitimate pathetic appeal. Mr. Spock's formal logic forbids emotion, while rhetoric encourages it. Most people can't bear the thought of abandoning a war in which citizens gave their lives. As long as you stay in the future tense and focus on the likelihood of victory, you still follow the lax rules of rhetoric.

In fact, a good rebuttal can use the same pathetic weapon.

> RHETORICAL YOU: Don't you dare talk about our soldiers dying in vain! By successfully ending the war, we'll be *honoring* our dead soldiers.

Notice how I changed the definition of "pulling out" from an ignominious disaster to a sort of victory. Pretty neat trick. Nixon used it to great effect in Vietnam. The logician will have a conniption over this, but deliberative argument, unlike logic, doesn't seek the truth—only the best choice. If changing the definition helps the audience decide whether to support a war, then your "fallacy" is no foul.

Consider the effect that a purer, more logically correct response might have on your audience.

> LOGICAL YOU: That's a fallacy! If the war effort fails, then many more soldiers will have died in vain.

This solid logical response risks making you look cold and heartless. Real deaths are more wrenching than theoretical ones. Besides, calling a foul here is like getting mad when someone bumps you in ice hockey. Don't expect an apology.

Spock for President

Take another logical fallacy that's good rhetoric: the appeal to popularity.

> KID: All the other kids make fun of me for taking the bus. They think I'm weird.

Instead of *logos*, the kid makes a pathetic appeal. It could actually work on some besotted parents. But the more rhetorically inclined might choose an unsympathetic response.

> PROPER RHETORICAL REPLY: Ridicule builds character. So does riding the bus.

▸ **Persuasion Alert**
It would have been more forthright to put fallacies in the "Advanced Offense" section. But a persuader has to start with what the audience believes, and few audiences consider the fallacy a legitimate offense.

You have just left the pure and noble realm of *logos* and wandered into the seedier neighborhoods of *pathos* and *ethos*—the terrain of emotional manipulation and ad hominem attacks, where rhetoric feels right at home. *Logos* alone rarely inspires commitment. And a tactic that wins a logical argument will almost certainly lose a political one. Michael Dukakis demonstrated this principle during the 1988 presidential campaign, when he gave a disastrous answer to a vicious question. Bernard Shaw, the moderator, asked Dukakis to imagine someone perpetrating a sex crime against his wife.

> SHAW: Governor, if Kitty Dukakis were raped and murdered, would you favor an irrevocable death penalty for the killer?
> DUKAKIS: No, I don't, and I think you know that I've opposed the death penalty during all of my life.

Why, no, Mr. Shaw, thank you for asking . . . What planet was that guy on?

The planet Vulcan, obviously. Dukakis already had a reputation as the Mr. Spock of politics, and his cool, reasonable response only confirmed that he was all *logos* all the time. Up to that point, Dukakis led in the polls. Pure logic may have cost him the election.

▸ **Useful Figure**
The *paraprosdokian* (pa-ra-proze-DOKE-ee-an) ("the planet Vulcan") attaches a surprise ending to a thought. The composer Harold Arlen used it when he said, "To commit suicide in Buffalo would be redundant."

TRY THIS IN AN ARGUMENT
When someone takes offense at what you said, try this neat little concession: "I'm sorry. How would you have put it?" Instead of getting defensive, you put your own words in her mouth.

So what should he have said? Should he have pointed out Shaw's blatant fallacy? After all, the question was a reductio ad absurdum, because it is extremely unlikely that Kitty Dukakis would ever suffer such a crime. But merely pointing out the fallacy, or responding like an automaton as Dukakis did, fails to persuade. Being in the right may make you feel noble, but being persuasive gets the rhetorical job done.

Dukakis would have done a much better rhetorical job by getting strategically angry.

RHETORICAL DUKAKIS: Mr. Shaw, I find that question offensive. That's just the kind of sleaze that's ruining politics today. You shouldn't bring my wife into this, and I think you owe me an apology.

Shaw probably would have apologized. You might call Rhetorical Dukakis's tactic a red herring, but it need not be one. Once he gained the higher moral ground, he could define the issue to his own advantage.

RHETORICAL DUKAKIS: Now, let's talk about the death penalty without getting personal about it. The death penalty isn't supposed to be about personal revenge—it's supposed to reduce crime. And you know that executing criminals has failed to reduce crime.

This approach would have made him look strong, passionate, and reasonable all at once—an *ethos* trifecta.

On the other hand, anything that constitutes arguing the inarguable counts as a rhetorical foul. Let's look at a few.

Foul: Wrong Tense

GOOD POLITICIAN: We need to figure a way to deal with the skyrocketing cost of elderly care so future generations can continue to take care of our seniors.

BAD POLITICIAN: You're attacking our senior citizens, and that's just wrong!

Unless the Bad Politician gets right back to the future, the argument is dead on arrival. If he actually does switch to the future tense, then he redeems himself rhetorically.

REDEEMED POLITICIAN: We shouldn't talk about seniors in isolation. Everybody should bear the burden of government expenses. So I propose a broader discussion of the federal deficit.

It's okay to use sermonizing, demonstrative rhetoric in a deliberative argument to get the audience on his side, but then the persuader should instantly switch to the future tense. This isn't just because Aristotle said so. It is simply more difficult to use the present tense to make a choice about the future. If your opponent insists on sticking to the present or past, call the foul.

TRY THIS IN A PUBLIC MEETING
The answer to the Bad Politician's "That's just wrong!" could be "Thanks for the moral lesson. But since when is it immoral to save taxpayers' money while helping our seniors?" It's another form of concession: grant the moral issue and restate your proposal in highly moral terms. Then it helps to restore the debate to the future tense: "Now can we stop being holy for a minute and talk about fixing the problem?"

YOU: Let's get beyond all the blaming and sermonizing. These folks want to know how we're going to deal with the issue.

Avoiding the future can really mess up your home life. For instance, whenever my wife wants to remind me of how clueless I am as a husband, she brings up the Evening Class Incident. Many years ago, Dorothy Senior casually mentioned over dinner that her twin sister, Jane, was learning ballroom dancing; Jane's husband had signed them up for classes. Taking the hint, I arranged for Dorothy and me to take an evening class, too—in computer programming. It was a great course, and we both got an A in it, but she remembers it as a less than positive experience.

DOROTHY SR.: I've never forgiven you for that. How romantic!
ME: You never said anything about romance. I heard "evening class," so I signed us up for a class.

DOROTHY SR.: In computer programming.

ME: I took the wrong hint. I apologized back then, and I remain sorry. So—want to learn ballroom dancing?

DOROTHY SR.: You just don't get it, do you?

> **Persuasion Alert**
> I'm writing in the
> past tense about
> my wife's failure to
> use the future
> tense. That puts me
> on shaky ground,
> both rhetorically
> and maritally. But
> we had this dia-
> logue a while ago;
> since then we've
> both learned to
> stop at "I'm sorry."

No, I didn't get it. I couldn't, because she made it
impossible. She would see any romantic attempt at this
point as unromantic. Besides, we were in inarguable
territory. I tried to change the conversation to the future
tense ("Want to learn ballroom?") and she wrenched it
right back to the sermonizing present ("You just don't
get it").

That same accusation became a feminist slogan during the Clarence Thomas hearings, when the judge's
allegedly sexist past threatened his nomination to the
Supreme Court. Feminists were outraged that the men
on the Senate Judiciary Committee grilled Thomas's accuser, Anita Hill, as
if she were a hostile witness. "They Just Don't Get It" became a rallying cry,
giving many women a feeling of solidarity. It was great demonstrative, present-tense rhetoric, but it failed to solve anything. Only a future-tense, deliberative slogan might have done that:

How will we make them get it?

That makes an inferior bumper sticker, admittedly, but it might have inspired women to work on one jerk at a time. Meanwhile, my wife's "You just
don't get it" got us nowhere. How to respond? I could call the foul.

RHETORICAL ME *(looking hurt):* You've proven you married an
insensitive fool. What are you going to do about it?

Whoa, that's extreme. But I mean it to be. By exaggerating her emotion,
I use the same pathetic device she often uses on me. It works, too.

DOROTHY SR.: Oh, you're not all that insensitive. I *love* being
married to you.

ME: Fool. I said "insensitive *fool.*"

DOROTHY SR.: Mmm-hmm.

I'll declare victory here, even if she did have to get in another dig. I probably deserve it. But we still can't dance.

Foul: The "Right Way"

This foul is closely related to avoiding the future, because it sticks to values—covering Right and Wrong, Who's In and Who's Out—instead of the main topic of deliberative argument, the Advantageous.

Dorothy Senior will not want me to mention this, but one of our longest-running arguments has to do with canned peaches on Christmas Eve. For years, she insisted on serving not just peaches, not some other kind of canned fruit, but *canned peaches* with our Christmas Eve dinner.

> ME: None of us particularly likes canned peaches. *You* don't like canned peaches.
>
> DOROTHY SR.: It's what we always had on Christmas Eve.
>
> ME: It's what *you* had when you were a kid. *We* had franks and beans, and you don't see me clamoring for weenies during the holidays.
>
> DOROTHY SR.: It's tradition, and that's all there is to it.
>
> ME: Why can't we start a new tradition? Like fresh pears, or single malt scotch?
>
> DOROTHY JR. *(getting into the spirit):* Or M&M's!
>
> DOROTHY SR.: If it's new, it isn't a tradition.
>
> ME: We're celebrating the birth of Jesus! A Christian tradition that began with . . . *a new baby.*
>
> DOROTHY SR.: Can't we just enjoy Christmas the right way, without arguing about it?

TRY THIS WITH A STUBBORN OPPONENT
When someone says, "There's a right way and a wrong way," and then tells you your way is wrong, bring up examples of when your opponent's way has failed, and say, "If that's the right way, I think I'll go with wrong." Call it the "If loving you is wrong, I don't want to be right" defense.

The "right way" precludes a choice; without choice you have no argument; and therefore it's a rhetorical foul. When your opponent commits one, you have several choices. You can call the foul.

ME: The "right way" would be a dish that makes everyone happy. Why don't we start a new tradition—one that our children can use to torture their spouses someday?

Or you can bring the argument to an abrupt close—take the ball away, if you will.

ME: If we can't have a discussion that gets us somewhere, there's no use in talking to you.

Or you can decide that marital relations have precedence over getting your way all the time. This is the option I took: I shut up and ate my peaches. Which, to my surprise, proved to be persuasive. Dorothy was so pleased she had won that, the following Christmas Eve, she served peach pie. It became the new tradition.

Five Good Reasons

If you stick to the present tense when you're supposed to make a choice, or if you talk only of Right and Wrong when the argument should be about what's the best choice, you commit a foul. Don't take me for a hypocrite here. Sticking to the present tense and to values is not wrong. It just makes deliberative argument impossible. You can't achieve a consensus; you can only form a tribe and punish the wrongdoers.

Another way to foul up deliberation is to argue for the sake of humiliating an opponent. This, too, is demonstrative, present-tense, I'm-one-of-the-tribe-and-you're-not rhetoric. Here's a good example of humiliation—from *The Simpsons,* of course.

LENNY: So then I said to the cop, "No, *you're* driving under the influence . . . of being a jerk."

TRY THIS WITH A SOPHIST
When someone tries to derail an argument with an insult, your response depends on who the audience is. If the two of you are alone, say something like, "This isn't recess. I'm out of here," and walk away. You're not about to persuade the jerk. But if there are bystanders, ridicule the insult. "So Bob's answer to the problem of noise in this town is that I'm a jerk. Was that helpful to you all?" You turn sophistry into genuine banter.

And another, from the same rich source:

CHIEF WIGGUM: Well let me ask you this: shut up.

Most of the time, humiliation is banter without argument. Humiliation seeks only to gain the upper hand—to win points or just embarrass its victims. You often hear it among thirteen-year-old boys, and it's probably good practice in wordplay. (It did wonders for me.) But humiliation rarely leads to a decision.

A more insidious kind of humiliation comes in the smiling guise of **innuendo.** If you object to it, you can look like a fool.

> **Meanings**
> Humiliation is a form of *ad hominem* attack, which formal logic calls a fallacy. But in rhetoric, most ad hominem arguments are in bounds. Attacking your opponent's *ethos* in order to win an argument is an important tactic. It becomes a foul when you insult someone simply to debase him, and not to persuade your audience.

> BOSS: It's nice to see you wearing a tie.
> ME: I always wear a tie.
> BOSS: *[Meaningful smile; obsequious chuckles from the sycophants in the room.]*

This kind of innuendo is an insulting hint. It puts a vicious backspin on plain, innocent truth, turning a favorable comment into a slam. I actually had a boss who used that innuendo. Saying he was pleased to see me dressed that way implied that I usually didn't. Which wasn't true, but he gave me nothing to deny. Talk about inarguable.

> **Meanings**
> *Innuendo* comes from the Latin for "make a significant nod."

I *could* have responded with a counter-innuendo:

> ME: Well, I'm just happy you're not wearing women's underwear this morning.

But I didn't. It's usually better just to play along with the boss.

> ME: If this is what it takes to get you to notice my ties, I'll wear this one every day.
> BOSS: Don't bother. *[Another smile at the snickering sycophants.]*

Innuendo can be particularly harmful in politics. The classic campaign innuendo makes a vicious accusation against an opponent by denying it.

Richard Nixon did it when he ran for governor against Pat Brown in 1962. He repeatedly denied that Brown was a communist, which of course raised the previously moot issue of whether Brown actually was a communist. Brown denied it, too, but his denials just repeated Nixon's innuendo.

The only decent rhetorical response would be to concede Nixon's argument.

> Even my opponent calls me anticommunist. If a guy like Richard Nixon thinks I'm tough on communism, then you should, too.

(As it turns out, Brown didn't have to answer Nixon. The ex-veep lost the election and gave his famous poor-loser statement, "You won't have Dick Nixon to kick around anymore." Innuendo doesn't always work, it seems).

TRY THIS WITH A SNIDE BOSS

It's doubtful that you can win points with a boss like mine. Console yourself with the likelihood that his peers in other companies consider him a jerk. On your next job interview, be deliberately tactful with a figure of speech called *significatio,* a sort of benign innuendo that hints at more than it says. Interviewer: "What do you think of your boss?" You: "He's very particular about his clothing."

It should be increasingly clear that most rhetorical fouls have to do with speaking in a tense that doesn't fit, arguing about values or offenses instead of choices, or forcing someone out of an argument through humiliation. It all comes down to a single foul: tribal talk instead of deliberative argument. But not all argument stoppers are as subtle as the innuendo. One in particular, the **threat,** takes tribalism to a sword-rattling extreme.

The threat is a no-brainer, literally. The Romans called it *argumentum ad baculum,* "argument by the stick." Lucy does it to her little brother, Linus, in *Peanuts.* "I'll give you five reasons," she says, closing each finger into a fist.

"Those are good reasons," Linus replies, reasonably. The problem is, she doesn't really give him a choice, and arguments are about choices. Parents spare the rod these days, but they still employ the rhetorical stick.

> You'll take piano lessons and you'll like them!

The tone determines whether that's a hopeful prediction or argument by the stick. Usually it's the latter. And that makes it the worst of all rhetorical fouls. It denies your audience a choice, and without a choice you have no argument.

The obscene gesture or foul language is a milder version of the threat, but it falls under the same rubric of tribalism. Not all obscenity is bad, from a rhetorical standpoint. Kurt Vonnegut had a character suggest an acrobatic copulation with a rolling doughnut—inspired banter, and even decorous under the right circumstance. Drivers in New York City seem to consider flipping the bird a form of salutation. But it hardly counts as deliberative argument. At its worst, it constitutes a threat. Either way, the only rebuttal is a similar gesture. Consider not rebutting at all.

I have to add another foul that doesn't really fall under tribalism: **utter stupidity.** As the expression goes, "Never argue with a fool. People might not know the difference." When Aristotle said that the better choice is easier to argue, he clearly wasn't thinking of debate with a moron. The most common stupidity in argument, aside from the gratuitous insult, is the arguer's failure to recognize his own logical fallacies. Take this classic Monty Python sketch.

M: Oh look, this isn't an argument.

A: Yes it is.

M: No it isn't. It's just contradiction.

A: No it isn't.

M: It is!

A: It is not.

M: Look, you just contradicted me.

A: I did not.

M: Oh, you did!!

A: No, no, no.

M: You did just then.

A: Nonsense!

M: Oh, this is futile!

A: No it isn't.

Similarly, there is no way to reach a successful conclusion to an exchange that goes:

▸ **Classic Hits**
THEY DID GIVE A FIG: According to the journalist-scholar Bruce Anderson, while our "bird" is phallic, the ancient Romans' obscene gesture mimicked a female organ. The *mano fico* ("fig hand") consisted of a thumb inserted between the first two fingers. It had the added advantage of forming a fist.

TRY THIS WITH A MORON
Again, if the two of you are alone, walk away. If you have an audience, consider throwing the fallacy back at your opponent. "I see. Purple is a fruit. So, since your skin is tan, that makes you a pair of khakis."

"That's a fallacy."

"No it isn't."

"Yes it is. Look, your premise doesn't lead to your conclusion."

"Yes it does."

Anyone who had a younger sibling during childhood has had bitter experience with the rhetorical foul of stupidity. When you find yourself back
in the realm of the inarguable, get out of there. Or if you're four years old,
hit him. Yes, it's another foul, but you may be doing him a favor.

The Tools

You now have the fallacies of formal logic, and the rhetorical argument
breakers. Strangely enough, I came up with seven of them—like the deadly
sins. But these rhetorical fouls aren't "wrong," since rhetoric has no real
rules. They simply make deliberative argument impossible; that's why I call
them fouls, in the sense that they lie out of bounds. The game cannot continue until you're back in bounds. (Grant me the annoying sports metaphor; I haven't used one in a while.) Rhetoric allows occasional sins against
logic, but it can't argue the inarguable.

The seven rhetorical out-of-bounds include

1. Switching tenses away from the future.
2. Inflexible insistence on the rules—using the voice of God, sticking
   to your guns, refusing to hear the other side.
3. Humiliation—an argument that sets out only to debase someone,
   not to make a choice.
4. Innuendo.
5. Threats.
6. Nasty language or signs, like flipping the bird.
7. Utter stupidity.

16. Know Whom to Trust

▲

PERSUASION DETECTORS
The defensive side of ethos

Virtue is a state of character concerned with choice, lying in a mean. —ARISTOTLE

You want the truth! You can't handle the truth! No truth handler you! Bah! I deride your truth handling abilities! —THE SIMPSONS

I wish I had been there when my mother bought a pool table. It was the single worst gift she could have given my father. He hated being indoors and was something of a cheapskate. He never wasted time knocking balls around; his idea of fun was to invent things. Our basement—the only room that could fit a pool table—was the envy of the neighborhood kids. It had fake palm trees, a volcano that lit up, and a waterfall that splashed into a pool with real goldfish. The place also flooded regularly and smelled like a sponge.

Mom found the table in a department store, when she went shopping for a shirt to give Dad on Father's Day. She got the pool table instead, and presented it to him after dinner, leading him down the steep basement steps with his eyes closed. The pool table sat where the Ping-Pong table used to be.

> MOM: Surprise!
> DAD: What the hell is that doing there?
> MOM: It's a *pool* table.

I considered it the best Father's Day ever. It was like *The Newlywed Game*, except that my parents had been married for almost twenty years. They weren't really fighting. They were just mutually bewildered. I sat on the basement steps, enjoying the exchange.

DAD: Well, I guess I could turn it into something.

MOM: You're supposed to play pool on it!

DAD: I don't *play* pool.

The table was gone the next day.

Why she got it in the first place remained a mystery for years. The salesman must have been brilliant. He worked with practically nothing but Mom's vulnerability to a good pitch. She *was* a bit of a sucker; she invariably agreed with the person who went last in an argument. But Mom wasn't stupid, nor was she an impulsive shopper. Years later, I asked her what happened.

MOM: There was something about that salesman. He made me think that a pool table would be perfect for your dad.

ME: But he didn't know Dad.

MOM: Well, he *seemed* to.

It sounds like some sort of *ethos* technique, so we return to its basic principles: **disinterest, virtue,** and **practical wisdom.** The same ethical tools that a persuader uses to sway his audience can serve you as a ready-made gauge of trustworthiness.

> **TRY THIS ON SALESPEOPLE**
> Doctors insist that the many gifts pharma salespeople bring have no influence on them; in reality, a doctor who receives gifts is four times more likely to prescribe that salesperson's drug. The technique works like this: The salesperson makes it clear she expects nothing in exchange for the gift—just friendship. The doctor thinks he separates the gifts from his drug decisions; but his relationship with the salesperson makes him more easily persuaded by her "information." Do you receive gifts at work? Don't worry about the gifts. Worry about the relationship. Refuse to discuss business face-to-face with any gift giver. Insist on getting all information by mail—snail mail and e-mail. Those media are more rational than face-to-face, as you'll see in a later chapter.

Mom's Heart's Desire

The salesman must have laid some major disinterest on Mom. According to the rhetorician Kenneth Burke, *ethos* starts with what the audience needs. The persuader makes you believe he can meet those needs better than you or anyone else. Advertisers and salespeople have a reputation for creating needs where they do not exist, but that is rarely true in a literal sense. In rhetoric, you *start* with needs; the manipulation part happens when the salesman or marketer makes you believe that his solution will meet those needs. A man responds to a beautiful woman in a car ad out of his need for—well, out of his need for a woman. But that was hardly the case with my mom. She simply wanted to please my dad. And she surely knew that a pool table wasn't the ticket.

> ME: What exactly did the salesman say?
>
> MOM: He didn't say anything particular that I can remember. He was very well-spoken, though. I do remember that.
>
> ME: You mean good looking?
>
> MOM: No, I mean *well-spoken*.
>
> ME: So you don't remember what he said, but you liked the way he said it?
>
> MOM: I don't know. Why are you asking me all this? I felt an instant connection, as if he really understood what I wanted.

TRY THIS AT WORK
Watch the best presenters in your company. What material do they start with—which audience resources do they use? If the talk is mostly rational, the foundation will be what the audience knows and believes. If it's emotional, the pitch will start with what the audience expects. If the speaker relies on her character, you'll hear about the audience's needs, and how she can meet them. Similarly, branding is an *ethos* strategy, and it relies on needs.

Now we get to the bottom of it. Because the salesman understood what Mom wanted, he had no need to know what *Dad* wanted. He knew Mom needed to feel a connection with a person, such as a well-spoken, polite salesman who seemed to understand her. They connected because he made her feel as if the two were Father's Day collaborators, sharing the same interest. My guess is, Dad was forgotten for a while. Eventually, I imagine the salesman delivering the classic line "I have just the thing." He seemed to sympathize with her needs, and he knew how to meet them. So how do you detect when this happens to you?

Here's a secret that applies to all kinds of rhetorical defense: **Look for the disconnects.** You already saw how logical short circuits can help you spot fallacies. When somebody tries to manipulate you through disinterest, look for a short circuit between his needs and yours; or if you're buying a gift, your needs and the recipient's. There was a three-way disconnect over the pool table: what Mom wanted and what Dad wanted were very different, and what the salesman wanted differed from what Mom and Dad each wanted. The salesman used his temporary warm relationship with Mom to cover up the disconnects in their needs. He doesn't give a fig about

▶ **Argument Tool**
THE DISINTEREST DISCONNECT: Is there a gap between your interests and the persuader's? Then don't trust without verifying.

TRY THIS BEFORE YOU VOTE
The Romans would ask, *"Cui bono?"* meaning, "Who benefits?" In modern political terms, the question is: Does the politician go after votes, or money? Access her voting record on www.vote-smart.org, and get her list of campaign donors from www.fecinfo.com. Does she consistently vote her donors' interest? Is she bucking public opinion when she does? Then when she says, "I don't just vote the opinion polls," what she really means is, "I prefer special interests to voters' interests." I'd vote for her opponent.

the commission! He just wants to make Mom—I mean Dad—happy.

Disinterest is simply the merger of your needs and the persuader's. Suppose the salesman were my mother's cousin. Then the two may indeed share the same needs—the guy might actually be disinterested. If he were my mother's ex-boyfriend, however, then things could get complicated. His interests might be split among making my mother happy, earning a commission, and getting revenge on my father.

Disinterest is one of the easiest rhetorical tricks to spot, because most of the time, interest is rarely far from the surface of a choice. Politicians will often couch brazen selfishness in terms of disinterest. South Dakota senator John Thune voted for a project that benefited a railroad he had lobbied for before he was elected. Thune defended himself piously:

> If you start banning elected officials from using their working knowledge on behalf of constituents, I think it would greatly erode our representative form of government.

You can see a red herring here; a politician accused of ethical sins will speak out against theoretical legislation that would ban it. You can also see the *ethos* disconnect. It is hard to know whether the railroad extension is good for the nation; but we certainly see where Thune's interest lies. He brazenly fails the disinterest test, and gets away with it. A constituency ignorant of the meaning of "disinterest" will hardly make it a political issue.

TRY THIS WHEN YOU BUY A CAR
Ask for references. While she makes you wait for the contract to be drawn up, call them—or pretend to. If she doesn't have a list ready to hand, walk away. A salesperson who maintains contact with customers has an interest in long-term profit that helps to balance out the desire for a quick buck.

Rhetorical defense is all about the disconnects. If someone pitches a logical argument, you do a quick mental inspection to find the short circuits in the argument's examples or commonplaces and the choices. If the argument lays some heavy disinterest on you—your salesman acts as if his only desire is to make you or your loved ones happy—then look for the disconnects between his needs and yours.

If my mother had been more rhetorically inclined, she could have spotted the salesman's goodwill disconnect and called him on it. Let's start
their conversation over.

> MOM: Can you tell me where I can find men's shirts?
>
> SALESMAN: Sure. I can take you there if you like. Shopping
> for Father's Day?
>
> MOM: I am. I know it sounds boring, but my husband needs a
> shirt.
>
> SALESMAN: Mmm, I'm afraid it *does* sound boring. I remem-
> ber my mother used to make a big deal out of Father's
> Day. Bigger than his birthday.
>
> MOM: What did she get him?
>
> SALESMAN *(as if he just thought of the idea):* May I show you
> something?

At this point the salesman has my mother in a vulnerable state. If she
had had her wits about her, Mom should have told herself two things:

1. He's a salesman.
2. He wants to show me something.

The combination rarely produces disinterest.

> MOM *(brightly):* What are you going to show
> me?
>
> SALESMAN: It's right over here. I think you're
> going to love it.
>
> MOM: Who's it for?
>
> SALESMAN: It's a really special Father's Day
> surprise.
>
> MOM: So it's for my husband?
>
> SALESMAN: Well, actually, it's for the whole family.
>
> MOM: If I look at it, will you take me to the
> shirt department?

When she asks who the surprise is for, the salesman dodges the question—a sure sign of a disinterest disconnect. Having spotted it, Mom brings the

> ▶ **Useful Figure**
> I mentioned the *litotes*
> earlier, but it's worth
> showing you another
> example ("rarely pro-
> duces disinterest"). In
> front of an intelligent
> audience, this ironic
> understatement can
> make you look cool
> and authoritative
> while your opponent
> looks like a blowhard.

> ▶ **Argument Tool**
> THE DODGED QUESTION:
> Ask who benefits from
> the choice. If you don't
> get a straight answer,
> don't trust that person's
> disinterest.

sales pitch to a crashing halt. Her failure to steer the conversation this way in real life resulted in a $2,000 pool table instead of a $30 shirt. And do you know how hard it is to return a pool table?

A Salesman, Lying in a Mean

The second characteristic of *ethos*, virtue, also has its disconnects, and it makes an especially good lie detector. Aristotle lets you put up a red flag even if you don't know the person, even while he talks. The secret lies in Aristotle's definition of virtue:

> *A state of character concerned with choice, lying in a mean.*

I know, I know. That hardly seems to define any kind of virtue you know. But the thing about Aristotle is, when you live with his idea for a bit, it begins to make a startling amount of sense. And you can use it to enhance your own reputation as well as evaluate the character of another person. Let's see how.

A state of character means rhetorical virtue, not the permanent kind. It exists only during the argument itself, and it adapts to the audience's expectations, not the persuader's. He could be a liar and a thief, but if you believe him to be virtuous, then he *is* virtuous—rhetorically and temporarily. That, for the moment, is his state of character.

TRY THIS IN A MEETING
Remember the *false choice* logical sin? If someone uses it, and seems to do it deliberately, don't trust his virtue. He's not interested in a reasonable argument.

▶ **Persuasion Alert**
I employ a version of the reluctant conclusion here ("it did to me at first"): I myself was once turned off by the term, but its value compelled me to change my mind.

Concerned with choice: Aristotle means that virtue comes out of the choices the persuader makes, or those he tries to sell you on. A persuader who tries to prevent a choice—through distraction or threats or by pitching the argument in the past or present—lacks rhetorical virtue.

Lying in a mean: That probably sounds Greek to you (it did to me at first), but the concept lies at the heart of deliberative rhetoric. To Aristotle, the sweet spot of every question lies in the middle between extremes. A virtuous soldier is neither cowardly nor foolhardy, but exactly in between. He chooses not to fling himself at the enemy; he lives to fight another day.

But he does fight. The virtuous person "lies in the mean" between patriot and cynic, alcoholic and teetotaler, workaholic and slacker, religious zealot and atheist. (If Aristotle had lived among us, I suppose he would have been an Episcopalian, or maybe a Presbyterian—some faith that lies midway between zealotry and atheism.)

If this person sounds like a Milquetoast, remember that deliberative argument deals with choices, and Aristotle saw the middle road as the shortest one to any decision. The mean lies smack in the middle of the audience's values. In short, virtue is a temporary, rhetorical condition—a state of character, not a permanent trait—and you can find it in the middle of the audience's opinions, or the sweet spot between the extreme ranges of a choice. A virtuous choice is a moderate one. Someone who chooses it has virtue.

How can you measure someone's virtue? One way is to see whether he finds the sweet spot between extremes. For example, when you walk into a department store to buy something for Father's Day, your mean lies in the middle of your budget. A virtuous salesman asks what you want to spend and sticks to that amount; a really virtuous salesman hits the sweet spot, taking your range of $50 to $100 and finding something that costs exactly $74.99. A salesman who fails to ask you for a range, or who tries to move your sweet spot to sell you a $2,000 pool table, lacks rhetorical virtue.

▶ **Argument Tool**
THE VIRTUE YARDSTICK: Does the persuader find the sweet spot between the extremes of your values?

Spotting a lack of virtue when numbers aren't involved is a bit trickier. Another way to evaluate a persuader's virtue is to ask yourself:

How does he describe the mean?

First, determine the middle of the road in any question. What is the mean in, say, child rearing? Aristotle would place it somewhere between severe beatings and letting the kid run rampant. You will want to fine-tune that mean according to your own lights.

Now imagine yourself a new parent asking people's advice on how to raise a child. (In actuality, you rarely have to ask for advice; people are all too happy to volunteer it.) Your advisers may suggest all sorts of help—prophylactic Ritalin, avoidance of "no," Baby Einstein tapes, strict discipline—and if you know absolutely nothing from kids, you might have trouble sifting

▶ **Persuasion Alert**
Personally, I
wouldn't take any
childrearing advice
that doesn't begin
with, "That depends
on the kid." The
practically wise
person uses "that
depends" as his
guide.

through all the theories. To test the virtue of the
people advising you, ask them what they think of main-
stream child psychologists like Dr. Spock or Terry Bra-
zelton. If they respond with extreme terms—"radical,"
"cruel," "abusive"—then beware of their advice. They
can disagree with the prevailing wisdom—that is the
whole point of persuasion—but if they describe it as
extreme, then they tag themselves as extremists.

Extremists usually describe the middle course as extreme.

Rhetorical virtue lets you leverage what you know, applying that limited
knowledge to areas where you don't have the facts. This is especially useful
with political issues, where the pundits and pols know
more than you and I. Politicians often pitch their own arguments as the mean between extremes, even in these
polarized days. They do that by making their opponents
appear to lie further from the middle than they actually
are. Conservatives can't say the word "environmental"
without following it with "extremist"; that makes anyone who expresses concern about global warming seem like a froth-at-the-mouth radical.

▶ **Argument Tool**
THE EXTREMIST
DETECTOR: An
extremist will
describe a mod-
erate choice as
extreme.

> CONSERVATIVE: Environmental extremists want to prevent a
> sensible energy policy, which is why they're trying to block
> careful, animal-friendly drilling in the Arctic National Wild-
> life Refuge.

Whenever you hear the word "extremists" or "special interests," consult
your own interests. Do you like the idea of drilling in the wilderness? If not,
does that make you an extremist? Take a look at the polls as well. Most
Americans don't want to drill in ANWR. So a group that opposes drilling
isn't, by definition, extremist.

Now, if you do support drilling, does that make you a member of the far
right?

> ENVIRONMENTALIST: He's on the conservative extreme that
> wants to drill Alaska so he can tool around in his SUV.

You'll often see people do the reverse of the extremist label, describing an extreme choice as moderate. Someone proposes marketing your product to teenagers. You know the teenage market, and you further know that appealing to it is a big risk. Yet the proposer describes it in moderate terms, showing a lack of rhetorical virtue. When he adds that the company should expand its advertising to cable TV, an area you know nothing about, assume that the decision would be just as radical. In other words, don't trust his choice. In the current feisty political climate, though, officials make "moderate" sound like a bad word.

As the Sophists liked to say, there are two sides to every question. Being on one side or the other does not make one an extremist. In fact, no rhetoric rule book forbids you from using the extremist or moderate label as a persuasive technique. If your own opinion lies outside the public's mean, you can describe that mean as extreme. Or you can label your own position as moderate. But the technique is tricky, to say the least. Most audiences don't appreciate being labeled as extremists. Usually, when a persuader labels an opponent as extreme simply because she disagrees with him, then he's probably the extreme one. Don't trust his virtue.

You see this kind of labeling among liberals and conservatives on almost every issue.

> LIBERAL: The extreme Christian right wants prayer in the schools so it can impose its religion on others.

Again, what are your interests? And what benefits the nation? Does allowing a small group to pray in a classroom really constitute established religion? Besides, given the country's other problems, should people even waste time arguing about school prayer?

> APPROPRIATE RHETORICAL REPLY: Most Americans support school prayer. If that seems extreme, what does it make you?

The old expression "There's virtue in moderation" comes straight from Aristotle. Virtue is a state of character, concerned with choice, lying in a mean. When moderates face scorn from the faithful of both parties, what does that make our country? You can do your bit for democracy, and your own sanity, with this pre fab reply:

I know reasonable people who hold that opinion. So who's
the extremist?

The Tools

"And, after all, what is a lie?" Lord Byron asked in his poem *Don Juan*.
" 'Tis but / The truth in masquerade; and I defy / Historians, heroes, lawyers, priests, to put / A fact without some leaven of a lie." Byron may exaggerate, but the truth is often difficult to suss out in an argument. Rhetoric
allows you to skip that problem and focus on the person as well as what
she says. In other words, *ethos* provides . . . not a lie detector, exactly, but a
liar detector—with basic tools for telling how much you should trust someone's sincerity and trustworthiness.

1. **Apply the needs test (disinterest).** Are the persuader's needs your
   needs? Whose needs is the person meeting?
2. **Check the Extremes (virtue).** How does he describe the opposing
   argument? How close is her middle-of-the-road to yours?

17. Find the Sweet Spot

▲

MORE PERSUASION DETECTORS

The defensive tools of practical wisdom

A companion's words of persuasion are effective. — HOMER

In the last chapter, we saw Aristotle's strangely sensible definition of virtue: a state of character, concerned with a choice, lying in a mean. Like virtue, practical wisdom also lies in the mean—or rather, the persuader's apparent ability to find the sweet spot. While you want to know how virtuous he is, you also want to assess his ability to make a good choice, one that fits the occasion. We're talking about Aristotle's *phronesis,* or practical wisdom, here. It recognizes that the sweet spot changes according to the circumstances and the audience. If my mother were shopping for a house, the sweet spot would lie a couple of hundred thousand dollars beyond the price of a pool table. The principle gets more subtle when we talk about politics or business. Then you want to see all of a persuader's *phronesis* kick in. Listen for two things.

First, you want to hear "That depends." The practically wise person sizes up the problem before answering it. Your adviser should question you about the circumstances first. If she spouts a theory without having a clue about your problem, then don't trust her judgment.

> ▸ **Argument Tool**
> "THAT DEPENDS."
> A trustworthy persuader matches her advice with the particular circumstances instead of applying a one-size-fits-all rule.

NEW PARENT: I'm reading conflicting advice about toilet training. What's a good age to wean a child from diapers?

UNWISE ANSWER: I don't believe in toilet training. Let the child determine when she's ready.

EVEN LESS WISE ANSWER: No later than age two.

PRACTICALLY WISE ANSWER: That depends on the child. Does
she show interest in toilet training? Are you willing to put
in the effort? Are diapers giving you any problem?

**TRY THIS IF YOU'RE
A PUNDIT**
Research shows that
experts on TV make
lousy prognosticators;
in fact, the more knowl-
edgeable the person is,
the worse the predic-
tions. Rhetoric provides
a reason: pundits tend to
overapply their experi-
ence to specific situa-
tions. A solution that
won't get you on talk
shows but will improve
your score is to do what
modelers do: describe
the likely outcome as
conditions change. Bad
Pundit: "China will be
the most powerful
nation by the end of the
century." Practically
Wise Pundit: "If we keep
borrowing money from
the Chinese, their eco-
nomic clout will balance
our military strength. If
we get the deficit under
control, we're likely to
remain on top."

I don't speak entirely rhetorically here. Dorothy
Junior, being our first, fell victim to all sorts of childrearing books. Thankfully, she has no memory of
our well-meaning abuse involving tiny plastic toilets
and panicky bathroom visits. It was a total failure.
Months later, she trained herself. Now that our kids
are grown, new parents think that my wife and I
must know something about children. And in fact
we do—about our own children. But what worked
for Dorothy Junior often was a disaster for George.
So whenever anyone asks me for generic advice, I
reply, "Don't listen to any advice."

I make no exceptions; which, come to think of it,
probably isn't very practically wise of me. A far more
sage person is my friend Dick. When my kids were
little, Dick and his wife, Nancy, moved overseas.
They were empty-nesters, having raised five great
kids and seen them through college. Dorothy and I
visited the couple on a vacation in Europe, and I remember sitting on their apartment balcony confid-
ing to Dick my frightening cluelessness as a parent.

ME: It seems that by the time I figure out how to deal with
one kid, she grows out of it, and then whatever worked for
her doesn't work for her brother. Sometimes I wonder if
I'm ready to be a parent.
DICK: I know what you mean. I'm *still* not ready to be a parent.

It was the wisest, most reassuring parenting help I ever got.

Phronesis divides the rules people from the improvisers and helps us understand politics today. George Lakoff misses the point with his theory of
"moral politics." Our country suffers more from a lack of perspective toward
rules and improvisation. George Bush, Howard Dean, and Nancy Pelosi are

▶ Persuasion Alert
Aren't swing voters moderate by definition? Calling Breyer a "liberal" and O'Connor a "conservative" exaggerates my point about their practical wisdom.

all rules people who think in the past and present tenses, forensically and demonstratively; they speak in terms of right and wrong, good and bad. On the other hand, it's no accident that the two recent swing voters on the Supreme Court, Stephen Breyer and Sandra Day O'Connor—a liberal Democrat and conservative Republican—were the only justices with legislative backgrounds. They're deliberative thinkers, and the ones with the most *phronesis.* Their written opinions use the future tense more than the others', and they tend to focus on the "advantageous," deliberation's chief topic. When you think about it, choosing a Supreme Court justice or a president isn't that different from choosing a spouse. Check out the candidates' disinterest, virtue, and *phronesis,* and you can make a reasonable prediction about how they will vote once they're in office.

▶ Persuasion Alert
Am I showing good *phronesis* here, or do you see a disconnect in my analogy? How much is a presidency like a marriage, really? The analogy may hold up better for the Supreme Court, where justices spend many decades in close quarters with one another.

Phronesis means more than good judgment; it also means having experience with the problem. So, **the second thing you want to hear after "That depends" is a tale of a comparable experience.** Suppose my mother began to think a shirt wasn't such a good idea but that the pool table was too expensive.

MOM: What about that bocce set over there?
PRACTICALLY WISE SALESMAN: That depends on your lawn. I've played with that same set, and the balls go all over the place if you have any stones or rough spots.

▶ Argument Tool
COMPARABLE EXPERIENCE: The practically wise persuader shows examples from his own life.

The practically wise salesman should also figure out whom the gift is really for. Father's Day may just be an excuse for my mother to buy a toy for herself. In which case the sale gets a whole lot easier.

Phronesis makes an especially good persuasion detector when you don't know where the sweet spot is—when you know too little about an issue, or have no idea what you want to spend. To determine whether you can trust the speaker's judgment, ask: has the guy figured out your needs—your real needs, that is? One of the most important traits of practical wisdom is "sussing" ability—the knack of determining what the issue is really about. Ideally,

▶ **Argument Tool**
"SUSSING" THE REAL
ISSUE: A trustworthy
persuader sees your
actual needs even if
you haven't men-
tioned them.

you want a pathologist like Greg House, the doctor on
TV with the worst bedside manner in history. House
homes in on the patient's real problem, and he does
it with an infallible accuracy that can come only from
scriptwriters. In one episode, a patient with bright
orange skin comes in complaining of back spasms.

HOUSE: Unfortunately, you have a deeper problem. Your wife
   is having an affair.

ORANGE GUY: What?!

HOUSE: You're orange, you moron! It's one thing for you not
   to notice, but if your wife hasn't picked up on the fact that
   her husband has changed color, she's just not paying
   attention. By the way, do you consume just a ridiculous
   amount of carrots and megadose vitamins?

[Guy nods.]

HOUSE: The carrots turn you yellow, the niacin turns you red.
   Get some finger paints and do the math. And get a good
   lawyer.

The patient defines the issue as a golf in-
jury. House produces a bigger issue: any wife
who doesn't notice her husband turn into a
carrot must be cheating on him. While the
AMA might not appreciate his Sherlockian
deduction, House shows the greatest *phronesis* abilities a persuader can have: to figure
out what the audience really needs, and what
the issue really is.

TRY THIS IN SIZING UP A
PRESIDENTIAL CANDIDATE
If the candidate touts experience
that's less than germane, and
makes it analogous to the presidency, vote for someone else.
Abraham Lincoln often spoke of
rural life, but he didn't describe the
White House as a log cabin. Nor
did he see the president as a corporate lawyer. His experience con-
tributed to his practical wisdom; it
didn't dictate his decisions.

The Right Mean People

Even if you're not buying anything, and you're not in an argument, *ethos*
principles can come in handy to size up a stranger. Suppose you evaluate an
applicant for a management job. Use what you learned in the last chapter
and this one; if her disinterest, virtue, and street smarts seem intact,
chances are you found the right person.

Disinterest: She should talk about what she can do for your company, not what your company can do for her.

Virtue: She should hit the sweet spot for the job: aggressive but not too, sufficiently independent but able to take orders. And her choices should lie within the mean, as Aristotle would say. How does she describe the company's future? Does her strategy lie within the corporate sweet spot—risk-taking but not too? Creative but practical?

Practical wisdom: Any candidate should have the right experience; you don't need rhetoric to tell you that. But how do you think she will use that experience? Is she stuck in the rut of her own background? Suppose she's a top saleswoman being considered for a vice presidency; the aggressive, elbows-out style that got her where she is may hurt her in management, where she has to get cooperation and teamwork out of her people.

College admissions officers might use the same criteria to evaluate young candidates. Think how disinterest, virtue, and practical wisdom might work to produce the ideal liberal arts student. Does he reflect the institution's values—or is he too zealous about them? What kind of education will fulfill his potential and make himself useful?

▶ **Persuasion Alert**
So how do you know you can trust me, the author? What if I just spun all these principles in a way that makes me look trustworthy? Boy, are you a tough customer. There's a reading list in the back.

Now let's talk relationships. You know those cheesy magazine quizzes where you measure your compatibility with your lover? *Ethos* can do that much better.

Disinterest: Do you share the same needs, and interpret them the same way? Good. But does your beloved consider your happiness second to his or her own? Then you have a serious disinterest problem. Mates can be disinterested only if they're willing to sacrifice their own needs to that of the relationship—in other words, if the relationship's stability is of greater value than their individual needs. You often hear about newlyweds' territorial problems. That's just another way of saying their disinterest is out of whack.

▶ **Persuasion Alert**
Aren't the *ethos* traits just supposed to make you *look* trustworthy? Rhetorically, yes. But we're on the defensive right now, and our job is to measure the gap between your lover's rhetorical ability and how much you can actually trust the person.

Virtue: Do you share the same values? Think about which ones will crop up in most of your arguments. And what do you and your lover consider "moderate" behavior? In every aspect of your relationship, what seems extreme? In *Annie Hall,* Woody Allen and Diane

Keaton go to separate analysts and talk about their marriage. Each analyst asks how often they have sex.

> HE: Hardly ever. About three times a week.
> SHE: All the time. About three times a week.

This is no mere communication problem, it's a rhetorical one—a matter of virtue. Their sweet spots lie too far apart. Aristotle's definition of virtue, "a matter of choice, lying in a mean," really makes sense here. The mean is your sweet spot on every issue.

Practical wisdom: Aristotle said that *phronesis* is the skill of dealing with probability—what is likely to happen, and what's the best decision under the circumstances. This combines two skills: the ability to predict, based on the evidence; and that of making decisions that produce the greatest probability of happiness. A partner should neither make things up as he goes nor be a rigid rule follower. Watch how your significant other responds to a problem you both face. Does your lover apply rules to everything? Does he or she think every choice constitutes a values question? If your lover asks what Jesus would do with whose turn it is to cook, you may have problems. (As far as we know, Jesus didn't leave any recipes.)

I can offer a personal example. When my wife and I decided to have children, we faced that classic choice of professional couples: which, if either of us, would stay home? I had this fantasy of playing the house husband, caring for the theoretical children and writing while they took their long, simultaneous naps. My wife was better organized, had superior social skills, and a higher salary as a fund-raiser; I figured she would earn most of the money. The problem was that Dorothy also had more domestic ability than I did. My idea of cooking was to throw raw hamburger into a pot of canned soup and call it stew. The other problem was that my wife hated her job.

All that was decided one morning in a startling way, at least for me, when Dorothy came into the kitchen.

> DOROTHY SR.: I hate asking people for money.
> ME: Boy, are you in the wrong profession.

I hadn't had my coffee, or I would have shut up right there. Instead, I asked what I thought was a rhetorical question.

ME: Why don't you quit?

She threw her arms around me, gave notice that very day, and two weeks later, our household income dropped by more than half. Dorothy had not seen my question as rhetorical. She didn't get a job, and I didn't write full-time, for the next twenty years.

Now, you could interpret my response to her complaint as both a success and a failure of practical wisdom. On the positive side, I had applied a value we shared in common—that people who hated their jobs shouldn't work in them if they could help it—to the particular situation. On the flip side, neither one of us actually deliberated over the decision, and one sign of *phronesis* is the ability to deliberate—to consider both sides of a question.

It could be that Dorothy didn't have much faith in my own wisdom, though she denies it. Maybe she knew that we both would be happier if I worked full-time and she reared the kids. She was right, of course. Plus she not only got what she wanted, she gave me the satisfaction of having proposed it in the first place. If she did it on purpose, it was with a time-honored technique: making me believe that her choice was really mine.

The Tools

Virtue and disinterest are only two legs of the *ethos* stool. A candidate may be the most pious, goodhearted, selfless woman who ever ran for mayor in your town, but she'll make a lousy mayor if she can't fix the potholes. Here's how to assess a person's practical wisdom:

> **The "That Depends" Filter.** Does the persuader want to know the exact nature of your problem? Or is she spouting a one-size-fits-all choice?
>
> **Comparable Experience.** This may seem painfully obvious, but it seems to escape voters regularly. How many times have we chosen the rich guy over the guy who's actually been in

politics? Comparable experience is less obvious when someone tries to sell you something. Then the question is, where did they get their information? From using the product themselves, or from company training?

"Sussing" Ability. Can the persuader cut to the chase of an issue?

ADVANCED OFFENSE

18. Speak Your Audience's Language

▲

THE RHETORICAL APE
Use words to gather a group around you.

CARL: *Let's make litter of the literati!*
LENNY: *That was too clever! You're one of them!*
[Punches him.]

—*THE SIMPSONS*

N ow that you know some of the workings of argument by character, let's get into the true black arts of *ethos,* the ones having to do with the people and things your audience identifies with. In this chapter and the next one, we'll deal with the **identity strategy.** It starts with getting the audience to bond with one another, and to see you as its ideal leader. Execute it adroitly, and the strategy can make the audience think

> ▶ Argument Tool
> THE IDENTITY
> STRATEGY: Get
> your audience
> to identify with
> your decision.

of your choices as expressions of the group. Anyone who chooses otherwise risks feeling separated from the pack.

In short, your word is their bond.

I Wanna Be Just Like You

What we humans do with words, wild chimpanzees do with lice. After every major dispute over food or sex, according to animal behaviorists, chimps devote extra time picking nits out of each other's hair. In the aftermath of an internal battle, they settle down to relationship mending. Prolonged bouts of grooming let the animals repair their social bonds.

Instead of nitpicking, we humans use present-tense, demonstrative rhetoric, persuasion that brings us together and distinguishes us from other groups. Demonstrative rhetoric exploits our instinct for forming tribes and rivalries, and our fear of being an outsider. "If men were not apart from one another," said the twentieth-century rhetorician Kenneth Burke, "there would be no need for the rhetorician to proclaim their unity."

The more people find themselves divided, the more they engage in demonstrative gestures—a great speech like the Gettysburg Address, or a heartfelt apology by a lover who nonetheless thinks he did nothing wrong. It can be a song, like the chants soldiers use when they march or the tunes kids swap on the Web. Even a common dialect—slang, jargon, or political code language—lets people demonstrate how they belong together.

That may explain why doctors have infamous handwriting. No good medical reason justifies it; the scribble is literally a code. The doc will probably tell you what the prescription is for, but the writing does the same thing that speaking in Latin once did for the medical community, distinguishing the illuminati from benighted laymen. The prescription scribble constitutes a kind of social grooming, like the nitpicking that chimps do to please each other. Call it **code grooming.** It will be our own exclusive term.

Even professional communicators practice code grooming through language and symbols impenetrable to anyone but themselves. Men and women who have dedicated their lives to clarity are just as guilty of code grooming as their scribbling doctors. Magazine editors call the beginning of a story the "lede," and refer to a caption as a "cutline." It's a bonding thing. They use "TK" to mean, "Fill in a fact here." It stands for "TO KOME" (the *K* makes it easier for proofreaders to spot).

Kids use code grooming in their instant messages. Look how fast they type—faster than some of them can think. Why is it all in lowercase? Surely they know how to use capital letters and punctuation; they probably could spell out entire words if they wanted to. What are they saying? You have no idea, and that's partly the point of all those weird abbreviations, acronyms, emoticons, and wds 2 tuff 2 rede, lol ("laugh out loud," for the uninitiated). Why do they IM one another in the first place? Ken-

> ▸ **Argument Tool**
> CODE GROOMING.
> Using insider language to get an audience to identify with you and your idea

> ▸ **Persuasion Alert**
> You could interpret my use of rhetorical terms in this book as a form of code grooming, welcoming you into an elite group. Strangely, though, the Greeks saw their rhetorical terminology as plain language. They knew the crisscross *chiasmus,* for example, as "the *X* figure." The figure of understated irony, the *litotes,* they called "the simple figure." *Litotes* means "plainness" in Greek. You and I will call it *litotes.* Why? Because we're cool.

neth Burke would know: teens feel insecure about their position in society, so they mutually groom like crazy.

From a parental standpoint, it does beat more physical versions.

Hearing Your Vision

When it comes to talking in code, however, teenagers don't hold a candle to politicians. Getting elected president of the United States doesn't always require great skill in formal, rational debate. The ranks of presidents have been filled—and will no doubt continue to be filled—with individuals whose rather uninspired speech has been transformed through the alchemy of rhetoric into political dominance. America's forty-third president, George W. Bush, deserves a special place in the rhetorical pantheon owing to his particular talent for code grooming. Future candidates may be more articulate than Bush, but they still have a lot to learn from the man. Pundits love to talk about his Christian code, but religion forms only a part of his grooming lingo. He also has his male code, his female code, and his military code. Bush speaks a pure demonstrative language of identity, favoring the present tense and using terms that resonate among various constituencies. When he speaks to the faithful, for example, he prefers "I believe" to "I think." In the summer of 2001 he used "believe" as a kind of fugue:

> *I know what I believe. I will continue to articulate what I believe and what I believe—I believe what I believe is right.*

Believe it. His repetitive use of code language extends to women. Before his reelection, Bush appealed to women with sentences that began, "I understand," and he repeated words such as "peace" and "security" and "protecting." For the military, he used "Never relent" and "Whatever it takes" and "We must not waver" and "Not on my watch." For Christians, he began sentences with "and," just as the Bible does:

TRY THIS AT A PROFESSIONAL MEETING
One of the best ways to bond a group is to tell a joke that only they would get. Steve Martin claimed he delivered one at a plumbers' convention that ended with the punch line "It says socket, not sprocket!" I tried something similar many years ago, when I gave a speech to a group of foresters. "What's one step lower than grade-three pulpwood?" I asked. "A carrot." It killed them.

*And in all that is to come, we can know that His purposes are just
and true.*

For men, he used swaggering humor that implied he personally pulls
the military trigger:

*When I take action, I'm not going to fire a two million dollar mis-
sile at a ten dollar empty tent and hit a camel in the butt. It's
going to be decisive.*

So what? Every politician uses codewords. What makes Bush different is
his masterful way of using codewords without the distraction of logic. He
speaks in short sentences, repeating code phrases in effective, if irrational,
order. "See, in my line of work you got to keep repeating things over and
over and over again for the truth to sink in," he once said, "to kind of cata-
pult the propaganda."

But he does more than just repeat things over
and over and over. He catapults his messages by leaving logic out of them. The result is what the poet
Robert Frost called the "sound of sense"—the meaning you intuit from hearing people speak in the
next room. You pick up the sense from the speakers'
rhythms and tone, and from an occasional empha-
sized word. If you ever played Sims on your computer, you know what I mean. The game's simulated
characters speak Simlish, a babble language invented by a pair of improv comedians. (An angry
character will exclaim something like, "Frabbida!")
You suss out much of what they say by their tone of
voice. Bush's strange statement "Families is where
our nation finds hope, where wings take dream"
makes almost poetic sense. It has the *sound* of sense.
He has a masterful way of combining repetition,
tone, and codewords unfettered by context.

▸ **Persuasion Alert**
My tongue is not as
far in my cheek as you
might think. Bushisms
offer a profound
example of code
grooming in politics;
Bush's illogic makes
the demonstrative lan-
guage that much eas-
ier to hear. His clumsy
rhetoric was at most
a minor obstacle to
election; in fact, by
making his speech
seem guileless—and
by allowing him to
repeat appropriate
codewords—Bushisms
may actually have
helped him win the
presidency.

*We look forward to hearing your vision, so we can more better do
our job.*

This is a classic Bushism, fractured syntax that seems to come out of a short circuit in the language center of his brain. You know what he means, though, don't you? If you heard it instead of read it, you would probably miss the "hearing your vision" part and come away with "look forward" and "hearing" and "vision" and "do our job." The resulting message conveys optimism, listening, and duty. Bushisms treat audiences like the dog in the *Far Side* cartoon.

> WHAT YOU SAY: Oh Ginger, that was a bad thing. You're a bad, bad dog, Ginger.
>
> WHAT A DOG HEARS: Blah Ginger, blah blah blah. Blah blah blah blah, Ginger.

Clearly, Bush didn't practice speaking Bushimistically. But he has done nothing to fix his syntax, probably because he benefits from it. Logic-free speech italicizes the words he wants to stick in our heads. When he says, "We'll be a great country where the fabrics are made up of groups and loving centers," he does not paint any sort of realistic picture of America. Nor does he intend to. The technique is not so much impressionistic as pointillist, dotting the rhetorical canvas with values to create a group identity. As Bush himself succinctly put it, "Sometimes pure politics enters into the rhetoric." He keeps everything else out of his more rhetorical statements, leaving only politically useful principles. "I'm a proud man to be the nation based upon such wonderful values," he says.

> WHAT BUSH SAYS: Part of the facts is understanding we have a problem, and part of the facts is what you're going to do about it.
>
> WHAT STICKS IN PEOPLE'S MINDS: . . . facts . . . understanding . . . problem . . . facts.

The distracted listener gets the impression of an engaged, knowledgeable leader.

Skeptical? Remember that you're receiving this argument in print, a logical medium. A good reader absorbs whole paragraphs, not words or phrases. Imagine hearing a Bushism on television while you make dinner and the dog barks and the kids argue over who got to use the PlayStation last and you wonder whether it's time to get an oil change. A great Bushism

is a work of art—neither an accurate representation
of reality nor an appeal to logic, but a series of impres-
sions that bring Bush closer to the group he wants to
appeal to.

▸ **Useful Figure**
The *polysyndeton*
(pol-y-SIN-de-ton)
makes a figure out
of a run-on sentence
by linking clauses
with a repeated
conjunction. I use
it here to convey
sensory overload.

> WHAT BUSH SAYS: I believe we are called to do
> the hard work to make our communities
> and quality of life a better place.
>
> WHAT STICKS IN PEOPLE'S MINDS: . . . believe . . . called . . .
> hard work . . . communities . . . quality of life . . . better
> place.

Bush attracts red-state voters by emphasizing the values of hard work,
quality of life, and making our community a better place. He also injects
the Christian codewords "believe" and "called" (a Christian is called by God
to fulfill his mission in life). He uses these codewords efficiently, with a
brevity impossible in a logical sentence.

Now you try it. Experiment on your own. Take rational, fully articulated
thoughts and reduce them to logic-free collections of values.

> RATIONAL THOUGHT: Boys, we can win this one. We're bigger
> in size, we've practiced harder, and we have the better
> game plan.
>
> LOGIC-FREE VALUES: Men, get out there. Be big. Be hard.
> Work the plan. Win the game.

> RATIONAL THOUGHT: Don't be scared. There aren't any mon-
> sters under the bed.
>
> LOGIC-FREE VALUES: You're safe. I'll be safe here, protecting
> you, in your own warm bed.

Avoid the Monsters

Am I proposing that we all speak like Bush? No. Probably even Bush doesn't
mean to speak like Bush. In fact, while eliminating the logic can make your
codewords stick better, you don't want to eliminate logic altogether. Code-

words tend to go along with present-tense, demonstrative, tribal rhetoric. To get what you want in a deliberative argument, you usually need a healthy dose of logic—spiked with values. Aristotle used the commonplace as the centerpiece of deductive logic, not a substitute for it. Commonplace words and codewords are often the same thing.

Straying more than a little from Aristotle, Bush takes those codewords and repeats them like a political mantra until they become like a song you can't get out of your head. But it can help you pull a tribe together. Repetition acts like a football cheer, or the refrain to a song, or a protest chant, making people feel part of a group—a group headed by you. These terms are the ties that bind Bush to his audiences; and the more ties, the better.

To speak in Bushisms or other effective code language, choose the words that work, and avoid denying words that trigger a bad response. You want to avoid repeating terms that hurt your argument. If you say, "Don't be scared," a kid may hear "scared." If you say, "There aren't any monsters under the bed," the kid hears "monsters under the bed." As we have seen, avoiding harmful words is especially important when you fend off an accusation. If you repeat the charge ("I am not a crook"), you may actually strengthen it in the audience's mind.

In fact, the reverse is true. You can use denial to mean the exact opposite of what you're literally saying, as Bush did when he described how Iraqis received our troops.

> WHAT BUSH SAYS: I think we are welcomed. But it was not a
> peaceful welcome.
> WHAT STICKS IN PEOPLE'S MINDS: . . . welcomed . . . peaceful
> welcome.

I call this technique **reverse words**—repeating the words that mean the opposite of what hurts your case. Instead of saying, "We hadn't anticipated the violent reaction to the invasion," Bush says, "We are welcomed. But it was not a peaceful welcome." A violent reaction turns into a peaceful welcome—with an incidental "not" in front of it.

You can use the same tool whenever an argument turns against you. Concede your opponent's point by admitting that the point is not its opposite. Queen Victoria

> ▸ **Argument Tool**
> REVERSE WORDS:
> Repeat the terms
> that express the
> opposite of your
> weakness or
> your opponent's
> stance.

said, in a famous understatement, "We are not amused." She did not say, "We are appalled."

> OPPONENT: Your department is failing to meet its goals.
> WRONG ANSWER: It's not really failing.
> RIGHT ANSWER: Well, we aren't breaking records yet.

> SIGNIFICANT OTHER *(looking fat)*: Does this make me look fat?
> WRONG ANSWER: No, not that fat at all.
> RIGHT ANSWER: It doesn't make you look thin.

Words like "failing" and "fat" generally do not make good codewords. "Breaking records" and "thin" do.

Code grooming is an excellent way to get an audience to identify with you. Blue-staters often have a hard time with it. They prefer a Bill Clinton or John Kerry, who can speak whole, logical, publishable thoughts. But John Kerry lost the election in part because he tried to win his arguments while Bush focused on identity. In a formal debate, as the ancients said, rhetoric is verbal jousting. In human society, as the modern rhetoricians say, rhetoric is social glue.

The identity strategy can do more than make your audience identify with you. In the next chapter you'll learn how to make them identify with your *choice*. You won't just win friends. You will truly influence people.

The Tools

There are some 2,800 languages spoken on earth at the moment, along with seven or eight thousand dialects. You can further divide dialects by regional accents, professional jargon, religious and political speech, and code language of all kinds. And these groups can split into the private jokes and secret words of families, friends, lovers. If you want to define a group of people—or rather, if you want to see how people define themselves—look for the language that makes them most comfortable. Code language determines who's in and who's out of our personal Venn circles. It reveals what we value.

We express the purest kind of present-tense demonstrative rhetoric in code—the words that we share within our own groups. The specific tools:

Code Grooming: Use language unique to the group, and as long as you don't apply it indecorously, you'll get in tight with your audience.

Logic-Free Values: Perfectly rational speech can not only be a turnoff for some audiences but actually distract them from a values message. This is one reason why Aristotle said that *logos* works better in an intimate setting than in front of a large crowd. Focus on the individual values words to bring a group together and get it to identify with you.

Repeated Codewords: Find those specific commonplace terms that make a group bond, and use them again and again and again.

Reverse Words: Find words that mean the opposite of the ones your opponent used. Avoid repeating your opponent's terms when you deny them.

19. Make Them Identify with Your Choice

▲

THE MOTHER-IN-LAW RUSE

Persuasion's most magnetic tool: identity

Rhetoric is concerned with the state of Babel after the Fall. —KENNETH BURKE

Learn to master the codes of your audiences, and you will go a long way toward winning their trust. Even better, you can get them to identify with your choice. If they're for it, they're in. If they're against it, they're out.

That is the purpose of this chapter: to take the **identity strategy** to its next level. We will employ a skillful mix of deliberative and demonstrative rhetoric, getting your audience to see your choice as something critical to your relationship. They will identify with what you want, and see the alternative choice, the one you oppose, as something alien to the relationship.

Sometimes identity is the sole purpose of an argument. As it is, few of us get to pitch our arguments on formal, organized occasions the way George W. Bush does. Our own arguments often come and go without any real resolution.

HE: So you think we should pull out of Iraq? I don't. We should finish the job.

SHE: What do you mean by "finishing the job"? You—[*Phone rings. She answers, returns eventually.*]

HE: Who was that?

SHE: My mother.

TRY THIS IN A PUBLIC DEBATE
When it appeared that Americans were torturing prisoners in Iraq and Guantánamo, the most effective argument against it was the demonstrative language of identity: "Americans don't torture people. That's not who we are." Similarly, when a group of taxpayers opposed giving raises to teachers in a wealthy school district near us—arguing that the district was already paying them 40 percent over the state average—a powerful rebuttal would have been demonstrative: "Salaries show concretely what we value as a community. A cosmetic surgeon in the local hospital makes five times what the average teacher earns." Then redefine the issue along deliberative lines: "The question shouldn't be about what we pay our teachers. It should be about what we demand from them. Let's raise their salaries and make them propose ways to boost our kids' advanced placement scores."

HE: You told her we weren't coming for Thanksgiving, right?
SHE: Well, I . . .
HE: You *didn't*? I thought we agreed to stay home for once.

A war debate thus turns into a quarrel over a family holiday. People often argue this way, sliding into points of view, getting interrupted, changing subjects, sometimes losing any discernible train of thought. How can you possibly stay on topic?

Much of the time, you can't. Many arguments—perhaps most of them—do not set about making rational choices; nor is that always such a bad thing. Besides helping you decide what to do, an argument can strengthen a relationship. Or weaken it. The difference lies in how you use code grooming.

The couple seems to have made a decision already; both agreed to stay home at Thanksgiving, at least until the woman was supposed to tell her poor mother they planned to abandon her this year. Future and present tenses get mixed; the man balances the pain of the trip (the disadvantageous, if you will) with the marital points the man would win for giving in gracefully. Call it deliberative argument: what choice will be to the family's best advantage? But their argument is not just about the "advantageous," is it? It's also about obligations, about keeping the tribe together. This is tribal talk, the language of demonstrative, present-tense rhetoric, whose main topic isn't the advantageous but what we value.

The man *could* weigh in with a strong demonstration of values:

HE: Hey, when I promise something, I stick to that promise. I don't change my mind because the sound of my mother's voice makes me feel guilty.

Then he could deliver a deliberative knockout blow that stresses the disadvantages of travel:

HE: And think of flying on the worst day of the year, only to eat institutional food at the senior center.

He could also toss logical grenades, mix in some *pathos* over his stress level at work, do a little *ethos* thing about the sacrifices he has made for the family over the years, offer a tempting vision of a happy, quiet Thanksgiving at home—and leave the woman speechless with his dazzling persuasion. He may even win and get to stay home. But the eventual result, most likely, is a Pyrrhic victory. By winning the argument, he risks loosening family ties. He may find himself doing relationship repair work for months to come, and his marriage could slide into such a parlous state that he ends up spending the night before Christmas with his feet hanging over the edge of a bed in his mother-in-law's spare room.

Which would you prefer: the family debating prize, or marital saint-hood? Sometimes winning an argument may not be your best goal. Relationships and values occasionally trump the advantageous and a rational decision. Ah, but is there a way for the man to have his Thanksgiving pie and eat it too? Possibly. Very possibly. With the identity strategy, he might. He needs to convince his wife that staying home strengthens the family, but flying for Thanksgiving weakens it.

Disclaimer: We're about to get into tactics involving naked, ruthless exploitation of a wife's feelings. If the man does it right, he will actually make her believe that stiffing her mother out of Thanksgiving is good for everybody, even her mother. This may seem inappropriate, especially in a chapter on defense, but I put it here for a reason: the identity strategy is one of the chief ways that advertisers, politicians, salespeople, and nearly every other nefarious element in society manipulate us. I place the weapon in your hands so we can dismantle it together, see how it works, and know when we're the victims.

In the identity strategy, *logos* can be a distraction. We saw that with Bushisms. Instead of weighing premises and offering compelling reasons, identification language simply brings your audience and your choice together in one tight, happy tribe. Let's resume the argument.

> HE: I thought we agreed to stay home for once.
> SHE: But you should have heard her. She's counting on seeing me—us.

Fumble! The husband *could* pick up the ball and run with it:

> HE *(looking hurt):* It'd be nice if you all considered me a member of the family.

But that would be too easy, and it would hardly help the relationship. Instead, the husband employs demonstrative rhetoric. He ignores the slip and gently imitates his mother-in-law, a Southern woman with Kentucky roots that stretch back to the Daniel Boone era.

> HE: You're comin' this Thanksgiving, ahn't you? When do the children get out of skoo'?

By mimicking the mother-in-law right down to her eccentric usage of "school'," the husband employs a time-honored technique that brings his audience inside the joke while distancing the victim. The wife laughs; she loves that he knows her mother well enough for a dead-on and yet gentle imitation. That brings the couple closer together, tightening the circle around the two of them. And it induces the wife to unconsciously leave her mother outside it.

▶ **Persuasion Alert**
Just as Virgil conducted Dante through the *Inferno*, I want to be your trusty guide through the persuasion underworld. So, just to keep my *ethos* intact here, I want you to know that I would never, ever do this to my own mother-in-law, and not just because she intends to read this book.

> HE *(looking serious):* You really want to go, don't you?

He's being quite sneaky, playing off his wife's sense of guilt; she doesn't want to go, but feels she should.

> SHE: Oh, I don't know . . .

Now he has the moral upper hand, and he uses it to groom her.

> HE: You know I love your mother. I'll support you in whatever decision you make.

"Love" and "support" are superb codewords that test well among women voters, sexist as that may sound; it's a bit risky to use it on the man's wife, though, especially if she earns the steady income. But by evoking her mother, he creates a forgiving environment that brings the couple closer together in love, harmony, and shameless manipulation.

TRY THIS IN THE OFFICE
You can employ a negative version of the identity strategy with an intentionally bad endorsement. Suppose your boss is leaning toward a decision that you oppose. Instead of arguing against the decision, you use your boss's despised predecessor as a weapon. You (innocently): "Larry would have loved that idea." The negative endorsement is risky, though. It could hurt your *ethos* by linking you with the wrong person.

> SHE: Oh, let's just stay home. I'll take a long weekend in early November and fly down myself.

The man will spend an extra couple of eons in purgatory eventually, but at least he won't have to fly six hundred miles for Thanksgiving.

Catching Code

Yes, code grooming has a dark side to it. What bonds one group excludes others. Exclusivity is part of the bond, after all. We lovers of language are loath to admit it, but some of our passion for "correct" grammar comes from an impulse not that different from a white adolescent's love of hip-hop lyrics: we grammarians know the code, which separates us from the others. When language changes, and we have difficulty keeping up with it, we feel some loosening of our social bonds. We feel ungroomed.

The misuse of the objective case ("He gave it to him and *I*," instead of the correct "him and me") breaks my grammatical heart every day. Yet no logical reason in our inconsistent, quirky old language exists for using the objective case. Proper grammar is elite, not "good," grammar. Still, learning it helps those who weren't to the office born. Anyone who interviews for a management job at a Fortune 500 company had better speak the corporate code, which puts the underprivileged at a disadvantage. On the other hand, if you give a black child from Watts a decent education, he benefits more than a privileged white kid from Greenwich—not because the Watts kid knows less (he doubtless has a wealth of knowledge denied the white kid) or because what he knows is less important, but because the black kid can pick up a language the white one already has.

In rhetoric, the persuader speaks the language of the audience. That may not be so easy. The nerdy white guy who mangles the dialect in the inner city ("Yo, ma niggah, sup?") is a commonplace in teen films, a variation of the *Beverly Hillbillies* shtick—outsiders meeting a different tribe and misusing the code, like rubes in L.A.

Your own tribe can be your family, age group, gender, religious denomination, socioeconomic group—anything that binds you with your very own words and images. When George Bernard Shaw referred to America and England as "two nations separated by a common language," he was making a rhetorical point: the same literal tongue can be used with subtle variations that combine and exclude.

One of those variants—and an effective code-grooming tool in its own right—is **irony,** the technique of saying one thing to outsiders and another to insiders. Wayne Campbell, Mike Myers's character in the movie *Wayne's World,* uses irony on a clueless inventor who comes on to their public-access show with the Suck Cut, a hair groomer that, as he puts it, "sucks while it cuts." Wayne concedes, "It certainly does suck."

▸ **Argument Tool**
IRONY: Bond with people by speaking a hidden language.

When you see irony as a form of code grooming, it makes sense that a time of deep societal division would be an especially ironic one. Feeling the social tension, people use irony as frantically as lousy chimps. They want to know who's in and who's out, and irony lets them strike a double chord that uses two dialects at once. Irony therefore makes the perfect rhetorical figure. It dresses in drag and then lifts its skirt. A kind of reverse password, it welcomes every member of the audience that "gets it."

Irony is at its best when some people *don't* get it. My daughter and I went to see the movie *Adaptation,* which has a scene that drips with irony. One of the characters says something especially sappy that the audience is not supposed to take at face value. It's meant to be funny. But a middle-aged woman sitting behind us said, "That is so *true.*" Dorothy and I looked at each other and cracked up. I'm grateful to that woman. She brought father and daughter closer.

You can use irony to sugarcoat messages to kids, even young ones.

YOU: Wow, what did you do to your room?
KID: It's not my fault.
YOU: No, I mean it's *fabulous.* I love the decor's studied sans souci. My dirty clothes would look *perfect* on this floor. Here, let me go get some . . .

▸ **Don't Try This in the Office**
While it's a great demonstrative tool for bringing a group together, irony can bollix up decision making. Action requires commitment, which in turn requires more emotional power than irony provides. This is why you'll find few ironic CEOs. Save the irony for people at your own level.

Well, it *could* work. At any rate, it might get a laugh—out of your spouse, not your kid. Just make sure that when you do use irony, it works for the audience you intend. When you have to say, "It's a joke," it's not a joke. I once spent the night at the home of a working couple with three small children. When Susan led me to my bedroom, she apologized for the mess. Thinking she knew what low standards I set as a housekeeper myself,

I replied ironically, "Well, you know, Susan, I find that a clean house creates the right moral climate for one's children. Clean house, clean mind."

Dead silence. Susan turned at the doorway and stalked down the stairs. "It's a joke," I murmured.

No, it wasn't.

Code grooming can work beautifully when you want to repair relationships or get your audience in sync with your mood and your ethos. But the identity strategy can hurt a group as much as it can help it. For one thing, overuse of identity leads to groupthink—where bonding, rather than the "advantageous," governs decisions. This is the danger of speaking demonstratively in the present tense. If the aim is identity, then the whole point of persuasion is to make everyone eager to belong—the ultimate source of yes-men and -women.

And as you have seen, code grooming can manipulate you in subtle ways. So you need to watch out for the particular codes that appeal to the groups you identify with, such as your education, gender, political leanings, age, looks, hobbies, and degree of optimism toward the world. Marketers slice demographic and psychographic groups into increasingly thin portions. Once they learn enough of your preferences and habits, they can predict your behavior with impressive accuracy. If you buy a Macintosh computer, you're more likely to vote Democratic. If you have an American eagle over your door, you're unlikely to drink single malt scotch. People who run three times a week spend a relatively small portion of their money on clothing. Along with these habits come code language, words that trigger an emotional response.

To construct a rhetorical defense against the marketing arts, list the words that make you feel good about yourself; for instance:

> ▸ **Argument Tool**
> CODE INOCULATION:
> List the codewords
> that appeal to you so
> you can be conscious
> when a persuader
> uses them.

> Educated
> Subtle
> Thoughtful
> Contrarian
> Sophisticated
> Cosmopolitan
> Learned

If an advertisement uses one of your words, congratulations: your group is getting marketed.

> McSnoot: The Educated Scotch
> The Jaguar Peripatetic: For the Contrarian Driver
> Grapefruit Juice: The Thoughtful Drink

The fact that I don't see those words must make me part of an extremely small marketing segment. Or a cheap one. I prefer to describe my group as "exclusive" or "highly select"—just like someone who reads this book. Feel sufficiently groomed?

The Tools

"Ideology" once meant the study of ideas; now it means a shared belief. Ideas become beliefs when people identify with them—when they help define the group itself. It would be difficult to describe what distinguishes Americans from other people, for example, without talking about what Americans value and believe in. To help turn an idea into a belief, these tools will get the audience to identify both with you and the idea:

> **Identity Strategy:** The surest way to commit an audience to an action is to get them to identify with it—to see the choice as one that helps define them as a group.
> A spin-off of the identity strategy is **irony:** saying one thing to outsiders with a meaning revealed only to your group.
> **Code Inoculation:** Be aware of the terms that define the groups you belong to, and watch out when a persuader uses them.

20. Get Instant Cleverness

▲

MONTY PYTHON'S TREASURY OF WIT
Figures of speech and other prepackaged cunning

I say they are as stars to give light, as cordials to comfort, as harmony to delight, as pitiful spectacles to move sorrowful passions, and as orient colours to beautify reason.
— HENRY PEACHAM

K now that feeling when you can't think of a clever retort until it is too late? The French and Germans, those connoisseurs of humiliation, each had a name for it *(l'esprit de l'escalier; Stehrwitt)*. Rhetoric invented figures of speech as a cure for these second thoughts; they arm you with systematic thinking and prefab wit so you never find yourself at a loss again. Figures help you become more adept at word play; they make clichés seem clever, and can lend rhythm and spice to a conversation.

Up until modern times, rhetoricians believed that figures had a psychotropic effect on the brain, imprinting images and emotions that made people more susceptible to persuasion. For all we know, they actually do; modern science hasn't disproved the theory. At the very least, figures add sophistication. They can attract the opposite sex (at least those who find a clever person sexy). Best of all, they form the coolest vehicle to persuasion, speeding the audience to your argument goals and blowing their hair back.

So let's pimp your rhetorical ride.

▶ **Meanings**
L'esprit de l'escalier and *Stehrwitt* mean "the spirit of the staircase" and "stair wit," inspiration that comes after one leaves another's apartment.

▶ **Persuasion Alert**
You may recognize a fallacy of ignorance in "Modern science hasn't disproved the theory"; because it hasn't been disproved, the fallacy goes, it must be true. But I'm saying we don't know either way, so I'll cut myself some slack here.

Those Scheming Greeks

The Greeks called them "schemes," a better word than "figures," because they serve as persuasive tricks and rules of thumb. While Shakespeare had to memorize more than two hundred of them in grammar school, the basic ones aren't hard to learn. Besides, you already use plenty of figures—analogy ("My love is like a cherry"), oxymoron ("military intelligence"), the rhetorical question (Do I have to explain this one?) and hyperbole (the most amazingly great figure of all).

> ▸ **Meanings**
> The Greek word for figures was *schemata*. Some rhetoricians use "schemes" to denote "figures of thought," but the Greeks did not make the distinction.

We spout figures all the time without knowing it. For instance:

> YOU: Oh, you shouldn't have.

If you really mean it—that if they give you one more ugly, ill-fitting sweater you'll have to kill them—then you have not used a figure. But if the gift is a new iPod, and you can barely keep from running off and playing it, then your oh-you-shouldn't-have constitutes a figure called **coyness.** Cheapskates who let others pick up the tab tend to use the coyness figure.

> ▸ **Useful Figure**
> COYNESS: The oh-you-shouldn't-have figure. Formal name: *accismus* (as-SIS-mus).

> CHEAPSKATE: No, let me . . . Really? Are you sure?

Teenagers are especially fond of the figure called **dialogue,** which repeats a conversation for rhetorical effect. A beautiful example appears in the first Austin Powers movie, when Dr. Evil asks his son how he's doing.

> ▸ **Useful Figure**
> DIALOGUE: Formal name: *dialogismus* (di-a-lo-JIS-mus). Use it to add realism to storytelling.

> SCOTT EVIL: Well my friend Sweet Jay took me to that video arcade in town, right, and they don't speak English there, so Jay got into a fight and he's all, "Hey quit hasslin' me cuz I don't speak French" or whatever! And then the guy said something in Paris talk, and I'm like, "Just back off!" And they're all, "Get out!" And we're like, "Make me!" It was cool.

▶ **Useful Figure**
SPEAK-AROUND, which uses a description as a name. Formal name: *periphrasis* (per-IF-ra-sis). The Latin-derived name, *circumlocution,* is more common among laypeople than among rhetoricians. "Periphrasis" is more insiderish.

When John Mortimer's fictional Rumpole of the Bailey refers to his wife as "She Who Must Be Obeyed," he uses a **speak-around,** which substitutes a description for the proper name. Prince Charles used it deftly when he referred to the leaders of China as "appalling old wax works." And a man who wants to sound like a Rat Packer uses a speak-around when he refers to women as "broads."

Allow me a parenthesis here (which, by the way, is a figure in its own right). A rhetorician who reads this may squirm at my use of "dialogue" and "speak-around" for *dialogismus* and *periphrasis.* But when the Greeks invented coyness, they called it coyness, not some name they couldn't pronounce. The Greek terms stuck, unfortunately. By the 1600s, rhetoric was sinking under their weight, to the point where the writer Samuel Butler complained:

> *All the rhetorician's rules*
> *Teach but the naming of his tools.*

I'll name the tools—in English *and* in Foreign. But you will find no final exam at the end of the book. Instead, this chapter covers some of the principles behind figures so you won't have to memorize a thing. Just use the tactics that sound best to you.

And God Said, Figuratively . . .

Figures come in three varieties: figures of speech, figures of thought, and tropes. Again, you don't have to know the terms; I use them just to show how they work.

Figures of speech change ordinary language through repetition, substitution, sound, and wordplay. They mess around with words—skipping them, swapping them, and making them sound different.

In the King James Bible, every verse in the first book of Genesis after "In the beginning God created the heaven and the earth" starts with "And."

TRY THIS IN A PRESENTATION
And have you noticed how political figures often begin their sentences with "And"? Many use it as a substitute for "Um" or "You know" while they think of what to say. "And" gives continuity and flow to oral speech. Use it too much, though, and you sound like a manic prophet.

And the earth was without form, and void; and darkness was
　　upon the face of the deep. And the Spirit of God moved
　　upon the face of the waters.
And God said, Let there be light: and there was light.
And God saw the light, that it was good: and God divided the
　　light from the darkness.

This technique is the **repeated first words** figure.
Monty Python and the Holy Grail uses repeated first words
in its own scripture, the Holy Book of Armaments.

> BROTHER: And Saint Attila raised the hand gre-
> nade up on high, saying, "Oh, Lord, bless this
> thy hand grenade that with it thou mayest blow
> thy enemies to tiny bits, in thy mercy." And the
> Lord did grin, and people did feast upon the
> lambs, and sloths, and carp, and anchovies,
> and orangutans, and breakfast cereals, and
> fruit bats, and large . . .
> MAYNARD: Skip a bit, Brother.
> BROTHER: And the Lord spake, saying, "First shalt
> thou take out the Holy Pin . . ."

Another figure of speech makes one noun serve a
cluster of verbs. Hockey announcers use this figure,
multiple yoking, when they do play-by-play.

> ANNOUNCER: Labombier takes the puck, gets
> it past two defenders, shoots . . . misses . . .
> shoots again, goal!

One of the most common figures of speech, the
idiom, combines words in an inseparable way that
has a meaning of its own. *The whole ball of wax* is an
idiom, for example. An idiom may be *Greek to you* (to
coin another idiom). *Joe Average* may not have the
foggiest notion of what a person is *getting at,* but take it
all with *a grain of salt* and *Bob's your uncle. Catch my
drift?* Listen carefully for idioms in conversation; they

> ▶ **Useful Figure**
> REPEATED FIRST
> WORDS: Formal
> name: *anaphora*
> (an-AH-phor-a).

> **TRY THIS IN A
> SPEECH**
> The anaphora
> works best in an
> emotional
> address before a
> crowd. "Now's
> the time to act.
> Now's the time
> to show what
> we can do. Now is
> the time to take
> what's wrong and
> set it right!"

> ▶ **Useful Figure**
> MULTIPLE YOKING,
> the play-by-play
> figure. Formal name:
> *diazeugma* (die-ah-
> ZOOG-ma).

> **TRY THIS IN A ONE-ON-
> ONE ARGUMENT**
> Multiple yoking lets
> you speak fast in a log-
> ical argument to over-
> whelm your opponent
> and bowl over your
> audience. "You failed to
> answer the question,
> used a whole string of
> fallacies, seem to have
> made up what few
> facts you used, and
> didn't even bother to
> speak grammatically."

make terrific code words. "Greek to me" comes from Shakespeare, and college graduates use it more than other people. If you hear someone say, "They're in a pickle," chances are she comes from the Midwest, where that idiom still gets served. When someone else suggests you "break bread" together sometime, the odds increase that he's a Christian. (George Bush's Christian code often relies on idioms like this to bring the tribe together.) And if someone warns against "changing horses in midstream," the commonplace idiom that helped get Bush reelected, you probably are not dealing with a risk taker. A good salesperson will listen for idioms and speak them back to you. If you say you want a stereo that "won't break the bank," for instance, you will probably hear the salesperson echo the idiom. Don't leave a good technique to the hawkers; try it yourself when you want to persuade somebody. It's one of the easiest figures to use in daily life.

▸ **Useful Figure**
IDIOM (ID-ee-om), which combines words to make a single meaning.

While figures of speech mess around with words, *figures of thought* are logical or emotional tactics—ready-to-hand schemes for using *logos* or *pathos* on the fly. Most of the tools you see in other chapters—from conceding a point to revealing an attractive flaw—qualify as figures of thought.

The rhetorical question is that sort of figure. Here's another: if you ask a rhetorical question and then answer it, you employ the **self-answering question.** Protesters use it all the time. ("What do we want? Justice! When do we want it? Now!") So does the Cowardly Lion in *The Wizard of Oz*.

What makes a King out of a slave? Courage.
What makes the flag on the mast to wave?
    Courage.
What makes the elephant charge his tusk in the
    misty mist or the dusky dusk?
What makes the muskrat guard his musk?
    Courage.
What makes the Sphinx the Seventh Wonder? Courage.
What makes the dawn come up like THUNDER?! Courage.

▸ **Useful Figure**
SELF-ANSWERING QUESTION: Formal name: *hypophora* (hi-PA-phor-a). For some reason this means "carrying below" in Greek.

Tropes swap one image or concept for another. The word is a bit jargonistic, but we use tropes all the time. **Metaphor** is a trope—it makes one thing stand for another. ("The moon is a balloon.") **Irony** is a trope as well, because it swaps the apparent meaning for the real one. **Metonymy** swaps a part for the whole ("bluehairs" for elderly women; "longhorns" for cattle). And **synecdoche** swaps a thing for a collection of things ("White House").

In short, figures of speech switch words around, figures of thought use argument minitactics, and tropes make a word stand for something different from its usual meaning. Rather than just name the tools, though, I prefer to show a few ways that let you coin figures in various real-life situations.

Grab a Cliché and Twist

If an opponent uses an idiom or cliché (the two are kissing cousins, to use a clichélike idiom), you can win the heart of an intelligent audience by **giving the expression a twist.** Too many people avoid clichés like the plague, but they're a great resource—they make the rhetorical world go round—but only if you transform them with your instant wit. You will find it easier than it looks. For instance, take your opponent's cliché and stick on a **surprise ending.**

> SIGNIFICANT OTHER: I want to look like her. She looks as if she was poured into her bathing suit.
> YOU: Yes, and forgot to say "when."

I confess, I adapted that line (practically stole it) from P. G. Wodehouse. While I'm swiping, I will steal a superb line from Rose Macaulay.

> FRIEND: It's a great book for killing time.
> YOU: Sure, if you like it better dead.

You don't have to wait for a cliché in order to mess one up. Just bring one of your own.

▶ **Useful Figure**
METONYMY (meh-TON-ih-mee), which uses a part to describe the whole. I use the original Greek or Latin names for some figures because that's what they're commonly called.

▶ **Useful Figure**
SYNECDOCHE (syn-EC-do-kee), which swaps one thing for a collection.

▶ **Meanings**
You might say all words are a kind of trope, in which we swap sounds or symbols for the things we're talking about. That's pretty much what Plato said. He saw our sense of reality as a kind of trope— a set of images that stand in for the real thing.

▶ **Argument Tool**
THE CLICHÉ TWIST: Concede your opponent's cliché and then mess it up deliberately.

▶ **Useful Figure**
SURPRISE ENDING: Formal name: *paraprosdokian* (pa-ra-pros-DOK-ee-an).

OSCAR WILDE: One must have a heart of stone to read the
  death of little Nell without laughing.

Well, sure, easy for Wilde, Macaulay, and Wodehouse—three of the
wittiest people ever. But here's a secret to make a cliché practically reinvent
itself: **take it literally.**

OPPONENT: Let's not put the cart before the horse.
YOU: No. We might try something faster.

Most clichés qualify as figures in their own right. Putting the cart before
the horse, for instance, is a metaphor. If you forget the figure and just take
the cliché at face value, you find yourself thinking about its weird logic.

OPPONENT: Let's not pour the baby out with the bathwater.
YOU: No, let's just pull the plug.

That baby-and-bathwater thing is a pretty shocking cliché when you
think about it. By responding to it literally, you agree with your opponent
even while you contradict him. Nice jujitsu.

Suppose your town proposes expensive new racquetball courts and hires an architect to design them.
The plans show that the courts will cost double what
the budget had predicted. The town council holds a
meeting, and you find yourself debating a racquetball fan.

YOU: We don't need racquetball. This town
  has other priorities.
RACQUET GUY: But don't *eliminate* the courts.
  We shouldn't throw out the baby with the
  bathwater.
YOU: No, you're right. Let's just pull the plug.

Most clichés are absurd when you take them literally, which gives you an excellent opportunity for wit.

OPPONENT: The early bird catches the worm.
YOU: It can have it.

**TRY THIS WHEN YOU'RE
FEELING SNARKY**
Just think of appropri-
ate clichés and then
reverse them in your
head to see if one
makes sense. My bat-
ting average is about
.200. Gossiping about
a nasty acquaintance's
new trophy wife:

ME: "In this case the
  early worm got the
  bird."
FRIEND: "Surely she
  had some say in
  the matter."
ME: "Well, that mysti-
  fies me. I'd like to
  brain her pick."

(No, I didn't actually
say these things; two of
them in a row would
make even me blanch.)

The Yoda Technique

You can also transform a banal idiom by switching words around.

OSCAR WILDE: Work is the curse of the drinking classes.

That reminds me of the clever anonymous soul who used Thorstein Veblen's theory of the leisure class to criticize the teaching load of a college faculty.

The leisure of the theory class.

But switching words around works with far more than clichés. One of the most effective devices can transform just about any kind of sentence. You saw it before: the mighty **chiasmus.** As I mentioned before, this is my favorite figure, partly because it sounds terrific, especially in a formal speech, but also because it does a useful bit of persuasion. The chiasmus presents a mirror image of a concept, rebutting the opponent's point by playing it backwards. Kennedy took a commonplace, "What's the country done for me lately?" and reversed it for his chiasmus. His speech wouldn't have been the same without it.

WITHOUT THE CHIASMUS: Instead of seeking help from government, you should volunteer for it.
WITH THE CHIASMUS: Ask not what your country can do for you, ask what you can do for your country.

The chiasmus lets you turn your opponent's argument upside down. Imagine you represent a corporation accused of playing fast and loose with tax breaks; one member of Congress has even claimed that your company cheats the government. You could make a figure-free defense.

YOU: We're being falsely accused in a grandstanding move so some prosecutors and bureaucrats can score some easy points.

Or you could put it in a *chiasmus.*

TRY THIS IN A PRESENTATION
Business clichés offer many opportunities for a figure. To make your point, choose a cliché that opposes it, and then flip the cliché in a chiasmus: "Let's not settle for swimming with the sharks. Let's make the sharks want to swim with us."

YOU: It's not a question of whether we're cheating the government. It's whether the government is cheating us.

As I wrote this, my son walked in looking unhappy. I helpfully made him even more miserable with a chiasmus.

GEORGE: My friends never call me.
ME: Do you ever call your friends?

Of course he does. My response was foolish, but I couldn't resist.

Besides countering an argument, the chiasmus lets you change the meaning of a word. Just play the clause in reverse.

KNUT ROCKNE: When the going gets tough, the tough get going.

This is hard to do spontaneously; but you could add some humor to your writing by, say, inserting a pun into a chiasmus. Suppose you give a surprise party for a friend who turns forty. The guy's mother gives you some old photos, including one that shows your friend at age two, splashing in a wading pool, buck naked. (Or the now common "butt naked," which is incorrect but makes more sense.) What phrase comes to mind that combines innocent nakedness with a birthday? Birthday suit! Is there a pun there? Why, yes, there is. "Suit" changes meaning when you turn it into a verb. So let's make a card out of a chiasmus.

Front of Card (respectable recent photo of Bob):
WHAT KIND OF PARTY SUITS BOB'S BIRTHDAY?

Inside Card (photo of naked, two-year-old Bob):
THE KIND WHERE HE WEARS HIS BIRTHDAY SUIT.

Smaller type could say, "Come as you are to Bob's surprise party." I admit, the chiasmus is far from perfect. Neither is the card. Well, think you can do it better? Okay, but you'd better do it well.

▸ Classic Hits
THE FIGURE OF SPEECH DEFENSE: The man credited for inventing figures of speech was a Greek Sophist named Gorgias (GOR-gee-us, but I like to call him "Gorgeous"). He once made a pretend defense of Helen of Troy, the runaway bride who launched those thousand ships. Gorgias declared beautiful Helen innocent by reason of figures; smooth-talking Paris used them to "drug" her into running off with him, so she wasn't responsible for her own actions. Which goes to show, even rhetoricians have their fantasies.

How Churchill Got Rhythm

When you're in a serious argument, wit and banter will only take you so far. Then the figures you need the most will be the simplest figures of thought. The most common take two points and weigh them side by side. You're either for us or you're against us. Or as Bush put it, "You're either with us, or you're with the terrorists." Cindy Sheehan, the woman who lost her son in the Iraq war, used a contrasting figure when she held up a sign in front of Bush's ranch.

SHEEHAN: Why do you make time for donors and not for me?

The official name for this either/or figure is the **dialysis,** which succinctly weighs two arguments side by side. You're either this or you're that. A close relative is the **antithesis.** No figure does a better job of splitting the difference. In fact, boxing referees use an antithesis at the beginning of every match.

> ▸ **Useful Figure**
> The *dialysis* offers a distinct choice: either we do this or we do that.

> ▸ **Useful Figure**
> The *antithesis* weighs one argument next to the other.

In this corner, weighing one hundred and seventy-six pounds, the middleweight champion of the world, Julio Fuentes. And in this corner . . .

Notice how my examples tend to use repetition and parallel structure—phrases with the same rhythm—as if the speaker were weighing a couple of plums, one ripe, the other not. This pattern can clarify things at home or in the office.

> **TRY THIS IN A FORMAL DEBATE**
> In an organized argument or a large meeting, use jujitsu in combination with an antithesis by repeating your opponent's expression and then changing its form. "The law wasn't weak until your administration weakened it." This actually produces another figure, called *antistasis.*

PARENT: You can do your homework now and come to the movies, or do it later with a babysitter.

EMPLOYEE: Our competition outsourced its call center, saved twenty percent, and lost ten percent of its customers; we kept things domestic, gained market share, and came out ahead.

WOODY ALLEN: Those who can't do, teach. Those who can't
teach, teach gym.

Each example does what too few people do in an argument: offer a
quick summary that shows who stands in what corner. Side-by-side figures
can be used for evil, though. Avoid them if you have more than two choices.
That's cheating (if you get caught, that is).

Say Yes and No at the Same Time

An antithesis is particularly effective when it makes you sound objective.
You carefully weigh things side by side, look at the results, and come to a

▶ **Useful Figure**
CORRECTION
FIGURE: Formal
name: *epergesis*
(eh-per-GEE-
sis), meaning
"explanation."

reasonable conclusion—or so the audience believes. Another way to achieve this rhetorical version of objectivity
is to **edit yourself aloud.** Interrupt yourself, pretend you
can't think of what to say, or correct something in the
middle of your own sentence. Bartender Moe does it in
The Simpsons.

MOE: I'm better than dirt. Well, most kinds of dirt, not that
fancy store-bought dirt . . . I can't compete with that stuff.

Actually, let's not use Moe as an example. Instead, look at these two ways
of berating a lover.

WITHOUT THE CORRECTION FIGURE: I've never been so embarrassed as I was watching you at the party last night.
WITH THE CORRECTION FIGURE: I never was so embarrassed as
I was last night. Actually, I *have* been that embarrassed—
the *last* time we went to a party together.

Correcting yourself makes your audience believe you have a passion for
fairness and accuracy even while you pile on the accusations. That particular example isn't great for a relationship, but if you intend to condemn
someone, at least do it eloquently.

In an earlier chapter we talked about how to redefine an issue during an
argument.

DANIEL BOONE: I've never been lost but I will admit to being confused for several weeks.

A great figure of thought for redefining an issue is a "no-yes" sentence.

LOVER: You seem a little put out with me this morning.
YOU: Put out, no. Furious, yes.

> **Useful Figure**
> THE "NO-YES" SENTENCE: formal name: *dialysis*. It repeats the opponent's word with "no" after it, followed by a new, improved word.

The "no-yes" sentence offers you wonderful opportunities for irony. Change one word and your audience will think you have an endless supply of catty wit:

FRIEND: He seems like a real straight shooter.
YOU: Straight, no. Shooter, yes.

Or:

COWORKER: She says they're using a new system.
YOU: New, yes. Systematic, no.

> **Persuasion Alert**
> Yes, I'm being defensive about my cleverness. Writing is far from the best medium for teaching rhetoric; even Aristotle's *Rhetoric* would go down easier if Aristotle was teaching it in a classroom (in English).

Funny, no. Witty, yes, especially if it comes out spontaneously. Remember, things sound much more clever when you say them aloud than they do on paper.

We Are Not Unamused

The antithesis and the correction figures lie mostly in *logos* territory. But some of the most effective figures of "thought" have to do with the emotions. You can use them to turn the volume up or down in an argument. The **litotes** is one of the most popular for calming things down. It makes a point by denying its opposite; the result is an ironic understatement, and an appropriate answer to a stupid question. When reporters asked O.J. Simpson why he made an appearance at a horror comic book convention, he answered with a litotes.

SIMPSON: I'm not doing this for my health.

Under the circumstances, "I'm not doing this out of good taste" would have made a better litotes. Still, showing up at a horror convention after being acquitted of a double murder certainly isn't healthy.

A litotes can make you sound more reasonable than your opponent, especially in an age when everyone else on the planet uses hyperbole as his sole figure . . . I mean, when understatement isn't exactly the current fad.

> TRY THIS IN A MEETING
> You usually hear "not exactly" at the beginning of a litotes, a tired usage that almost turns it into a cliché. Try "I don't expect" or "I hope" instead. My wife and I went to the ballet, where a male dancer performed a staid minuet while two women spun and whirled around him. "I hope he doesn't strain himself," Dorothy said, a bit too loudly. It seemed to be the highlight of the evening for an alarming number of people.

> DAUGHTER: I'm going to school. Bye.
> FATHER, WITHOUT A LITOTES: You're not going anywhere dressed like that.
> FATHER, WITH A LITOTES: You're not exactly dressed for the part.

The litotes goes against the grain in these bloviated times, when most people assume an argument must consist of insults and exaggeration. Still, turning up the volume isn't such a bad thing at times. The ancients were big on "amplification"—figures that make an argument seem bigger than life. A particularly effective one orders your points so that they build to a climax. This figure, called (wait for it) **climax,** uses the last part of a clause to begin the next clause.

> BEN FRANKLIN: A little neglect may breed great mischief . . . for want of a nail the shoe was lost; for want of a shoe the horse was lost; and for want of a horse the rider was lost.

> ▸ Useful Figure
> CLIMAX: Formal name: *anadiplosis* (an-a-di-PLO-sis), meaning "climax."

The climax's structure works like a pyramid, with each part overlapping the next. It can lend an ominous pathos to a highly logical bit of narration: this happened, which led to this, which led to this. The climax also makes a terrific plot summary.

> JOAQUIN PHOENIX in *Gladiator:* They call for you: the general who became a slave; the slave who became a gladiator; the gladiator who defied an emperor. Striking story.

You can also use a climax for comparison, organizing things from least to most or vice versa. Humphrey
Bogart chose most to least in *The Caine Mutiny*.

> CAPTAIN QUEEG: Aboard my ship, excellent per-
> formance is standard. Standard performance
> is substandard. Substandard performance is
> not permitted to exist. That, I warn you.

The climax lends a rhythm that an audience gets
into—even when it disagrees with your point. The listener mentally fills in each next piece. This works so
well that it makes an efficient means of manipulation; a climax can lead an
unwary audience step by step straight into the slippery slope fallacy. Supreme Court justice Clarence Thomas tried just that in a law school speech.

> THOMAS: If you lie, you will cheat; if you cheat, you will steal;
> if you steal, you will kill.

As with any rhetorical tool, take good care of it, use it wisely, and try not
to hurt anyone.

TRY THIS IF YOU'RE THE BOSS
The climax can seem dramatic and quiet at the same time, making it an ideal business line. "Reach across departments and form teams. Teams boost creativity. Creativity boosts productivity. And productivity is what we are all about."

In Praise of "Like"

Now comes the fun part, which I saved for last. We have covered some basic
techniques for coining figures of speech and thought. For the rest of the
chapter, let's break some rules. We will start by using a figure of speech to
make up new words. This is dangerous in high school or a government
agency, where verbal originality often gets duly punished. You might also
face condemnation from people who consider novel usage a linguistic im-
purity. But the words will come, whether we want them to or not. Better you
and I should invent them than some adolescent on the street or, worse,
some adolescent behind a computer.

The figure I'm talking about is called **verbing.** Language conservatives
who want to close our lexical borders hate this figure, because it's a prodi-
gious neologizer. Calvin in *Calvin and Hobbes* dislikes the *anthimeria* (he's

▸ **Persuasion Alert**
Neologizer? That's a
neologism—I just
made it up. I call the
anthimeria "verb-
ing" because that's
its most common
use, but the figure
applies to any novel
change in a word's
use—noun to verb,
verb to noun, noun
to adjective. I like
"neologizer." It's
very neologous.

surprisingly conservative for a six-year-old). "Verbing weirds language," he says.

It certainly does. But our language can use some weirding. It freshens things up. Shakespeare certainly thought so. He used verbing to form "bet," "compromise," "drugged," "negotiate," "puking," "secure," "torture," and "undress," among many others, and he created even more words by changing verbs to nouns and nouns to adjectives. In an age when the average person had a vocabulary of 700 (today's college grad averages 3,000), Shakespeare's exceeded 21,000. He accomplished this by weirding language. If weirding was a turn-on for him (to use a once-popular *anthimeria*), it positively ecstacizes me.

You can Shakespearicate with some ease simply by turning nouns into verbs or vice versa. I'm not sitting at a desk. I'm *desking*. Like any kind of wordplay, verbing can distract instead of persuade. But if you need to attentionize an audience, it makes a pretty good tool.

> YOU: The next set of slides show our strategy in detail—so much detail that you might have trouble reading some of the charts. Don't try to get through them all. I just put them in to give you the big picture. It's a technique I call PowerPointillism.

Usage abhors a vacuum, and verbing can fill it. For years, grammarians frowned at the use of "contact" as a verb, as in, "I'll have my secretary contact your secretary." But words often enter common usage out of need, not ignorance. "Contact" is shorter than "get in touch," and more general than "call," "e-mail," "write," "meet with," or "bother." If you don't care how the secretaries talk to each other (assuming people still have secretaries), have them achieve contact.

"Impact" gets similar frowns, some of them deserved, when it is used as a verb. A meteor impacts the earth. A defensive lineman impacts the quarterback. I'd even accept a tax cut that impacts the economy—that runs smack up against it, for better or worse. But when

▸ **Persuasion Alert**
"PowerPointillism"
may exist already,
but I can't find it
on the Web.
Believe me, I
didn't spend a lot
of time thinking it
up. Fellow execs
would groan if I
whipped it out at
a meeting, but
deep down they'd
think me a witty
chap. Even the
most threadbare
figure comes off
as terribly clever
when it seems
to be spoken
spontaneously.

people overuse "impact" as a stand-in for "harm," I get impatient. "The bird flu impacted South Asia the hardest." This is metaphornication at its worst. A virus could impact something minuscule, perhaps, just as sperms impact eggs. But I'm sorry, microscopic viruses do not impact South Asia.

Verbing has a subspecies (called, technically, *parelcon*)—a word that gets stripped of its meaning and used as a filler. "Y'know" (we'll call that a word) is an example, and a bad one. "Y'know" means, um, y'know. I mean, it means "um."

The word "so," when used unnecessarily, is another misuse of an *anthimeria:*

> HE: So when are you coming?
> SHE: Well, so I was going to come tonight.
> HE: So are you bringing Lamar?
> SHE: So who's asking?

This is empty, fruitless talk that only reaps all its "so's."

In most cases, "like" commits the same crime. Even the brightest college students toss in "like" liberally, like a heart patient oversalting his fries. It's unhealthy. It impacts language wellness. But we shouldn't banish the place-filling "like" altogether. In fact, let's call it the *rhetorical "like."* Used judiciously, the rhetorical "like" serves many subtle purposes. You may not appreciate this next example, but bear with me:

▸ **Not So Useful Figure**
THE "LIKE" FIGURE:
Formal name: *parelcon*
(pa-REL-con), meaning "redundancy."

> SHE: I told him I was dating Wen Ho, and he was like, "You're *what?*"

In this case, "like" serves as a disclaimer of accuracy. ("The following quotation is an approximation, and only an approximation, of my ex-boyfriend's rhetorical ejaculation.") Young people often use "like" in this fashion to be ironic. It means, "He said that but not really." It also expresses ironic distance. ("The views expressed by my ex-boyfriend are not necessarily those held by me.") So, let's stretch things a little.

> HE: So are you, like, freaking or something?

This makes even my teeth hurt a little. But the "like" does serve a purpose—a couple, actually. It inserts a pause, like a rest in music, to place more emphasis on the sentence's key word, "freaking." And it gives "freaking" a broader connotation, as in, "Are you something in the nature of freaking?"

So: even meaningless words have meaning. Place fillers tend to change from generation to generation. "Y'know" was my generation's, and "like" is the filler of choice for the generation coming of age today. Why the evolution? Maybe my generation was (rightly) uncertain about its ability to communicate. "Y'know" meant, "Are you with me? Do you get what I'm saying?"

"Like," on the other hand, reflects a group too timid to stand firmly on one side of anything. This generation is an ambiguous one, which, from a rhetorical standpoint, may not be so bad. But if you want a consensus, irony eventually has to give way to commitment. Otherwise it's, like, so wishy-washy.

The Tools

William Shakespeare seems not to have enjoyed the endless list of figures he had to memorize at the Stratford grammar school. His plays contain a number of unflattering references to the likes of "Taffeta phrases, silken terms precise, / Three-pil'd hyperboles, spruce affectation, / Figures pedantical" *(Love's Labour's Lost)*. Yet Shakespeare stitched figures into speech better than anyone else, ever. His reluctant education in rhetoric lent rhythm and color to his compositions. While he ridiculed his education, he served as education's ideal.

> ▸ **Useful Figure**
> As Shakespeare was undoubtedly aware, he used a figure in this abuse of figures: the *asyndeton* (a-SYN-de-ton), which eliminates the conjunctions between phrases for poetic or emotional effect.

> ▸ **Useful Figure**
> "Get all Stratford Grammar on you" employs yet another figure: the *metallage* (met-ALL-a-gee) takes a word or phrase and uses it as an object within a sentence. ("I've heard enough 'Nos' for today.")

You'll see a larger list of figures in the back of this book, but the point of this chapter is not to get all Stratford Grammar on you with figures to memorize. Now that you see the ways that preplanned devices can work in speech, you will find yourself noticing figures all around you and, I hope, begin to freshen your own language with them.

Twist a cliché: Clichés make the world go round, and your job is to screw up their orbit. Ways to undermine clichés include **taking them literally** and reducing them to absurdity, attaching a **surprise ending,** and **swapping words.**

Change word order: Besides doing this with clichés, you can coin my favorite figure, the **chiasmus,** which creates a crisscross sentence.

Weigh both sides: This category of figure sums up opposing positions and compares or contrasts them. The **either/or** figure (dialysis) offers a choice, usually with an obvious answer. The **contrasting** figure (antithesis), on the other hand, can be more evenhanded. These side-by-side figures sum up an argument on your own terms, allowing you to define the issue.

Edit out loud: Correcting yourself midsentence allows you to amplify an argument while seeming fair and accurate. Another editing figure is the **redefiner** *(correctio)*, which repeats the opponent's language and corrects it.

Turn the volume down: The ironic understatement called **litotes** can make you seem cooler than your opponent.

Turn the volume up: The **climax** uses overlapping words in successive phrases to effect a rhetorical crescendo.

Invent new words: Verbing *(anthimeria)* does this easily by turning a noun into a verb or vice versa. The **"like"** figure *(parelcon)* also transforms the usage of words, most often by stripping them of meaning and using them as a rhetorical version of the musical rest note.

21. Seize the Occasion

▲

Spot and exploit the most persuasive moments.

A time to rend, and a time to sew; a time to keep silence, and a time to speak . . .
—ECCLESIASTES

....

As far as I know, my mother played exactly one practical joke in her entire life. She did it to teach my father a lesson, though neither one ever told me what Dad had done. It must have been egregious; Mom was not the joking type. She had a great sense of humor, but not the kind that needs a victim—except for this one time. It was as if she had waited all her life just to spring one joke and then retire in triumph. The joke went like this.

Dad comes home from work one Friday evening to find a dive mask, snorkel, fins, and a tiny Speedo laid out neatly on the bed.

▶ **Persuasion Alert**
Why am I suddenly using the present tense? For the same reason jokes often do. The present conveys *enargeia*, the sense that you're right here, right now.

DAD: What's that for?

MOM: It's for the party tonight.

DAD: I thought it was just dinner.

MOM: No, it's a costume party.

DAD: What for?

MOM: The women just thought it would be fun to have the men wear something wild.

DAD: Where's your costume?

MOM: I'm wearing a dress. The women won't be in costume.

You're thinking, what chump would fall for something like that? But it was inconceivable that Mom would know how to pull off a joke, even if she wanted to. It was unprecedented, and that was what made Dad fall for it. So Dad puts on the Speedo, grabs an overcoat from the closet, and drives her to the party. There he dutifully sheds the coat and dons the gear before flopping up to the host's front door and ringing the bell.

> DAD: What are the other men wearing?
> MOM: Oh, we're not supposed to tell. That's a surprise.
> DAD: What do you mean, a—

The door opens to reveal a formal crowd of women in dresses and, of course, men in coats and ties. Dad told me later that he was too much in awe to be angry. After all, she used remarkable patience and timing to make her husband look like an ass. Whatever it was he had done to her, I doubt that he did it again.

Rhetoricians would appreciate Mom's mastery of time and occasion. The ancients had a name for it: **kairos,** the art of seizing the perfect instant for persuasion. Just as educators have their "teaching moment"— an opportunity to make a point—persuaders have their

> ▸ **Argument Tool**
> *KAIROS:* Rhetorical timing, an ability to seize the persuasive moment.

persuasive moment. A person with *kairos* knows how to spot when an audience is most vulnerable to her point of view, and then exploit the opportunity. When someone sees you all dressed up and wants to know what the occasion is, he asks a *kairos* question: what timing and circumstances warrant that outfit? Snorkeling gear at an evening cocktail party is bad *kairos*. Knowing the perfect occasion to make your husband wear inappropriate snorkeling gear: that's good *kairos*.

A race car driver with *kairos* knows how to spot an opening and cut off the car ahead. (The ancients referred to chariots. Same thing.) A kid with *kairos* can tell precisely when her father is most vulnerable to a request for ice cream. *Kairos,* in short, means doing the right thing—practicing your decorum, offering the perfect choice, making the perfect pitch—at the

> ▸ **Classic Hits**
> WE CALL HIM "NICK OF TIME": The Greeks made *kairos* into a god, and sculpted him as an athlete, beautiful in front and bald in back, to show the persuasive moment as fleeting. The Romans changed his name to *Occasio*—"occasion." He survives in the expression, "Fortune is bald behind."

right time. The ancients made a big deal of *kairos,* because those fleeting moments are essential to changing an audience's mind.

Many arguments fail simply because of bad timing. A husband wants to talk his wife into buying a satellite radio but finds her paying bills—not a good moment to talk about spending money. Or he approaches her just as she starts crying over the novel in her hands. Or he tries to talk to someone about the election just when the guy has to leave work to pick up his kid at school. You could have the best argument in the world, but it won't get anywhere with these audiences. Not at the moment.

Josef Stalin, on the other hand, was a master of *kairos*. According to biographer Alan Bullock, Stalin would sit mute until the very end of meetings. Finally, if there was any disagreement, he would weigh in on one side or the other and settle the matter. He did this so often that comrades would look at him toward the end of every meeting, waiting for his judgment. In a party of equals, he made himself more equal than anyone else, despite being a coarse, ill-dressed peasant among well-bred colleagues. Stalin was the Eminem of *kairos*, a man who used his rhetorical skill to persuade an unlikely audience.

TRY THIS WITH A NEW IDEA
You're used to doing outlines. You can research an idea. And (perhaps with the help of this book) you know how to present it. But do you know your way around an occasion? Consider making an occasion plan, consisting of (1) the specific people who need to be convinced; (2) the best time (of year, week, and day) to convince them; and (3) the perfect circumstances (restaurant, office, gin joint) for persuasion.

If it worked for the mass-murdering dictator, it can work for you. In your own meetings, when do you speak up, and when do you shut up? When is it a good idea to procrastinate with an e-mail? When are the best times to broach a touchy family subject? And can *kairos* improve your sex life? (Of *course* it can!)

When the Commonplace Picks Up and Moves

If your audience is self-satisfied and unanimous, perfectly content with its current opinion, then you lack a persuasive moment. But few attitudes stay intact forever. As circumstances change, cracks begin to form in your audience's certainty.

> **When an audience's mood or beliefs are on the move, you have a persuasive moment.**

You'll find a persuasive moment in a time of uncertainty, change, or need, when a mood shifts or the audience sees evidence that challenges its beliefs—such as when the latest news conflicts with a commonplace. In the seventies, a significant portion of the population held the commonplace "Drugs

▶ **Argument Tool**
MOMENT SPOTTER: Uncertain moods and beliefs—when minds are already beginning to change—signal a persuadable moment.

are a victimless crime," right up until crack cocaine hit the streets and caused a crime wave. That was a great persuasive moment for those who wanted to get tough on drug crimes. When the evidence challenges the commonplace, beliefs begin to migrate, and you have a persuadable moment.

Some opportunities pop up in the middle of a meeting. Beliefs can migrate when people are simply sick of talking. Look at this scenario: A college considers changing dining services, so it follows academic tradition by holding a series of committee meetings involving every campus constituency. You agree to go to one, because the campus food tastes awful and it costs more than the fare offered by competing bidders. The meeting begins badly, from your point of view.

TRY THIS AT A TOWN MEETING
Why do the last speakers have the persuasive advantage? (Lest you doubt that they do, research confirms it.) One reason: the earlier speakers can cause opinions to begin migrating. Take advantage of this by restating the opinions of the earlier speakers, including opponents. The uncertain audience can be as vulnerable as the half-persuaded one.

TENURED PROFESSOR: I think we should stick with what we have. The service went out of its way to celebrate Martin Luther King Day this year—soul food, posters in the dining halls . . .

YOUNG INSTRUCTOR: I thought that was demeaning. I mean, fried chicken and collard greens!

TENURED PROF: That was entirely appropriate . . .

INSTRUCTOR: Do they serve spaghetti on Columbus Day?

PROF: I reject your analogy. Italian Americans don't represent a cohesive cultural minority.

DEAN: And we don't celebrate Columbus Day. The Native Americans . . .

SECRETARY: What do you mean Italian Americans aren't cultural?

TRY THIS WITH A NEW BUSINESS IDEA
Does your idea require an investment, or does it save money immediately? If it costs money, wait to propose it at the end of a successful fiscal year, when there may be money left in the budget and the forecast looks good for the next one. If your proposal saves money, time it for midyear. That's when execs get most nervous about making their numbers.

People? People? Can we please talk about the food? The temptation to yank the meeting back on track is awful. But you have a notion to try out your *kairos,* and this does not exactly seem like a persuasive moment. So you do the proper rhetorical thing: look concerned while doodling in your notepad. Eventually, the chair does her duty.

> CHAIR: Clearly, diversity will be important in the college's decision. What other issues do we need to consider?
> BUDGET OFFICER: We have four bids, and one of them is twenty percent lower than—
> TENURED PROF: Local. We should use local produce.
> SECRETARY: And organic.
> CHAIR: Okay, organic and local . . .
> BUDGET OFFICER: I really think price ought to be . . .

And then the lone student in the room brings up quality.

> STUDENT: The food sucks. It's, like, unidentifiable defrosted meat with rice maggots in gravy. Or veal parmesan that looks like scabs picked off elephants . . .
> SECRETARY: Ooh, thanks for sharing.
> STUDENT: Sorry. So I'm, like, just give me anything else. *Anything.* Hot dog venders. Pizza Hut. I don't care.

That reminds the dean of the time the food service served melted Popsicles for dessert at the trustees' dinner. The secretary wonders why they don't serve greener salads. The prof begins doodling in his notepad, and the instructor glances at the clock. Now is your persuasive moment. Cultural considerations are temporarily forgotten and the current service doesn't look quite so lovely. The only person who hasn't spoken is you.

> ▸ **Argument Tool**
> ANOTHER MOMENT SPOTTER: Are the other arguers petering out? Now's the time to sum up opinions in a way that favors yours.

> YOU: Here's what I'm hearing.

Good start! You can now sum up the consensus in your own terms.

> YOU: We are what we eat, which, from your descriptions *(glance at the student)* is not a pretty picture. So let's start

with the lowest bidder. *(Budget officer gazes with love in his eyes.)* Try out the food. If it's good, then we negotiate over cultural events and local produce. If it's not, we move on to the second lowest bidder.

> ▸ **Useful Figure**
> "You are what you eat" becomes clever only when you stick something onto the end of it. That's a *paraprosdokian*, the surprise ending figure.

The chair writes that down, the meeting adjourns, and many, many months later you eat better food. You performed first-class *logos*—defined the issue, conceded the others' points, spoke in the future tense . . . you even used a commonplace. "You are what you eat" is no mere cliché when the student's description remains fresh in people's minds. And you did good *kairos,* waiting until the opinion in the room began to shift.

Wait Till You See the Red in Their Eyes

The *pathos* side of a persuasive moment is similar to the *logos:* the time is ripe when the circumstances begin changing your audience's mood. The husband whose wife is crying over a romance novel needs to conduct some serious diagnostics before he pursues a little sexual healing. Do the tears come from the inevitable part of every sappy novel where the hero and heroine seem to be separated forever? Or from the part where the inevitable jerk mistreats the woman in a way that reveals the abuse all too common to his gender? Best not to find out. Hang back. Leave her alone, and then subtly check in on her a half hour later. No tears? Now is a good time to sit next to her and say, "Are you all right?"

TRY THIS IN A MEETING
Wait until late in the meeting, then speak in the tone of the reluctant conclusion (implying that sheer logic, not personal interest, compels you). You will seem like a judge instead of an advocate.

TRY THIS WITH A MAJOR E-MAIL
Most people send out important e-mails—big announcements, major ideas or proposals— late in the day. But office workers tend to multitask when they read e-mails at the beginning and end of the day. At lunchtime, Internet use soars as people focus on surfing and their latest mail.

SHE: Why?

HE: You just seemed a little upset awhile ago.

SHE: Oh, it's this stupid book. The heroine's lover accidentally kills her brother. *(Slight embarrassed smile.)* It's all very sad.

HE *(resisting urge to say, "Wasn't that a musical?"):* That's what I love about you.

SHE: . . .

HE: You went through labor without any drugs, twice, without shedding a tear. *(Uh-oh. Mention of parturition not a good mood setter.)* And yet you tear up at a sentimental novel.

SHE: You don't love that about me at all. It drives you crazy.

HE: You cried watching *Superman!*

SHE: His parents had to send him to another planet when he was just a baby. And *you* thought it was funny!

HE: . . .

He shouldn't have let the discussion lapse into the past tense: *You cried watching* Superman*!—You thought it was funny!* When you disagree in the past or present tense, you're not having an agreeable moment. The future tense is the one you want.

The man made a decorum mistake also with his highly improbable that's-what-I-love-about-you line. It caused him to lose credibility. The husband might have tried this approach instead:

HE: You know, that crying thing used to drive me crazy.

SHE: Doesn't it still?

HE: No. It doesn't. You went through natural childbirth. *(D'oh! Again with the birthing!)* And I've seen too many other instances of your bravery to think you're a softy. You're not sentimental. You're an empath. A loving person.

SHE: Are you trying to tell me something?

> ▶ Classic Hits
> "TIME FOR BED" IS ANOTHER *KAIROS* POEM: The biblical Ecclesiastes— "There is a time to, etc."—is a *kairos poem.* The original Hebrew term for "Ecclesiastes" means politician or orator. Set in the present tense, it's a bravura example of demonstrative rhetoric, the language of values.

You try doing better. It may not be the argument that fails him, but the moment. If she were in the right part of the book—where the man and woman, having been kept apart for 422 pages, finally get it on—then her husband might have a highly persuadable moment. She might tackle him before he says a thing. In sex, as in comedy, timing is everything.

But enough about sex. I want a satellite radio. (My mentioning one earlier was no accident.) My wife earns the steady income, and I find it wise to get her consent. But when I go to talk to her about it, there she is on the living room floor, sorting through the bills. Clearly, the mood isn't right. So instead of waiting for a persuadable moment, I try to make one. Heading to the kitchen, I whip up some grilled cheese sandwiches and tomato soup, her favorite lunch. (She's a Midwesterner, all right?) I wait until the aroma attracts her, and then turn the heat down. She stands, salivating, for a good ten minutes until I finally slide the spatula under the sandwiches. *Then* I make my satellite radio pitch. My wife's mood will be on the move, from frustrated frugality to hunger. Research will back me on this. Studies of consumer buying habits show that people spend a lot more money when they're hungry—not just on food, but on other necessities, such as satellite radios. At any rate, she may have forgotten about the bills temporarily.

TRY THIS WITH YOUR CREATIVE WORK

As you saw in earlier chapters, belief and expectation create or enhance moods. Cooks invented the appetizer as a *kairos* enhancer, getting the juices flowing like Pavlov's dog and creating the perfect moment to eat. You can do the same thing with your work; preview your idea with coworkers, taking care to reveal just a bit of what's to come. I used similar appetizers with my Web site, gradually putting up more of my book in a kind of reverse striptease. Internet sales data show that large doses of appetizers sell more books, just as long movie trailers attract more filmgoers than short ones.

> ME *(offhandedly):* Satellite radios are half the price they were six months ago.
> DOROTHY *(paying half attention):* Mmm.
> ME: So I was thinking. That may be the solution to the reception problems you've been complaining about. [*D'oh!*] I mean that you've been having.
> DOROTHY: I haven't been complaining about it. You have.
> ME: We live in the middle of nowhere. It's impossible to get decent radio. Ordinary people get to listen to all kinds of stations. We don't.
> DOROTHY: So what?

I let that one lapse into the present tense, didn't I? And I failed to use a strong commonplace. "Satellite radios are half the price," I said, implying, "which makes them a real value." Dorothy is a big believer in values, but since she never wanted a satellite radio in the first place, it's not a value from her point of view. *Kairos* alone won't hack it. So here I offer a far better commonplace:

> ME: You know what they've got on satellite radio now?
> DOROTHY: Mmm?
> ME: The Weather Channel. Twenty-four seven.

Now we're talking! Being from the Midwest, Dorothy finds the weather infinitely fascinating. Her parents—educated, accomplished people—would sit and watch the Weather Channel for an hour or more during prime time. They would pass up *Friends* and *Seinfeld* and even PBS specials in favor of stalled weather fronts and a drought in south Florida. The idea of getting the Weather Channel on radio would be irresistible to Dorothy.

> ME: And I can get a satellite radio at half price, plus a monthly
>   subscription for twelve bucks.
> DOROTHY: So you want a satellite radio.
> ME: No, I . . . I was thinking *you* . . .
> DOROTHY: And is that why you made lunch?

Well, sure. But after twenty-four years of marriage, Dorothy is totally onto me. When it comes to any kind of cool gear, I lack the disinterest essential to the trustworthy persuader. No *kairos* can get past that. I did get the satellite radio, by the way, using the unrhetorical method long favored by the male sex: I gave it to her for Christmas.

Let *Kairos* Fix Your *Ethos*

True geniuses at *kairos*, and I'm certainly not one, can turn their *ethos* liabilities into assets. When Martin Luther King went to prison, jail was a scandal, not the honor it can seem today. But he had a marvelous instinct for *kairos*, and he knew that white America—at least a sizable portion of it—was ready to consider a black man in prison something of a martyr. Cassius Clay used a similar *kairos* sleight of hand when he recognized before most people that white kids were beginning to listen to black musicians, that the generations were growing apart, and that the decorous world defined by Emily Post and John Wayne was about to change. The time was ripe for a Muhammad Ali, an overtly sexual, self-referential boaster, the original trash talker, a fighter turned peace activist, the world's first (and maybe only) ironic pugilist. Muhammad Ali was masterful in violating just about every element of middle-class, early-sixties decorum. He succeeded because he had a fighter's timing and an entertainer's decorum. He started out as a poorly educated black man from Kentucky and became the coolest man on the planet, occupying the very heart of the new decorum.

On a less profound level, when Bill Clinton was president, I saw him speak in the White House to a group of Democrats from New Hampshire. He treated them as his greatest political allies, and he spoke fondly of the state's first-in-the-nation primary in 1992. But he had lost that primary! New Hampshire Democrats spurned Clinton and chose a little-known Massachusetts senator named Paul Tsongas. Undeterred, Clinton had clawed his way back up in opinion polls and began to win the primaries that followed. He called himself the "Comeback Kid." And he thinks back on New Hampshire as the little state that started it all. Talk about a positive attitude; positive to the point of delusion. But a *kairos* lesson lies at the end of that story: if the decision isn't going your way, you can choose another persuasive moment.

TRY THIS IN POLITICS
In an unscientific study, I looked at every presidential campaign from 1960 through 2004 to see if there was a correlation between the national mood and the degree of smiling optimism each party's nominee seemed to show. I found that when voters think the country is headed in the wrong direction, Democrats tend to nominate sunny candidates (Humphrey, Clinton), while Republicans choose relatively gloomy ones (Nixon, Dole). The opposite holds true when voters like the country's direction; the Dems nominate frowners (Mondale, Kerry) and the GOP picks optimists (Bush and Bush). As I'm writing this, the country is in a terrible mood, which predicts a cheerful Democrat versus a grim Republican in the next election.

You could also say that Clinton simply switched audiences, from judgmental Yankees to people more amenable to his Bubba charm. The campaign did that for him. Where the primaries went, so did he, and after New Hampshire, they went south. Switching audiences can turn an unpersuadable moment into a persuadable one. Marketers spend millions to find susceptible audiences open to these moments.

Unfortunately, you and I don't always have that luxury. If one's lover is not in the mood, one generally should not seek a more amenable audience next door. Generally, you have to take the audience you are given, and if you want to persuade them, you usually need to wait for the right occasion. But not always. *Kairos* is the art of seizing the occasion, remember. Timing is only half of an occasion. And the other half? The medium. That's the next chapter.

The Tools

Just to make sure we have it all down:

Changing circumstances or moods often signal a **persuadable moment.**

You can create a persuadable moment by **changing or pinpointing your audience.**

22. Use the Right Medium

▲

If you want a symbolic gesture, don't burn the flag, wash it. —NORMAN THOMAS

Most men, but not all, know that it is a bad idea to propose marriage at a baseball game. It takes a strange mix of shyness and exhibitionism to ask a woman to marry you via JumboTron. If your proposal requires any persuasion, you may find yourself standing embarrassed in front of thousands of highly entertained fans. In short, you have chosen the wrong medium. The medium can make or break a persuasive moment. Say the right thing at the right time over the right channel, and the world is your rhetorical oyster.

You know the hazards of saying the wrong thing, and of persuading at the wrong time. The medium can be just as important. A guy where I used to work speculated about the sex lives of a couple of office mates in what he thought was a private e-mail to a coworker, and ended up sending it to the entire company by mistake. He is no longer employed with that company. Another guy I know commented enthusiastically on the breasts of a coworker in a manufacturing plant, unaware that his intercom was set for "Broadcast." He, too, is no longer with his company. Uncle Wip, host of a popular 1940s kiddie show on Philadelphia's WIP Radio, won idiotic immortality when he said, thinking he was off the air at the end of a program, "That ought to hold the little bastards." And you know about Paris Hilton's romp with a video camera.

> ▸ **Persuasion Alert**
> Look at my *logos* strategy here. I use extreme examples to prove my conclusion: the right medium is crucial to your *kairos*. Half of them are personal, because experiences bolster my *ethos*.

In each case, the fool in question performed in front of an unintended, if often appreciative, audience. This is nothing new. For eons, private letters have been intercepted and conversations overheard; technology now just makes it much, much easier to address the wrong crowd, or the wrong number, or to do it at the wrong time.

Which would you use to propose marriage: Face-to-face? The silent proffer of a ring? Letter? E-mail? Text message? Blog? PowerPoint presentation? Skywriting? Announcement at a ball game? Initials carved in a tree? Hallmark card? ("Our marriage is sure to be beautiful. Best wishes.")

The choice seems fairly obvious, though not to everyone, apparently. The face-to-face approach works best because it throws in all three appeals, by logic, character, and emotion. Skywriting and JumboTrons just don't convey the same pathetic appeal. And failing to show up for your own proposal certainly lacks *ethos*.

You should consider several factors in choosing a medium: timing, the kind of appeal (*ethos, pathos,* or *logos*), and the sort of gestures you want to make.

What's the timing? In other words, how fast a response does your audience expect? And how long should the message last? Paris Hilton might have been happier in the long run if her boyfriend had used a mirror instead of a video camera.

Which combination of *ethos, pathos,* and *logos* would persuade best? Each medium favors one appeal over the others.

What gestures will help your appeal? I mean "gestures" both literally and figuratively. In rhetoric, gestures can constitute everything from a shrug to a bonus check. A smile, a protest march, the boss's game attempt to wear a Hawaiian shirt on casual Friday, the subtler kinds of body language—all count as gestures. Rhetoricians went nuts over them in the eighteenth and nineteenth centuries, thanks to the "elocution movement." The old social structures were breaking down, and one's birth was becoming less of a prerequisite for aristocracy. Education could help earn a place in the gentry. But one also needed decorum—the manners and mannerisms of a gentleman or a lady. You can imagine the demand for books that taught how to act like gentlefolk. A whole category of best sellers sprang up around the teaching of elocution, which combined voice and gesture. In 1829 a speech instructor at Harvard even made himself notorious by teaching "exploding" vowels and devising a bamboo sphere for use in practicing gestures. The sphere tortured students until it was hung from a barber pole in Harvard Yard. Nonetheless, publishers were rapidly putting out books with engravings that showed gestures to convey every possible emotion.

Sensing Persuasion

What does all this have to do with the medium you choose for your message? Everything. Each sense has its own persuasive quality, and the medium using that sense carries the same sort of persuasion.

Sound is the most rational sense in regard to the spoken voice (though a voice can convey a lot of *ethos*). When the sound is music, *pathos* takes over.

Smell is the most pathetic. A bit of perfume, a whiff of gunpowder, or the stench of a diaper can trigger a strong emotional response.

Sight leans toward the pathetic, because we tend to believe what we see—and as Aristotle said, what we believe determines how we feel. But sight becomes almost purely logical when it encounters type on a page.

Touch: Pathos, of course. That's literally what we feel.

Taste: Pathos again, naturally.

Isn't it interesting that the spoken voice should be a rational medium? Television confuses things, because images trump sound; that makes TV lean toward the pathetic. Rhetoric naturally favors the logical approach; that's why persuaders try to convey vivid imagery; just as sight beats sound, *pathos* tends to trump *logos*. Radio reporters were on the front lines throughout the Vietnam War, but who remembers them? It was TV that ended that war—emotionally.

Okay, but what about reading type? That involves sight, doesn't it? No. Well, yes, it does involve the eyes, but the act of reading is more sound than sight—you receive voices, not mere type.

If you want your *kairos* to work properly, you need to know the rhetorical qualities of each medium. Take e-mail, for instance. As a medium of type, it conveys *logos* for the most part, with a bit of *ethos*. This makes it very bad for expressing an emotion. Because your audience can't see your face or hear your voice, your feeling becomes disembodied.

TRY THIS WHEN YOU SELL A HOUSE
A realtor will tell you to bake bread or put a few cinnamon sticks in a warm oven before an open house. This isn't to cover smells; it's a pathetic gesture that takes advantage of the smell receptors' proximity to the region of your brain dedicated to memory. Baking smells give potential buyers the comfortable feeling they had when they were kids—or think they had.

▸ **Classic Hits**
THEY WOULD HAVE BEEN POPULAR ON THE SUBWAY: The Greeks and Romans all read aloud, even when they were alone. It didn't occur to them to read silently. Words on a page were like a recording; the reader's job was to play it back in his own voice. A group of readers must have sounded like a classroom of first-graders. No wonder they had a love-hate relationship with writing.

Then there's the weird timing of e-mail, both instantaneous and potentially permanent. An e-mail stays angry, sitting there like a bomb in your
audience's in-box, long after you have calmed down. E-mail humor can be
tricky for the same reason. The secret of comedy is timing, right? E-mails
don't *have* any particular timing. And remember the problem of the unintended audience?

In fact, you should avoid e-mailing any message that smacks of *pathos*.
Why do you suppose most people choose not to pray over e-mail? They may
receive prayers, sure. But why don't they e-mail God for forgiveness and to
smite the Dallas Cowboys next Sunday? Because God lacks an Internet
service provider? No. Because praying is *pathos*, with a little *ethos* mixed in,
and e-mail is mostly *logos*.

**TRY THIS IN YOUR
OFFICE E-MAILS**
Want to gain a respect-
able *ethos* through
your notes? Make them
shorter when you
address people at your
level or below. Don't get
too brief when you man-
age up, though. Higher-
ups in a company write
shorter e-mails, implying
that they don't have to
justify their choices.
(God's e-mails would be
very, very short, in the
nature of "Cut it out.")

You might expect me to say that e-mail is a fairly
poor way of showing gestures as well. But if you see it
in the broadest, rhetorical sense, the length of your
note is a form of gesture. The longer the note, the
more *logos* it conveys. The shorter the note, the more
its flavor becomes *ethos*. As Cicero noted, gestures
help determine your decorum. The more understated the gesture, the higher your apparent position in society. This notion is by no means out of
date, as business e-mails prove.

You would think that instant messaging would
work the same way; but it doesn't, for two reasons:
IM-ing is even more instantaneous than e-mail, and
it has very little to do with what the civilized world knows as "writing." Plus,
unless you're on an FBI watch list, the instant message is ephemeral. It has
the life span (and intellectual content) of a moderate belch. Yet the literal
medium is type. The IM can't be much of a *pathos* medium, or there would
be no need for those weird, mimelike frowny-face emoticons or obnoxious
acronyms like "LOL." Instead of actual laughing, it's a text message of
laughing. So, absent *logos* and *pathos*, what does instant messaging have left?
Ethos. All *ethos* all the time. The IM is all about identity. It takes place almost
entirely in the present tense, and its language is packed with code grooming.
An IM is to written text what a walkie-talkie message is to an oration. In fact,
the instant-message medium *is* a walkie-talkie, for all rhetorical purposes—
rapid-fire, used merely to locate people and keep in contact, and spoken

mainly in code, IMHO (In My Humble obnoxious Opinion). You can use it to find out where someone is, or whether he is ready for lunch. But the primary user of the instant message is the teenager, who lives for demonstrative rhetoric—telling who's in and who's out of the tribe.

Go ahead and laugh at teenagers, but perhaps the rest of us could use more of this friendly gesturing. Adults have lost something since Victorian times, when gentlefolk would come calling and leave their cards— messages that usually consisted of nothing but their own names. I can't think of a modern parallel, except for the just-touching-base voice mail . . . and the adolescent's IM.

TRY THIS WITH YOUR KIDS
If you and your children each have a computer with an Internet connection, insist that they make you their IM "buddy." That way you can tell when they're on. When you travel, IM them. Because you're on as long as you stay connected, an IM gives kids a sense that you're there. My own children seemed to like it when I became their buddy.

The instantaneous quality of the Internet explains why it has not turned out to be the great cauldron of democracy its inventors and Al Gore had hoped it would be. If any aspect of the Internet would foster democracy, you would think that the "blogosphere," an egalitarian universe of voices, would be at the very heart of the movement. But like the instant message, the blog does little more than bring together extremely like-minded people. Whether it's the daily lament of a tragically pimpled sixteen-year-old or the dishings of network journalists, a Web log is a diary. It is not like a ship log, which is a permanent record of the ship's journeys. A blog serves mostly as an ephemeral reflection of the events in a person's life, profession, or field of interest. Blogs do offer a democratic opportunity to get attention through sheer writing talent, as the Wonkette, a stay-at-home Washington blogger, proved. But few blogs contribute much to deliberative discourse; their main purpose is bonding, not choices. Even the Wonkette consists mostly of gossip and potty humor.

TRY THIS WHEN YOU WANT TO SELL SOMETHING
To test a new product, set up a blog and link it to appropriate pages on Wikipedia, the Internet's volunteer encyclopedia. It lets you pull together a community of a few hundred subscribers in as little as several weeks. You can send them your product or ask for suggestions in marketing it. I did this with my own rhetoric blog, and had a dedicated community of thousands of subscribers who gave me advice for my book.

As a committed blogger myself, I learned the medium's demonstrative qualities the hard way. Every day in Figarospeech.com I take something that somebody said in politics, sports, or entertainment and parse it as a figure of speech, revealing the rhetorical tricks and pratfalls. I thought that, like this book, the blog would teach the many wonders of rhetoric that I was learning. And I like to think that it does, a little. But my fellow "figurists," as I call them, like to think of themselves as a community. In response to one particularly innocuous entry, one subscriber thanked me for "fighting the good fight." This is demonstrative language par excellence, and it helps explain why the Internet has failed to bring everyone together under its big, friendly, blogospheric roof.

The Logical Telephone

So much for the World Wide tribal Web. Let's look at the more traditional media. Take the phone call. In earlier eras, voice was the dominant way people communicated; hearing is the most logocentric sense. This is why the conference call is such a rational exercise—and why businesspeople spend billions to avoid them by hopping on airplanes. If human communication were completely logical, the major airlines would be out of business. The telephone limits rhetoric to just one appeal, *logos*. Humans need doses of *ethos* and *pathos* to form teams and sustain relationships.

Okay, so why do telecoms sell mobile phones with such pathetic ads—the young mother who holds the phone up to the newborn so Grandma can hear it? Because a picture of an Aristotelian debate wouldn't sell telephones. Besides, ads about telephones do not use phones as their medium. They use TV, magazines, newspapers, and the internet—media that mix all three appeals, with a heavy emphasis on *pathos* (Grandma) and *ethos* (gorgeous movie star handling cell phone).

Is the phone really that rational a medium? The notion stretches credulity when you see a teenager phone a friend. Indeed, any medium can be used for *ethos*—as a means of touching base. Have you ever observed a girl or boy call up their first love? The surprising part is not what they say to each other; it's the long silences when the couple says nothing at all. The phone call is a connection, not a conversation—not really a call at all, but a

TRY THIS WITH A MEETING

If you don't want anyone to feel like an outsider, avoid meeting in a conference room unless everyone can attend in person. Otherwise, set up a conference call where each individual phones in. That keeps the meeting on solidly logical ground. Otherwise, callers can sense the significant looks people shoot one another, and might feel they're being excluded from the tribe.

different medium altogether, an electronic connection. This explains why the IM has largely replaced the phone for that purpose: because the Internet lets adolescents wire up with a network, not just one person.

The phone call still counts as one of the most rational media—if the phone is used to make an actual call, with people actually talking. You would think that the newspaper op-ed essay would be more rational, but it's not. Type on a page does indeed emphasize *logos*. But the op-ed is less rational than it looks. More important than the logic behind the message is the author behind it: a political solon, celebrity journalist, the newspaper's own editor, or one of the powers that be. The modern op-ed page is a real departure from newspapers of old. Madison and Hamilton published the essays that later became the *Federalist Papers* as op-ed pieces in New York newspapers. But in those days, essayists were anonymous. Modern newspaper opinionists have big names that give them ready-made *ethos,* so they don't have to cultivate it through their writing.

All the other media follow the same *ethos-pathos-logos* pattern, depending on which senses you use to receive them. Letter writing? Rational. Gift giving? Very emotional, provided that the gift is tangible, not a check. Gifts carry a great deal of *ethos* as well, cementing relationships and showing off the means of the gift givers. In other words, giving makes a terrific gesture. Smoke signals? Sight: rational. Perfume? What do you think?

The senses and their persuasive appeals explain why you can give a perfectly rational speech just by standing up and talking. But when you want to persuade a group of people, as you will see in the next chapter, you need to use more than your voice.

The Tools

When you seize the moment, make sure you use the **right medium** for your argument—one with the proper emphasis on *ethos, pathos,* or *logos,* with perfect timing for the moment.

To judge a medium for its rhetorical traits, ask yourself which physical senses it uses.

> **Sight** is mostly *pathos* and *ethos.*
> **Sound** is the most **logical** sense.
> **Smell, taste,** and **touch** are almost purely **emotional.**

ADVANCED AGREEMENT

23. Give a Persuasive Talk

▲

THE OLDEST INVENTION
Cicero's five canons of persuasion

The highest bribes of society are at the feet of the successful orator. All other fames must hush before his. He is the true potentate. —RALPH WALDO EMERSON

Now that you have the basics of offense and defense, we're ready to bring out the big guns, Cicero's five canons of persuasion: **invention, arrangement, style, memory,** and **delivery.** While he devised them for formal orations, they also work beautifully in less formal settings such as presentations to a boss or a book club. We'll pull together a talk of our own, with the help of the five canons.

Cicero put them in a particular order—invention, arrangement, style, memory, and delivery—for good reason. This is the order you yourself should use to make a speech. First, invent what you intend to say. Then decide what order you want to say it in; determine how you'll style it to suit your particular audience; put it all down in your brain or on your computer; and finally get up and wow your audience.

I would be the last person to contradict Cicero, so we will start with inventing our speech. Let's say I want to propose a noise ordinance for my town that would consign leaf blowers and their heedless, gas-wasting, polluting owners to the innermost circle of hell, where they belong.

Sorry about that. I feel better now.

Suppose the town has called a special meeting, and the board of selectmen has given me fifteen minutes to state my case. Then an opponent of the noise

▸ **Persuasion Alert**
Call this technique "modest name-dropping." I refer to a respectable source so you're aware of my knowledge, then coyly ask who I am to question the authority. The best bragging wears a cloak of modesty.

ordinance will get equal time. After that, the audience can ask us questions or state their own opinions. Finally, the town will hold a voice vote on whether to put the ordinance on the agenda for town meeting in the spring.

Instead of just sitting down and writing the speech, I walk outside, scuffle my feet through the dead leaves, and figure out what everybody wants, starting with me. That's the first part of invention: what do I want? Is my goal to change the audience's mood, its mind, or its willingness to do something?

Well, what I really want is for citizens to rise up and destroy every leaf blower; but what I want for my *speech* is to change the audience's mind—to convince my fellow townsfolk that we need a new noise ordinance. What kind of rhetoric do I need for that: past (law and order), present (values), or future (choices)? We're talking about the future here—about making a choice—so the rhetoric is deliberative. I'll bring in values, but only those the audience already has, and I won't blame anybody for the noise.

Having decided what I want from the audience, next I nail down the issue itself. Cicero tells me to ask whether it is simple or complex. If complex, I should break the question down into smaller issues. But in this case the issue is really very simple. The town either wants a noise ordinance or it doesn't.

Cicero says I should be prepared to argue both sides of the case, starting with my opponent's pitch. This means spending some time imagining what he will say. I'm guessing he will talk about values a lot—the rights and freedoms that a noise ordinance will trample upon. This little debate in my head helps determine the crux of the argument, the point to be decided. What is this argument really about? Why did I propose the ordinance in the first place? Is it about noise, or about leaf blowers? I think it's about noise in general—the leaf blowers are just the last straw, adding to motorcycles, guns (it's a rural town), teenagers squealing their tires, and all the other acoustic tortures of life in modern America.

But as I watch a private plane buzz overhead, I think: Maybe it's about whether we mean to hole ourselves up inside our homes, with our windows closed and our kids hooked up to their PlayStations. Do we intend to be a bunch of family-sized bunkers, or a real community?

Nah, the point about isolation is too vague. It's about noise.

Having decided on the goal and the issue, now I need to think about the audience's values. The previous year, we ratified a town mission statement. (Even towns have to have a mission now; apparently it's not enough to state that the purpose of Orange, New Hampshire, is to exist.) Our mission statement includes "the quiet, rural nature of our town" among our values. On the other hand, one of the commonplaces you hear the most in these parts is "A person has a right to do what he wants with his property." The motto on our state license plate, "Live Free or Die," sums up the general attitude.

Therefore, when I come up with my central argument packet (Aristotle's enthymeme), I should talk about rights instead of quiet; I already know that my opponent will focus on rights, and it would be nice to take the rhetorical wind out of his sails. So my argument packet will go something like, "We need to cut back on noise because it's ruining our chance to enjoy our own property." So much for deductive logic. Then I'll talk about how the deer seem to be shyer than they used to be, and how Mrs. Ferson down the road can't nap on her porch the way she used to. Next I can cover cause and effect, describing what our town will be like if we let the volume of noise build—a whole community of deaf-mutes, or a bunch of homebodies in an area people used to live in for its outdoor recreation. So much for townsfolk enjoying their property, unless their machines are louder than their neighbors' machines. I could seal the point by asking for a show of hands: how many people think that noise from leaf-blowers and other loud equipment keeps them from enjoying their property?

> **Meanings**
> Most of rhetorical invention really isn't invention at all. The Latin *inventio* means "discovery" as well as invention in the modern sense. Your job in this stage of the speech is to discover, or invent, the "available means of persuasion," as Aristotle put it.

Arrangement

Having invented my basic argument, I now need to arrange it. Rhetoricians came up with many variations on the organization of a speech, but the basics have remained the same for thousands of years. Essentially it comes down to this rule of thumb:

> *Ethos* first.
> Then *logos*.
> Then *pathos*.

Start by winning over the audience. Get them to like you through your shared values, your good sense, and your concern for their own interest. Make them identify with you. All the tools of *ethos* apply here.

Then launch into your argument, stating the facts, making your case, proving your point logically, and smacking down your opponent's argument.

End by getting the audience all charged up, through patriotism, anger—any of the emotions that lead to action.

If you really want to follow a classical outline, structure your speech like this:

> **Introduction:** The *ethos* part, which wins you "the interest and the good will of the audience," as Cicero puts it. (He calls this section the **exordium.**)
>
> **Narration,** or statement of facts: Tell the history of the matter or list your facts and figures. If you have time, do both. This part should be brief, clear, and plausible. Don't repeat yourself. State the facts in chronological order, but don't begin at the beginning of time—just the part that is relevant to the immediate argument. Don't startle the audience with "believe it or not" facts—this part should be predictable. What they hear should sound usual, expected, and natural.
>
> **Division:** List the points where you and your opponent agree and where you disagree. This is where you can get into definitions as well. It's a biological issue. It's an ethical issue. It's a rights issue. It's a practical issue (what benefits our society the most?). It's a fairness issue.
>
> **Proof:** Here is where you get into your actual argument, setting out your argument packet ("We should do this because of that") and your examples.
>
> **Refutation:** Destroy your opponent's arguments here.
>
> **Conclusion:** Restate your best points and, if you want, get a little emotional.

You can do all this pretty easily in fifteen minutes; technically, you can do it in two. The introduction could be something humorous about the height of the microphone, or a quick thanks to the arrangers and the audience for letting you speak. The facts could take a minute or two, and so could the division—the points of agreement and disagreement. The proof would take the longest in a short talk, because you want to bring in all your strengths of examples and premises, as well as causes and effects. The refutation could refute just one point that your opponent made, or is likely to make. And the conclusion could consist of just one sentence.

Applause. Sit down.

In my case, I have a bit of an *ethos* problem with my fellow townsfolk. In New England, people consider you a newcomer if you weren't born in their town; they might begin to tolerate you after a couple of decades. I moved to Orange two years ago, though I had lived in New Hampshire for many years before. So it's best not to talk much about me. I show up dressed the way most of my audience dresses, with a clean old flannel shirt and work pants, and I take care not to talk too fancy; that takes care of the *ethos* part. I offer thanks for letting me speak, then launch right into my statement of facts—noise levels steadily rising, according to tests a geeky friend has done around the town.

For the division part, I list the options, including doing nothing. My opponent agrees about the increasing noise level, but we disagree on how much that matters, and whether a noise regulation interferes too much with our individual rights.

Division can actually help your *ethos*, if you use the **reluctant conclusion:** when the audience seems against you, pretend that you came to your decision reluctantly. Talk about your deep belief in property rights, but then define those rights in broader terms than your opponent does. The right to enjoy your property may include the right to peace and quiet.

Then comes the proof, where I put together my argument packet.

> ME: Most of us live here because Orange is a special place. And what makes it special, as our town plan puts it, is its "quiet, rural character." Well, it can't be quiet, and it can't be rural, if we start importing a lot of new recreational machinery.

My refutation then anticipates what my opponent will say:

> ME: Bill will tell you it's a matter of rights. And I'll go along with that. It *is* a matter of rights: my right to enjoy my property—working on my trails, splitting firewood, watching the beavers—versus the rights of a home owner to do

whatever he wants with *his* land. But when that includes playing with loud toys, then his right screws up my right—while doing harm to the character of this town.

Finally, the conclusion. I restate my strongest points and then describe the town as it would be with a noise ordinance, where people can use their chain saws to cut firewood, enjoy their ATVs and snowmobiles—just within certain times. And the rest of the time we can live in the town we love for the reasons we love it—natural beauty, quiet, and all the things that set us apart from people who live in the city or the suburbs. This being the land of the Yankee, I have to take care not to be too emotional. That doesn't go down big in our town. But there is nothing wrong with exploiting the emotion of pride a little bit, recalling to the audience what makes us special and sets us apart from the folks in the rest of America.

▶ **Classic Hits**
THOSE RHETORICAL SCIENTISTS: Articles in modern research journals follow a strict outline that comes straight out of Cicero: theory (exordium), methods (narration), discussion (proof and division), conclusion.

Arrangement tends to get short shrift among rhetoricians, but it's especially important today. Most of our arguments—even personal ones—take place at disconnected times, in various places, over more than one medium. When do you focus on your character? When on logic or passion? You can see that some of the principles of arrangement work even when you're not giving a speech. Remember that *ethos, logos,* and *pathos* work best in that order. Begin with your strengths—whether your facts or your logic. And put your strongest resources both at the beginning and at the end.

Style

Having invented and arranged my thoughts, now is the time to decide what sort of words I want to express them with—the style I want to use. Rhetorical style has to do with the way we speak or write, much like our modern literary style. But where we moderns celebrate self-expression, rhetoric stresses the *audience's* expression. Like Shakespeare's Prospero, a persuader's style "endows thy purposes with words that make them known." In the modern sense of style, we want to stand out from the crowd; in the rhetorical sense, we want to fit in. The ancients came up with a set of virtues and vices for style, and they'll work well for me at the town meeting.

Virtue number one is **proper language**—words that suit the occasion and my audience. In my case, that means no foreign words or any other language that shows off. I want to follow the principle of eighteenth-century rhetorician Christoph Martin Wieland: "To be not as eloquent would be more eloquent." Aristotle said that uneducated people speak more simply, "which makes the uneducated more effective than the educated when addressing popular audiences."

▸ **Meanings**
The word "style" comes from the Latin *stilus,* the sharp stick Romans used for writing. The word didn't enter our lexicon until the Renaissance, when rhetoric became in part an effete art of letter writing.

> WRONG: There are those among us who prefer the roar of the internal combustion engine and the echo of their sound waves upon the surrounding hills. Then there are those who seek the quiet spaces to renew our spirit, much as Odysseus did when he set out upon the silent vastness of the sea.
>
> RIGHT: Some of us like to use our land for ATVs and snowmobiles, and others like to do more quiet things.

The second virtue, **clarity,** should be obvious. Alan Greenspan sounded like the Oracle of Delphi when he was chairman of the Federal Reserve, and that worked for him. It would not work for me.

> WRONG: The quasi-constitutional argument by my opponent contains an internal contradiction that comes to light when you apply the principle of *stare decisis.*
>
> RIGHT: Does the town have the right to restrict noise? Yes, it has that right.

The third virtue, **vividness,** is a bit trickier, and cooler. It has to do with the speaker's ability to create a rhetorical reality before the audience's very eyes. The Greeks called it *enargeia,* which means "visibility." *Enargeia* works best in the narration part of a speech, where you tell the story and give the facts.

> WRONG: People have been impacted by all the noise.

RIGHT: Mrs. Read tells me when she goes to visit the beaver
lodge down by the brook at her place, they sometimes
don't swim up to her. She walks all the way down, a half
mile from her house—you know where it is—with an
apple in each hand, and whistles like this. When it's quiet,
they come. Some of you have seen them eat out of Mrs.
Read's hand. But when the beavers hear the sound of an
ATV, they smack their tails in the water and make a dive
for their lodge.

The fourth virtue is the most important: **decorum,** the art of fitting in.
My accent is a bit too mid-Atlantic for Yankee ears, but I will not try to
change it to talk about the loud "cahs" on the mountain road. An unsuccessful attempt to fit in may entertain the audience, but it won't make you
persuasive. Instead, I'll talk about the same things the locals talk about.

WRONG: I ain't gonna tell you what you can and can't do. No
sir! Why, I cut a few trees myself and make a helluva racket
doing it, too!

RIGHT: I make noise, too. I felled and bucked seven cords of
wood this past fall, running two chain saws in tandem, and
I'm sure you could hear it all the way to
Orange Pond.

The fifth and final virtue, **ornament,** has to do
with the rhythm of your voice and the cleverness of
your words. In my case, nakedness works best, but
maybe I could get away with a nice chiasmus toward
the end:

ME: It comes down to this: we can either control the noise, or we can let the noise control us.

That might work. Tricky language can be hard to
remember, though. The ancients had a solution for
that, too.

TRY THIS WITH A MEMO
Apply a "style filter" to
your writing, using
Cicero's checklist of style
virtues: (1) *Proper lan-
guage:* Is your prose just
grammatical enough for
the audience? (2) *Clarity:*
Would the least informed
reader understand it?
(3) *Vividness:* Do your
examples employ all
the readers' senses?
(4) *Decorum:* Do the
words fit the audience?
Are there any anachro-
nisms, sexist terms, or
PC language that might
mark you as an outsider?
(5) *Ornament:* Does it
sound good when you
read it aloud?

Memory

Cicero called memory "the treasure-house of the ideas supplied by invention." Like other rhetoricians, he had his own methods for creating an inventory of thoughts and ways of expressing them. The ancients had wild ideas about memory, employing pornography, classical architecture, primitive semiotics, abusive classroom techniques, and exercises that orators continued throughout their lives.

It went like this: every rhetoric student would construct an imaginary house or scene in his head, with empty spaces to fill with ideas. One rhetorician was extremely specific about it:

> *The backgrounds ought to be neither too bright nor too dim, so that the shadows may not obscure the images nor the lustre make them glitter. I believe that the intervals between backgrounds should be of moderate extent, approximately thirty feet; for, like the external eye, so the inner eye of thought is less powerful when you have moved the object of sight too near or too far away.*

It might take years to create a personal memory house or landscape, but the resulting mnemonic structure could last a lifetime. The student then created his own mental images to fill each space. Each image would stand for a concept, an ideal or commonplace, or a figure of speech. Imagine an indoor shopping mall with stores that hold figures, commonplaces, particular concepts, and argument strategies. Some of the stores never change their merchandise, while others supply ideas that can serve a particular speech. You arrange the stores according to the classic outline of an oration, with items useful to your introduction, narration and facts, division, proof, refutation, and conclusion. For example, the introduction section can have all the devices of *ethos* in them. One of them, the "doubt trick" *(dubitatio)*—the one where you pretend not to know where to begin—can be a mirror in the shape of a question mark. Another, the one where you seem to have come to your choice reluctantly, after considering all the opponent's arguments, can be a painting with a picture on both sides of the canvas. Each picture can stand for an opposing argument. If we really wanted to follow the ancient practices, we would make the picture pornographic, and fill some of the stores with naked men or women doing very interesting

things. Rhetoric teachers found that their students—all young males—tended to remember
these images especially.

Even if they didn't have to give a speech,
Roman gentlemen were supposed to walk through
their "memory villas" at least once a day, visiting
each section and imprinting the images in their
heads. Then, when he did have to speak, the Roman could simply walk through the villa and visit
the sections he needed. Instead of memorizing
an outline and phrases, the way we might, he
only had to remember the route for that particular speech, along with a few new images—stored
in the appropriate places—that spoke to the particular issue.

Strange as this may seem to us today, we do
have parallels to this architectural memory. Take
PowerPoint, for instance. Each slide often contains an image—a picture, chart, or graph—that
conveys a particular concept. By looking at the
slide along with the audience, the speaker can remember what to say. If
you had the time and the inclination, you might experiment by combining PowerPoint with the ancient memory technique. Write down all your
thoughts. Now put each thought on a PowerPoint slide. Find or create a
graphic for each slide. Print the slides in thumbnail view and cut them
out with scissors. Now create a kind of board game,
like Snakes and Ladders, where you follow a path
through a kind of landscape and encounter each
slide. Place the slides in the order you want along
the path, beginning with the introduction and finishing with the conclusion. Stare at your "board
game" for an hour or two, focusing on the pictures
(you won't be able to read the type anyway). Could
you give the speech without notes or slides? At any
rate, that's what the Romans did, only they had the
advantage of years of practice.

In my case, since my talk is only fifteen minutes

long and I intend to speak plainly, I can do it without notes or rhetorical mnemonics. But the Romans had to speak for hours, and their audiences interrupted them constantly. In a pinch, they could always duck into their memory houses and pull out something, well, memorable.

Delivery

If I did my job properly with invention, arrangement, style, and memory, the fifth part should be a slam dunk. That's delivery—*actio*, the Romans called it—the act of acting out the speech. Delivery has to do with body language, along with your voice, rhythms, and breathing.

> ▸ **Meanings**
> The ancient Greek word for delivery was *hypokrisis*. It shows history's ambivalence toward persuasion; the word eventually became our *hypocrisy*.

People were crazy about it during the Renaissance and early Enlightenment. I found a best-selling book from the era, John Bulwer's *Chironomia,* in the Dartmouth College library stacks. It has engravings linking positions of the hands and fingers with facial expressions and rhetorical emotions, along with useful explanations. To express admiration, for instance, you were supposed to hold your hand out, palm up, fingers together. Now spread your fingers while cocking your wrist and turning your palm to face the audience. Admiration! Commoners studied books like this to imitate the gentry's mannerisms. Act like gentlefolk, and you're more likely to become gentlefolk. Thomas Jefferson did the opposite when he became president. He wore corduroy pants and rode horseback instead of taking a coach. He was making a rhetorical gesture, signaling the un-European common-man simplicity of America.

> ▸ **Meanings**
> What we call theatrical acting, seventeenth-century Elizabethans called "playing." Acting was what orators did.

> **TRY THIS IN A LARGE ROOM**
> When asked what was the single best advice to give a beginning actor, the drama coach at Dartmouth during the 1960s answered, "Speak louder." It works especially when you're nervous. Focus on speaking loudly—making sure the microphone is tuned in advance—and your voice will automatically take on a confident tone and rhythm.

But the original idea of delivery had to do with speeches, not political symbolism. Let's start with voice. The ideal voice has **volume, stability,** and **flexibility.** Volume is the ability to project. Stability means endurance. For really long speeches, speak calmly during the introduction to save your voice, and avoid speaking shrilly. As for flexibility, you need to be able to vary your tone according to the occasion. The rhetoricians delineated a bunch of tones—the dignified, the explicative, the narrative, the facetious, tones for conversation, debate, and emphasis—but these days we speak almost entirely conversationally.

Still, varying my voice can help me. I can punctuate my speech with softer tones—a great way to convey the *enargeia* of woodland quiet—and get louder toward the end. I should also speed up and slow down according to the thoughts and imagery I convey—again, slow in the woods, fast when I describe all-terrain vehicles.

TRY THIS IN PUBLIC
Ronald Reagan's longtime speechwriter, Martin Anderson, said that his boss would stand erect, with hands slightly cupped and thumbs aligned with his pant seams. It feels uncomfortable, the president said, but it makes you look relaxed.

As for physical movement, rhetoricians tell me not to call attention to my gestures. To emphasize a point, I should lean my body a little from my shoulders, for example. But it's better to avoid gestures altogether than to do the wrong ones. So I'll focus on my facial expression—again following Cicero, who said, "The eyes are the window of the soul." They make the most eloquent gestures of all, with the generous help of my rather bushy eyebrows.

Okay, I'm ready. I walk into the spare white room, and a floorboard creaks alarmingly underfoot. New Englanders don't make the most encouraging audiences, but this one is attentive at least. I look out at the forty or fifty faces in the room, and my momentary terror is relieved by the ammunition I'm packing: the argument I invented, the right arrangement, a sense of the proper style and tone, an outline I remember because I use it for every speech (intro, narration, division, proof, refutation, conclusion), and the confidence that if I talk a bit loud, I'll feel confident. Most of all, though, I have Cicero backing me. And not just his theory, either. Once, during an important trial in the Roman Forum, he stopped in terror, just frozen with stage fright. And then he ran away. The greatest orator in history, the man brave enough to defend the Republic against Julius Caesar himself, ran away. However embarrassing, it was one of his greatest contributions to rhetoric because ever since, a speaker can calm his butterflies with the knowledge that it happened to the best of us.

The Tools

Poor Edward Everett. He delivered the real Gettysburg Address, and no one remembers him. But at the time, people considered Lincoln's little 268-word number a tad embarrassing. It was rather plain for its day, and Lincoln's high, nasal voice did not carry well in an outdoor setting. Everett, on the other hand, was the main attraction. Daniel Webster's heir apparent as the national orator, he could hold a crowd rapt for two hours—and did on that day. A dedicated Ciceronian like Webster, Everett consciously used the five canons. And so should you and I in any speech or presentation.

Now that you've seen me give a speech, it's time to watch a master at work. Read on . . .

Invention: Dig up the materials for your speech. ("Invention" comes from the Latin *invenire,* "to find.") Just about all the logical techniques you encounter in this book go here. You'll find the specific *logos* tools in the Appendices.

Arrangement: Introduction (lay on the *ethos* here), narration, division, proof, refutation (those four middle parts should be heavy on *logos*), conclusion (where you can get emotional).

Style: The five virtues of style are proper language, clearness, vividness, decorum, and ornament.

Memory: This is the canon hardest to adapt to modern speechifying. The ancients started their students on memory drills when they were small children, and as adults they constructed "memory villas" and filled the rooms with topics. Fortunately, we have PowerPoint, which works a lot like a memory villa.

Delivery: Here you actually act, in both the theatrical and active senses. Think about your voice—are you loud and confident enough for the room?—and gesture. Cicero included the eyes (both eye contact and expression) as an aspect of gesture. A confident voice and expressions that start with the eyes: those are the chief secrets of *actio*.

24. Wow Your Audience

▲

THE OBAMA IDENTITY
Steal the tricks of a first-class orator

I brought the house down. — MARCUS TULLIUS CICERO

People who think grand oratory is dead should have been watching on July 27, 2004, when a man gave a speech that literally changed the course of history.

"Barack who?" people asked when the senate candidate with a strange name took the podium of the Democratic Party convention as its keynote speaker. As he waved to the audience, TV reporters read off their cheat sheets: Three-term Illinois state senator, first African-American president of the Harvard Law Review, author of out-of-print book titled *Dreams From My Father*. Had made unsuccessful bid for a seat in the U.S. House of Representatives four years before, couldn't even get a VIP pass to the 2000 convention. Recently won Democratic primary for U.S. Senate seat. Republican opponent dragged down by sex scandal. Barack Obama suddenly a rising star.

I didn't bother to watch the speech at the time. Who wanted to sit through some nobody's windy oration to a shrieking hall of silly-hatted Dems?

My mistake.

The last time a speech by a relative unknown led directly to the presidency was in 1860, when a hick lawyer from Illinois named Abraham Lincoln mesmerized an elite audience in New York City with his famous Cooper Union address. Lincoln had to convince a relatively small group of skeptics that he had the brains and savvy to be president. Obama merely had to prove he was a political rock star. Both of them succeeded.

Obama's speech made his book a sudden bestseller and gained him thousands of adoring fans. He went from political novelty act to presiden-

> **▶ Persuasion Alert**
> I counter an opposing point of view, not by arguing against it, but by suggesting that people on the other side are merely clueless. If only they had my facts, why, they couldn't help but agree!

tial contender overnight. The next time he addressed the convention, in 2008, he was accepting his party's nomination.

Let's see how he seduced us in his keynote speech and in a few of the more memorable ones that followed. His tricks will come in handy if you plan to rule the free world yourself—or just your own small part of it.

Copy Cicero's Outline

You'd think Obama went to rhetoric school. He follows Cicero to a tee, organizing the speech in the good old classical way: introduction, narration, division, proof, refutation, conclusion.

Introduction: Like a good Ciceronian, Obama establishes his character right at the beginning of his convention speech: "My presence on this stage is pretty unlikely." Nice modesty ploy that provides a smooth segue into his narration.

Narration: He tells the story of his parents—a goatherd who went on to study in America, a woman born "on the other side of the world, in Kansas"— and ends with a moral that links his character with the American Way: "I stand here knowing that my story is a part of the larger American story," he says. "This is the true genius of America, a faith in the simple dreams of its people."

Division: The good orator uses the division to represent both sides—his own in the most glowing terms, and his opponents' . . . well, you don't want to be too obvious about condemning the other side. Far better to sound disappointed in the opposition's total wrongheadedness. That's Obama's tack: "I say to you tonight: we have more work to do." What he really means is, "*After four years of Bush and Cheney,* we have more work to do." Use the division to sound more reasonable than the other side, implying that you're the *nice* one.

Proof: To back up his point about how much needs doing, Obama uses that classic rhetorical device, the catalogue: jobs being shipped overseas, oil companies holding America hostage, our liberties sacrificed in the name of safety, faith used "as a wedge to divide us," and a badly run war.

> ▸ **Argument Tool**
> CATALOGUE:
> Support your argument with a list. Start with the merely awful and build up to the truly shocking.

Refutation: Here's the fun part—the out and out attack on the opposing side. But here's where Obama also strays a bit from Cicero's playbook. Instead of going after the Republicans directly, he attacks "the spin masters and negative ad peddlers" who seek to divide Americans. And then he delivers the biggest line of the night. Up till now he has kept his voice steady, reasonable, even clipped. Now it takes on the volume and cadence of a pulpit-thumping minister: "Well, I say to them tonight, there's not a liberal America and a conservative America, there's the United States of America!" It became the sound bite heard around the world.

Conclusion: The end of a great speech does double duty as both a summary and a call to action: "In the end, that's what this election is about. Do we participate in a politics of cynicism or a politics of hope?" ("HOPE!" yell the delegates, happily answering a rhetorical question.) Having dealt with all the logos stuff, Obama can surf the waves of applause with a string of "ands." He calls his audience to action by describing a happy future: ". . . and John Kerry will be sworn in as president, and John Edwards will be sworn in as vice president, and this country will reclaim its promise, and out of this long political darkness . . ." Each clause gives the audience another goose, and the crowd gets louder and louder until the hall becomes so deafening you have to read his lips for the obligatory "Thank you and God bless you."

▶ **Useful Figure**
You won't see a better use of the anaphora, the drumbeat figure that uses the same word to begin succeeding sentences or clauses. Obama's "ands" are spaced precisely to build up the applause of a large audience.

Although Kerry did not end up being sworn in as president, Obama's speech was a smashing success—for Obama. Cicero would have been proud.

Yell at an unseen enemy

▶ **Try This in Your Class or Book Club**
Can't imagine yourself using this device (its unpronounceable name: prosopopeia)? Suppose you wish this book had a more serious tone. Instead of merely stating that opinion to the others in the room, tell it to my absent self: "Come on, Jay, do you have to make a joke about everything?" Thanks for the constructive criticism.

OBAMA: We will not apologize for our way of life, nor will we waver in its defense, and for those who seek to advance their aims by inducing terror and slaughtering innocents, we say to you now that our spirit is stronger and cannot be broken; you cannot outlast us, and we will defeat you.

Nothing brings the tribe together better than a common foe, and the best way to portray yourself as leader of the good guys is to issue the bad guys a stern warning.

Obama isn't really talking to the enemy. He's talking to voters. Instead of urging us to be patient—a tough thing to tell a notoriously impatient country—he brags about our resolve. We'll outlast the enemy, because we're tough!

Turn a problem into a noble test

Despite what far too many after-dinner speakers seem to think, you can't make people eager for the tasks ahead by simply calling a problem an opportunity. Nor can you just call a problem a "challenge," though even Obama is guilty of this cliché now and then. Instead, tell the audience that they're being given a chance to prove themselves. That's what he did in his inaugural speech.

> OBAMA: Let it be said by our children's children that when we were tested we refused to let this journey end, that we did not turn back nor did we falter; and with eyes fixed on the horizon and God's grace upon us, we carried forth that great gift of freedom and delivered it safely to future generations.

Keep in mind that his audience considers the men and women who fought World War II to be the "greatest generation." I have friends who seem downright jealous that they didn't live through that war. They missed the chance to prove that they, too, could be the greatest. People will do a lot to prove their virtue; even, at times, to the extent of risking their lives.

> ▸ **Argument Tool**
> The appeal to virtue is one of the best ways to call your audience to action. But make sure you're appealing to the right virtue. Telling a high-school class that they could prove themselves "the most hygienic of all time" may not inspire quite the same reaction.

Admonish your audience by flattering it

> OBAMA: America, we are better than these last eight years. We are a better country than this.

Every rhetorically minded parent knows this technique. Instead of telling your little miscreant that she's a bad girl for plastering the wall with baby food, you tell her that she's acting out of character.

YOU: Oh, Sadie! You don't do things like that. You're a *good* girl.

Essentially, that's what Obama did when, in his acceptance speech at the 2008 Democratic convention, he talked about America being "better" than the previous eight years. Except, of course, he was accusing the Republicans, not his daughter, of flinging slop.

Describe the Outcome of your Choice as a Dream

OBAMA: What if it was as easy to get a book as it is to rent a DVD or pick up McDonalds? What if instead of a toy in every Happy Meal, there was a book? What if there were portable libraries that rolled through parks and playgrounds like ice cream trucks? Or kiosks in stores where you could borrow books? What if during the summer, when kids often lose much of the reading progress they've made during the year, every child had a list of books they had to read and talk about and an invitation to a summer reading club at the local library?

This speech, delivered at a librarians' convention, must have sounded to his audience like a bookish Eden. Okay, so it's not the most memorable "dream" speech given by an African-American leader. But Obama went beyond simply describing a utopia; he used the scene setting as a way to float specific ideas past the audience: jingling book trucks, in-store libraries, and the like. Want to sound like a visionary? List your proposals in the form of a vision.

Use Movie Techniques for Drama

OBAMA: One march was interrupted by police gunfire and tear gas, and when the smoke cleared, 280 had been arrested, 60 were wounded, and one 16-year old boy lay dead.

This historical mini-narration captivated a labor convention when Obama was still a U.S. senator. Its secret lies in the cinematic order of events, as if the speech were a movie scene that began with a wide-angle shot and gradually zoomed in. First you see the march, and the cops on the move. Now we zoom in a bit to find heavy smoke and gunfire. Zoom in more, and the camera moves over anonymous bodies. Then a close-up to show the lifeless face of a teenage boy. Heartbreaking.

> ▶ **Try This Test**
> Rewrite Obama's sentence and reorder the sequence. Suppose he had followed the usual M.O., working his way up from the smallest number: "one 16-year-old boy lay dead, 60 were wounded, and 280 had been arrested." Why does Obama's original order make a better climax?

Simplify with a Balancing Figure

In the spring of 2008, the presidential primary race had narrowed to a close match between Obama and Hillary Clinton. A scandal on either side could tip the balance. And that's just when Obama's minister, Jeremiah Wright, appeared all over YouTube, calling damnation upon America. Up to that point, race hadn't been much of an issue in the campaign; nobody could win from using it.

This time, Obama had no choice but to answer the preacher. But instead of just distancing himself from the loose canon, the senator audaciously took on the whole issue of race. It was as if he repaired a broken-down car by turning it into a rocket ship.

> ▶ **Useful Figure**
> The **enantiosis** (eh nan tie OH sis) lists a series of opposites side by side. Charles Dickens used it to begin *A Tale of Two Cities*. ("It was the best of times, it was the worst of times . . .") Use it when you're arguing against oversimplification of an issue.

OBAMA: The church contains in full the kindness and cruelty, the fierce intelligence and the shocking ignorance, the struggles and successes, the love and yes, the bitterness and bias that make up the black experience in America.

Obama attempted to show that the minister's extremism was just one part of a very complicated story. But how do you tell a complicated story without getting too . . . complicated? With a figure of speech that pairs contraries in succeeding clauses. The figure lets him show the brighter side of a tarnished coin by implying that the Reverend Wright actually blesses America—when he isn't damning it.

To Emphasize a Point, Interrupt Your Sentence

OBAMA: Our challenges may be new. The instruments with which we meet them may be new. But those values upon which our success depends—honesty and hard work, courage and fair play, tolerance and curiosity, loyalty and patriotism—these things are old.

▶ **Useful Figure**
The official name for this technique—changing grammar in mid-sentence—is anacoluthon

▶ **Persuasion Alert**
What's the point of mentioning all the speeches I've sat through? By portraying myself as a one-man tough crowd, I throw more weight behind those goosebumps. You could also call the device a form of reluctant conclusion (See chapter 8)

Why didn't he just say, "Those values . . . are old?" That would be more concise, and even pretty. But by inserting another subject into the end of the sentence, Obama pauses for a beat, and then boldfaces each of those final words: "These. Things. Are. Old." Notice also that the four words end a long, singsong list. The pressure builds and builds, phrase by phrase, until its release in that last clause. I've sat unmoved through a great many speeches, but this part gave me goosebumps.

Connect Unalike Things with Alliteration

OBAMA: This is the price and the promise of citizenship.

Sacrificing together, meeting challenges—these are the themes of inaugural speeches, including Obama's. There's just one awkward thing about making a speech like that. All through the campaign he has pandered to us, claiming there really is such a thing as a free lunch. *I'll fix healthcare, build up the military, pour money into education, and lower your taxes! Not only will I defy the law of gravity, I'll get Congress to change that law, too!* Once Obama got safely past the election, he could remind us that there actually is a price to citizenship. But wait: the price and the glory, he says, are two of a kind. To help make the connection, Obama subtly uses sound-alike words.

Beware that a liberal allowance of like letters can leave us all loony. But a pair of "p's" in the middle of a sentence can marry unlikely rhetorical cousins.

Link a Bad Choice with the Impossible

OBABA: I can no more disown [Jeremiah Wright] than I can disown the black community. I can no more disown him than I can my white grandmother—a woman who helped raise me, a woman who sacrificed again and again for me, a woman who loves me as much as she loves anything in this world, but a woman who once confessed her fear of black men who passed by her on the street, and who on more than one occasion has uttered racial or ethnic stereotypes that made me cringe.

> ▸ **Useful Fallacy**
> One form of the false choice fallacy pretends that two things belong together when they actually don't. But isn't this bad? No more than any other fallacy. In rhetoric, you're harmed only if you're fooled.

People often tell me what a logical guy Obama is. And indeed he is, when he wants to be. But at the center of these inspiring words lies a glittering core of illogic. Not only *could* he disown Wright, he more or less did. The two men apparently haven't spoken since. On the other hand, disowning the woman who helped raise him is a good deal more difficult. But the takeaway for you here is the "I can no more [insert bad choice] than I could [insert impossibility]" figure. It's a rhetorical form of guilt by association, linking two things that don't naturally belong together. Instead of just making an assertion, as a lesser orator would do—"I'm not going to disown the guy, and that's all there is to it"—you attach the opposing choice to something virtually impossible.

Sum Up with One Memorable Word

OBAMA: Virginia, I have just one word for you, just one word. Tomorrow. Tomorrow.

Saying this the night before the presidential election, Obama imitated the obnoxious guy in *The Graduate* who says, "I want to say one word to you. Just one word . . . Plastics." Obnoxious, yes, but memorable. Obama could have said, "This whole campaign comes down to one day: election day!" But he used repetition and a one-word summary to make tomorrow sound like the fulcrum on which the future of humankind rests. All while making a great pop-culture reference.

Show Grit by Ending a String of Negatives with a Positive

Right after he was sworn in as president, Obama used his inaugural address to channel another of his political heroes, John F. Kennedy.

▸ **Useful Figure**
The epiphonema
(e-pih-fo-NEE-ma)
gives a pithy,
memorable summary
of your case.

OBAMA: Today I say to you that the challenges we face are real. They are serious and they are many. They will not be met easily or in a short span of time. But know this, America—they will be met.

Those three sentences follow a "narrative arc," as writers like to say. First, we're told that the problems (sorry—"challenges") are a big deal. Then we're told we're going to walk a long, tough trail to the end. Finally we get to the happy ending. Obama rhetorically rehearses the classic heroic fable: hero gets mission, meets obstacles, overcomes all. And just who are the heroes of this morality play? We are! For a moment, the audience gets seduced into being almost glad the obstacles are so great. How else could we prove our mettle?

Channel a Great Character

During his presidential campaign, Obama gave a first-rate speech at Martin Luther King Jr.'s Ebenezer Baptist Church. The senator occasionally slipped into wonkish arrhythmia, with clunky phrases like "empathy deficit," but he got the crowd amen-ing when he picked up the imagery and figures of speech that MLK used himself.

OBAMA: In the struggle for peace and justice, we cannot walk alone. In the struggle for opportunity and equality, we cannot walk alone. In the struggle to heal this nation and repair this world, we cannot walk alone.

▶ Useful Figure
The **symploce** (SIM-plo-see) repeats everything but the middle of each clause. Use it to make your audience anticipate the changed parts—in this case, "peace and justice," "opportunity and equality," and "heal this nation and repair this world."

Repeating the beginning and end of successive clauses made a kind of hymn—a beautifully pathetic way of saying, "I'm one of the faithful, like you, and I'm carrying the torch that the Reverend King once held."

If you're ever asked to speak at the retirement or funeral for a good soul beloved by friends and family, see if you can pick up your subject's rhythm, speech pattern, or expressions. It's not only a fine way of ingratiating yourself to the audience; by implying that his spirit lives on, you do the person honor.

The Tools

Soon after taking office, Obama toned down his demonstrative rhetoric. Some of his oratory-loving fans were disappointed, but the president knows that his power ultimately rests on competence, not speeches. Still, you can bet that Obama will get demonstrative again each time the nation faces an immediate crisis or tragedy. Talk that brings the tribe together can temporarily trump deliberative speech—and even actual competence. Can you think of any recent examples?

While Obama is a much more deliberative guy than his predecessor, you'll find a lot of great demonstrative talk in his speeches. Teddy Roosevelt didn't call the White House a "bully pulpit" for nothing. Leaders reserve their best speeches for sermonizing, reminding us of the values we hold in common. That's why Obama uses so many identity tools, along with first-rate figures of speech and thought.

Cicero's outline: Introduction, narration, division, proof, refutation, conclusion.

Identity strategy: Distinguish your audience from outsiders. Then make them believe they'll be better people if they do what you want them to.

Enargeia: Describe your choice's happy outcome as a dream. And dramatize your narration using cinematic techniques.

Figures of Speech: A balancing figure can make the complex seem simple. Emphasize a point by summing it up in one word ("Plastics!") or by starting a new sentence without finishing your last one. Use alliteration to make the unalike seem alike.

Figures of Thought: Make something seem impossible by connecting it in the audience's eyes to something else that's impossible. Want to show determination? Follow a string of negatives with a sure-fire short, positive clause.

Channeling: Associate yourself with the audience's heroes—not just by praising them, but by sounding like them.

25. Use the Right Tools

▲

THE BRAD PITT FACTOR
The instruments for every occasion

A great ox stands on my tongue.

—AESCHYLUS

You are well on your way to becoming an argument adept, with a whole slew of persuasive tchniques. Admittedly, chances are excellent that you and I will never acquire the eloquence of an Obama. But then, we don't have to. Opportunities to address a giant political convention seldom arise. You'll probably put your new-found tools to use with smaller audiences. This chapter will help you by walking through several situations that have to do with landing a promotion and selling ideas.

Having seen the many techniques rhetoric has to offer, you might feel like the beginning skier who gets too much advice: "Bend your knees, hold your hands above your waist, lean into the uphill ski, press with your toes, and remember to keep your shoulders perpendicular to your skis at all times!" You could suffer the same vertiginous feeling in an argument. Quick, should you use code grooming or a redefinition strategy first? Do you emphasize character, or emotion? What are the right commonplaces to use?

One way to get a feel for the tools is to watch the arguments around you and try to determine the techniques people use—or fail to. Dorothy Senior loves to come home and tell me about the rhetoric she heard on NPR.

> DOROTHY SR.: The attorney general pulled off a perfect Eddie Haskell Ploy, and the interviewer didn't even call him on it!

▶ **Argument Tool**
To refresh you on the Eddie Haskell Ploy, which we encountered in Chapter 6: When it seems that a decision won't go your way, endorse it as proof of your disinterest and virtue. Short of open bribery, it's the greatest sucking-up tool ever invented.

Unlike Dorothy, of course, you haven't been learning the art with me for seventeen years. (Thank your lucky stars.) You may not have the Eddie Haskell Ploy on the tip of your tongue. Don't worry about it. Even if you can't think of the names for the tools, you will find yourself spotting the persuasion.

To help, let's slot the 136 tools in this book into a few memorable groups:

> *Goals*
> *Ethos*
> *Pathos*
> *Logos*
> *Kairos*

The appendices contain a cheat sheet with the tools organized into these areas. But you probably already know how to conduct a basic rhetorical analysis on the fly, even without cribbing. When you hear an argument, ask yourself:

> **Goals:** What does the persuader want to get out of the argument? Is she trying to change the audience's mood or mind, or does she want it to do something? Is she fixing blame, bringing a tribe together with values speech, or talking about a decision?
> ***Ethos, pathos, logos:*** Which appeal does she emphasize—character, emotion, or logic?
> ***Kairos:*** Is her timing right? Is she using the right medium?

Selling uses the widest variety of these skills. I mean "selling" in the broadest sense: taking a product and making your audience desire it badly enough to do something about it. That product could consist of a thing, an idea, or you. If you happen to hold a job, or live with another person, or belong to the human race, then you have done your share of selling. The question is just how good you are at it, how comfortable with it, and whether you want to do it better.

The Proper Way to Suck Up

Let's start by selling *you*. Suppose your immediate superior quits, and you want to make a bid for the position without arousing the jealousy of your peers. Your goal is easy: to get the top boss to give you the job. This is a deliberative argument, since it has to do with a choice. Values language may help your argument, and if you're the walk-over-your-own-grandmother type, you could use some forensic language to smear the other potential candidates. But you want to speak mostly in the future tense, focusing on what you can do to benefit your company or organization.

Now, which of Aristotle's three appeals do you emphasize—*ethos, pathos,* or *logos?* You can eliminate *pathos* pretty quickly; the strongest persuasive emotions, such as anger and patriotism, work poorly in an office. Any emotion you do employ is best saved for the end, when the boss is ready to make a decision and you want him to commit to you.

Ethos or *logos?* Since the boss is evaluating you, character should be your main appeal. Logic can certainly help. You could write a bang-up memo telling how the job could be done better. But even that would serve to show off your character, by revealing an abundant supply of practical wisdom.

Remember the three *ethos* traits? Practical wisdom is one. Virtue and disinterested goodwill are the other two. You show virtue by aligning yourself with the organization's values. Describe how you will save money or bring in business or members—whatever the company values most.

▶ **Persuasion Alert**
Do the tools really work in this situation? They did for Dorothy Senior. I wrote this scenario from a real-life experience. Little more than a year after she resumed her career, her boss resigned for health reasons. After a national search, her employer chose the internal candidate: Dorothy. They made her a VP. She credits rhetoric with helping her make her best pitch.

As for disinterested goodwill, think of your audience, which in this case is just one person: the boss. One of the best "goodwill" lines to use on a superior is, "What do you need?" As overly simple as this sounds, in all my years of managing people I rarely heard the expression from my direct reports. Dorothy Senior says it's the single best piece of advice I gave her when she went back to work. She asked me what she should keep in mind during her weekly one-on-one meetings with the boss. "When you're done updating him on what you're doing, ask him what he needs," I said. She became indispensable within a couple of weeks. (She actually followed up on those needs, which is something I rarely got around to when I was employed.)

How Bush Senior Became President

Another stupidly simple piece of goodwill advice: thank people in writing. Congratulate them in writing. Commiserate in writing. Write notes—e-mails, handwritten cards, whatever seems appropriate. George Bush Sr. was famous for his thoughtful letters, which he would peck out on his manual typewriter. An intern of mine, who was no fan of Republicans, once wrote an article that mentioned the president. He received a short note from Bush praising his writing (and disputing a point in the piece). The intern became one of his many personal fans. Bush made himself a paragon of disinterested goodwill by taking some of his precious time to write a note to a young stranger. Use this note-writing habit to manage up, down, and sideways at work.

Assuming you are such a paragon yourself, you have already taken care of goodwill with your boss. All right, so then you write a detailed strategy memo to show off your practical wisdom and to prove you have more virtue (in the rhetorical sense) than any other candidate. This is where *kairos* comes in, by the way. To show that you can turn on a dime, write the memo as fast as you can without being sloppy, and send it ASAP.

First, though, think how you want to present that memo. Should it be printed and bound with a clear plastic binder? Or e-mailed as an attachment? If the boss is no reader, would he let you give a PowerPoint presentation? Or e-mail one to him? That's *kairos* again—timing plus medium.

While you wait for the boss to get back to you, what other *ethos*-boosting tool can boost your chances? Decorum! If you don't already dress at the level you aspire to, start now. Use code grooming, picking up the jargon and commonplaces that the top boss uses. And you might try to employ an identity strategy. How can you make the boss identify with promoting you? One of the easiest ways is to make him identify with *you*—to see you as a junior version of himself, the way Robert Redford cast his doppelganger, Brad Pitt, in *A River Runs Through It*. Business sociologists say that managers do tend to hire people with personalities similar to their own.

Some of your coworkers may see your identity tactics as first-class sucking up, so decorum has to work in all directions. If you want to suck up to the boss, suck up to your peers at the same time. Make a point of socializing with them during this period. Take time for them. Sing their praises to people who will report back to them.

Now, assume that your strategy works to the point where the boss calls you in for a job interview. You don't need a memorized script, or figures of speech on the tip of your tongue. Just focus on your *ethos* strategy: practical wisdom (you know what is good for the company, and you have the skills to carry them out), virtue (you share the company's values and will do what it takes to support them), disinterested goodwill (you're loyal to the boss and want to make his job easier). Get your decorum down, with the proper dress (for the supervisor's role) and code language that pleases the boss.

Let's run the strategy through some dialogue and see how it pans out.

> BOSS: Why do you want this job?
> YOU: Because I see the way you mentor people, and I'm ex-
>   cited about the opportunity to bring people along in their
>   own careers.

Great! I assume the boss is big on mentoring and often uses the "learn-ing experiences" commonplace. Your answer shines with both disinterested goodwill and virtue. You also used an excellent ethical backfire tactic, emphasizing a weakness as a strength. Alas, your boss sees right through that one.

> BOSS: Do you think you're ready to mentor people? I see from
>   your résumé that you haven't supervised many people in
>   your career.

This may sound like an *ethos* question, but it may take some logic to con-vince him. How can you reveal your mentoring skill while sitting alone with him? One way is to come up with examples—inductive logic. Suppose you don't have any supervisory experience, though. Remember that facts com-pose only one of three kinds of examples, the other two being comparison and story. Time for some storytelling!

> YOU: Well, there's a reason why other employees come to
>   me with advice. Just to give you one example: Jaime over
>   in accounting had a terrific idea for a word-of-mouth
>   promotion—he swore me to secrecy, so I can't tell you
>   what it is. He asked me how to approach you, and I helped
>   him put together a short presentation and booked the
>   time on your calendar. You see him next Tuesday.

Well done. By telling a story, you put the boss in your shoes. Whenever you can get the audience to see through your eyes, and experience what you experienced, you put them in a receptive mood. The boss talks about the strategy in your memo, you go over your particular strengths, and it's time to wrap things up.

> BOSS: So, is there anything else you'd like to add?
>
> YOU: Yes, there is. I'm sure you have other great candidates. But nobody will put more heart into it than I will. Give me a chance, and I'll meet your expectations and then some. And I really want that chance.

> **▸ Persuasion Alert**
> Who said anything about coworkers coming for advice? You're using a slightly risky but useful technique: speak of an unproven point as if it's already a given. It's risky because your audience—the boss—might call you on it, requiring some serious backing and filling.

Nice peroration. You leave the room with a palpable emotion. Now, some bosses might be put off by this sort of display; some might prefer candidates who play a bit harder to get. But a little emotion at the end of a job interview is usually a good thing. Cicero said so (he was talking about an oration, but it works the same way). And you know I never second-guess Cicero.

Wielding the Book Club

Selling an idea uses much the same tools. Suppose you're so excited about rhetoric that you want to get your book club to read this book. Here it's a matter of getting the club to make a choice, not take an action. Therefore, emotion bears less of a burden.

Another difference from a job interview: the product's *ethos* counts even more than your own, unless your group has loved every book you have recommended. But suppose for the sake of this argument that this is the first book you present. Where do you start?

> YOU: I have a book that's going to surprise most of you. It surprised *me*, at least.

Um, okay. Where are you going with this?

> YOU: I picked it up in the bookstore because I was curious about the title *(holding book up)*. When I found it was about argument, I was going to put it right back on the shelf.

Oh, I get it. The reluctant conclusion. Very nice. It establishes your disinterest and walks the audience through your reasoning.

> YOU: But then I flipped the book open. Let me read you what I read. *(Read passage from the introduction about my rhetorical day.)* This isn't stuffy scholarship, or a cheesy business book. It's funny, and it actually teaches you how to argue. But that's not why I'm proposing that we read this together. It offers even more than that.

> ► **Persuasion Alert**
> Oh, for crying out loud. Not only do I just happen to use my own book in a sample argument, now I'm even having you praise it. I bank on my identity strategy. Throughout the book, I have attempted to put you in my shoes, playing back dialogues, winning and losing arguments, in the hope that I can get away with an occasional abuse of authorial privilege.

Oh joy, a *dirimens copulatio,* the but-wait-there's-more figure! Now you're just pouring it on. You use inductive logic to read an example, employ the definition strategy—it's not a scholarly or biz book—and promise something even better. Your group leans in to hear what comes next.

> YOU: It shows how argument isn't just a matter of dominating people. It's about getting what you want, of course. But it's also a way of avoiding fights and nastiness of all kinds—in politics as well as at home or work. This club likes to focus on serious books that make a difference in people's lives. Well, actually, this book is too entertaining to be purely serious, but it has a really serious purpose. And that's to get us back to what the author calls our "rhetorical roots."

Very nice. You mention the club's core values and show how the book sticks to them—a way of touting its rhetorical virtue. You even switch to the future tense at the end.

FELLOW CLUB MEMBER: Is the author an expert on rhetoric—
a what-do-you-call-it?
YOU: Rhetorician.

Uh-oh, a practical wisdom question. Does the author have a clue about his subject?

YOU: No, he's not an academic.

An excellent use of the redefinition tactic. Your fellow member asked if the author was an expert, not an academic. The club avoids scholarly books. Still, that fails to solve the practical wisdom problem. Where are you taking this?

> **Useful Figure**
> "Bob's your uncle" is an *idiom*, a set of words that convey a single meaning. Idioms are a rich source of common-places, being a close relative of the cliché. In this case, though, I deliberately use an anachronistic idiom to sustain a light tone. ("Bob" was Robert, Lord Salisbury, a British prime minister who in 1887 promoted his nephew.)

YOU: But he spent many years in publishing as a manager and a consultant, and he's also a journalist—not to mention being a husband and father—so he's able to apply rhetoric to real-world situations.

The very definition of practical wisdom! I couldn't have said it better myself. Head right to a summing-up sort of peroration, and Bob's your uncle.

YOU: So I can't imagine a better book for this club. It tells a personal story while it teaches useful social and intellectual skills that we didn't learn in college. If you have any more doubts, I'll be happy to read you a couple more passages.
BOOK CLUB LEADER: I don't think that'll be necessary. Do any of you? All right, let's have a vote!

Congratulations. You won a good argument, employing the book's own *ethos* to make it look good; wielding induction and redefinition; and making the group identify with the choice by employing values language. Oh, and thank you so much.

Franchising Charm

While a prepared pitch is relatively easy to deliver—you could memorize your little book club speech if you really wanted to—you may find it harder to be rhetorically nimble when someone raises an objection. Let's take an idea and put it—you—in an awkward situation.

You need to raise money to franchise a chain of standardized bed-and-breakfasts, so you give a terrific PowerPoint presentation to a venture capital firm. The proposed chain, Bed & Breakfast & Beyond, has all the charm, comfort, and value of regular B-and-Bs while adding quality assurance and branding. "We're the Starbucks of boutique hotels," you say. "An intimate experience, backed by a reliable brand."

Cue the lights.

One of the venture partners has a puzzled look. Uh-oh.

> VENTURE CAPITALIST: Standardized B-and-Bs? Isn't that an oxymoron?
> YOU: So is "venture capital."

Love the snappy answer! But remember that thing called decorum? Your job is to make the audience identify with you and your decision. Poking fun at the audience's profession does not constitute good decorum. Try again.

> YOU: It's more of a paradox.

Strike two. Mr. V.C. clearly loves to show his erudition, so arguing about terminology lacks decorum. We'll give you one more try.

> YOU: That's a great point, and it illustrates the genius of B&B&B. We take a mature industry and create a whole new sales category: assured uniqueness. That may look like an oxymoron, but it actually eliminates the flaws of two mature industries: the standard hotel chain and the independent B-and-B property. The visitor is guaranteed a unique experience—no two properties will look alike—while being assured of a high level of quality. This kind of

selective branding should produce an ROI north of eighty percent within five years.

Now you're talking. You use VC code language ("mature industry," "property," "ROI"—meaning "return on investment") to show you understand the venture capital world. And you refer to the firm's most cherished commonplace, profit through risk. Keep this tactic in mind: when you find yourself in trouble, you can often buy time with appropriate code language.

Concession makes an even better instant response, especially if your challenger and the audience are one and the same. Your answer to Mr. V.C. constitutes an excellent concession, a neat jujitsu move that turns a hostile question to your advantage.

Can I really expect you to have such a snappy answer at the tip of your tongue? No. A concession is not always snappy. If you can't think of anything else, agree with your opponent.

When in doubt, concede.

Like the code-grooming tactic, concession buys you time. If you can't follow up with a great jujitsu line, using your opponent's argument against him, you can still switch the tense to the future, and the main topic to the advantageous.

I'm going to put you on the firing line again. You want to sell another idea—a political opinion this time.

> YOU: I think we need to increase the Head Start budget. A
>   third of the kids in this country live below the poverty line,
>   and unless we can give them a decent breakfast and some
>   early education, we're just asking for trouble when those
>   kids grow up.
> OPPONENT: Well, I think just the opposite. We should cut aid
>   to poor families. Welfare mothers are lazy and a drain on
>   society.

How do you answer? You could call him a bigot, but that would end the argument. You could try to reason him out of his prejudice by offering macroeconomic structural explanations, then follow up with an appeal to *pathos*—emotional examples of hardworking mothers making $6 an hour. If your real audience is a group of liberal intellectuals, that response just might work, though your opponent probably would remain unconvinced. Besides, it's awfully hard to pull such an answer—practically a full-fledged oration—out of your hat. Your alternative? When in doubt, concede.

> YOU: Yeah, I'm sure there are lazy people on welfare.

The best kind of concession redefines the issue without appearing to. Here you shift the generic "welfare mothers" to a limited number of "lazy people." Plus you depersonalize the bad guys in the story. "Welfare mother" implies a slattern who shoots up to entertain her boyfriends while the kids terrorize the neighborhood. "Lazy people" conjures up a hazier, less specific image.

Still, concession alone won't win an argument, so you follow up by changing the tense and the issue.

> YOU: But the question is, how can we spend the least federal
> money over the long run? A kid in Head Start is much less
> likely to end up in prison. I'd rather the kid got a job than
> to have to support him behind bars.

By shifting the tense, you move the conversation away from tribal talk and into something arguable. Plus you use a conservative commonplace, "Spend Less Money." Will the argument succeed? It might, especially if the audience includes more than just your opponent. The advantageous is a powerful topic.

It can even work in an election—provided you have a savvy audience. Suppose your rhetorical ambitions get so fired up that you run for local office. At a public debate, the incumbent holds up an old photo of you as a teenager wearing a shirt that says TOKIN' MALE.

> INCUMBENT: My opponent abused drugs. And drug abusers
> do not belong in public office!

Ouch. All the heads in the audience now swivel in your direction. What do you do?

1. Deny you ever smoked. Say you bought the shirt off a young reforming addict who needed money for the church collection plate.
2. Say you didn't inhale.
3. Attack your opponent.

> YOU: My opponent has fathered three children out of wed-
> lock. Now, I like a man with family values. He may not have
> many values, but he sure has a lot of family!

Well, a character attack has its virtues (in a rhetorical sense), but is that
why you run for office? To make fun of people? Denying you smoked or
inhaled should be your last resort. Even if you never did smoke, and you
wore the shirt in high school to disguise your lack of hipness, a denial
would repeat the charge in the audience's mind. (Remember the logic-free
values talk in Chapter 18. Values-laden terms tend to stick better than logical points do.)

Instead, try conceding.

> YOU: I cannot tell a lie. I did wear that T-shirt in high school.
> And I admit my hair looked like that.

Nice use of humor to lighten the audience's mood. What's next?

> YOU: And I sewed some wild oats as a kid. And as a respon-
> sible adult with children of my own, I regret it. But do you
> want to discuss old T-shirts, or can we talk about how to fix
> the pothole we all had to step over when we walked from
> the parking lot?

There are plenty more answers where that came
from, and maybe some alternatives would test better
with focus groups. But any concession that changes
the tense from the past (accusation) and present (tribalism) to the future (the advantageous) will win the
attention of your audience.

"Sure," says the talk-radio-saturated, attack-ad-
battered, politically fed-up reader. "And what planet
are *you* on?"

▶ **Persuasion Alert**
I use the correction
figure here ("not a
planet, a nation"),
repeating my (imag-
inary) opponent's
term and substitut-
ing another one.
The best correction
makes you look
more virtuous than
your opponent by
using a term that
the audience values
more.

It's not a planet, it's a nation. It used to be a rhetorical one. And it can be one again.

The Tools

In this chapter, we pulled together the whole arsenal of rhetorical weapons.

For offense, think of your goal, set the tense, and know your audience's values and commonplaces. Then use *ethos, logos,* and *pathos,* usually in that order.

For defense, when you don't know what to say, try conceding, then redefining your concession. ("You could say it's spinach, yes. Others would say it's broccoli.") Finally, switch the tense to the future. ("But the question is, how are we going to get that vegetable down you?")

And for specific tools, turn to page 297.

26. Run an Agreeable Country

▲

RHETORIC'S REVIVAL
An argument for the sake of argument

Where there is much desire to learn, there of necessity will be much arguing . . . for opinion in good men is but knowledge in the making. —JOHN MILTON

"**Y**ou know why Americans are so fat? They drink too much water."

It was late at night on the Italian Riviera, and I was eating with two local entrepreneurs, Gianni and Carlo, in the beautiful seaside town of Sestri Levante. We had already debated politics, the state of education, even the fish population in the Mediterranean (we were in a fish restaurant, and the owner jumped in)

Gianni took up the subject of water after a couple of hours and too much wine. "I went to America last month, everybody is with a bottle of water. And"—he leaned significantly across the table—"*everybody* is fat." This launched an argument that took us through another bottle or two of (nonfattening) wine. You could hardly call it high discourse, and I doubt that Gianni even believed what he said. But he was following the age-old European custom that turns argument into a bonding experience.

If it weren't for the wine, I would have shrunk in embarrassment. People at other tables were *looking* at us, and they were laughing—with us, most likely, but still. Here in the States, only the rude, the insane, and politicians disagree.

Then again, our aversion to argument is part of our tradition, right? Not if you go back before the mid–nineteenth century. Europeans who visited the States early in our history commented on how argumentative *we* were. What happened?

What happened was that we lost the ability to argue. Rhetoric once formed the core of education, especially

▸ **Persuasion Alert**
I organized this chapter along the lines of a Ciceronian oration. This part is a classic *exordium,* or introduction, which stresses *ethos* and defines the issue.

in colleges. It died out in the 1800s when the classics in general lost their popularity and when even academia forgot what the liberal arts were for: to train an elite for leadership.

You have seen how powerful the art is for personal use; and you doubtless understand why hundreds of generations learned it as an art of leadership. But rhetoric reserves its chief power for the state—which leads me to the burden of this final chapter:

Rhetoric could help lead us out of our political mess.

I intend to show you the indispensable role that rhetoric played in founding the American republic, and how its decline deprived us of a valuable tool of democracy. At the end, I'll offer a vision of a rhetorical society, where people manipulate one another happily, fend off manipulation deftly, and use their arguments wisely. It won't be as hard as it sounds. I've been practicing on my family for years.

> ▸ **Persuasion Alert**
> I end this first section with a bit of self-deprecation to balance the lofty (some would say pretentious) tone. Early in this "oration," I need to work some *ethos* mojo. Plus, Cicero said that a good oration should flow nicely from part to part. Mentioning my family allows a smooth transition to the next section, which mentions my family.

My Big Fat Rhetoric Jones

My kids say I sound like the father in *My Big Fat Greek Wedding*. Just as that dad claimed the Greeks invented everything, I have an annoying habit of seeing rhetoric behind everything. At church once, my wife had to shush me when I leaned over and explained the origin of the Christian mass.

ME: It's taken right from a rhetoric-school exercise called the *chria*.

DOROTHY SR.: Shhh.

ME: Students would repeat something historically important, playing the main characters themselves.

GEORGE: So who gets to play Judas?

DOROTHY SR.: Will you please be quiet?

ANOTHER PARISHIONER: Shhh.

> ▸ **Persuasion Alert**
> Speaking of pretension, I need a device to lay some more cool rhetorical facts on you without turning you off. So I resort once again to self-deprecation, nerdily reciting rhetoric facts in a dialogue that has me nerdily reciting rhetoric facts. Ooh, weird.

Another time, I was explaining to Dorothy Junior the etymology of the medical terms she loves as an aspiring med student.

ME: Dialysis—a figure of speech.

DOROTHY JR.: That's nice.

ME: It's where the speaker puts both sides of an issue next to each other in a sentence. Like the one-two beat of a heart, see.

DOROTHY JR.: Dad, I . . .

ME: Doctors stole a bunch of figures at a time when rhetoric held a higher status than medicine—metastasis, antistasis, epitasis, metalepsis . . .

DOROTHY JR.: Dad, I don't care!

Then just the other day, while flying back from a consulting trip in North Carolina, I found myself lecturing on rhetoric to my startled seat mate, a young woman who had just graduated from journalism school.

ME: Do they still teach you to cover "who, what, when, where, how, and why" in a newspaper story?

SEAT MATE: Yes, they do.

ME: Journalism got that right out of classical rhetoric. Know who Cicero is?

SEAT MATE: Um, I think I . . .

ME: He said that the orator should cover all these bases during the "narration" at the beginning of a speech.

SEAT MATE (*giving frozen smile*): . . .

> **Useful Figure**
> This self-editing figure, the *metanoia* ("change of heart"), corrects an earlier phrase to make a stronger point. It's a faintly ironic way to spruce up a cliché like "Don't get me started."

And don't get me started about the birth of the American republic. Actually, do get me started.

Channeling Cicero

You often hear about America's founding as a "Christian nation," but its system of government owes a greater debt to rhetoric—even though the discipline was on the decline before the Revolution. In the 1600s, Britain's Royal Society of leading scientists called for "a close, naked, natural way of

▶ **Persuasion Alert**
Now we're into the
narration, which
uses storytelling to
establish the facts.
You can make a
concept into a
character by intro-
ducing opposing
ideas and their
advocates as vil-
lains. That nasty
Royal Society!

speaking" that would "approach Mathematical plain-
ness." It issued a manifesto urging speakers of English
"to reject all the amplifications, digressions, and swellings of style; to return back to the primitive purity,
and shortness, when men deliver'd so many things,
almost in equal number of words." The society's ideal
of a one-to-one word-to-thing ratio probably hadn't
been achieved since humans lived in caves, but their
plea helped scrape off some of the gilding from that
day's overelaborate speech.

Of course, among those who employed amplifications, digressions, and
swellings of style were Christopher Marlowe and William Shakespeare. But
every movement has its casualties.

Nonetheless, sheer academic inertia allowed rhetoric to maintain a
large presence in higher education up through the eighteenth century,
and everyone who attended the American Constitutional Convention had a
thorough grounding in it. John Locke, the modern philosopher who inspired the founders the most, occupied a rhetoric chair at Oxford. Late in
life, Jefferson credited Locke, along with Cicero and Aristotle, with helping
inspire the Declaration of Independence.

The founders were absolutely mad about ancient Greece and Rome. They
lived in knockoff temples, wrote to each other in Latin, and commissioned
artists to paint them draped in togas. The founders did more than just
imitate the ancients, though; they virtually channeled their republican fore-
bears. Admirers called George Washington "Cato," after a great Roman senator. When they bestowed the "Father of our Country" label on Washington,
they actually quoted Cato—who called *Cicero* the father of his country.

It seemed as though everyone wanted to play the part of Rome's greatest orator. Caustic, witty John Adams liked to consider himself the reincar-
nation of witty, caustic Marcus Tullius Cicero. Adams even recited the
Roman orator as a sort of daily aerobic workout. "I find it a noble Exercise,"
he told his diary. "It exercises my Lungs, raises my Spirits, opens my Porrs,
quickens the Circulation, and so contributes much to [my] health." Alexander Hamilton liked to sign his anonymous essays with Cicero's nickname,
Tully. Voltaire called Pennsylvania leader John Dickinson a Cicero. John
Marshall called Washington a Cicero. But some people thought Patrick
Henry, who spoke fluent Latin, was the Cicero who beat all Ciceros (except

the original one). Witnesses say that when he shouted, "Give me liberty or give me death," he threw himself on the floor and played dead for a moment. It brought the house down.

All during the Revolution, theatergoers flocked to performances of Joseph Addison's smash hit, *Cato*. Its plot—a noble democrat struggles to save the republic from tyranny—paralleled their own cause. Cato-esque George Washington saw it many times, and to cheer the troops he had the play performed at Valley Forge, twice. When his officers threatened to mutiny, Washington imitated the rhetorical techniques that the Cato in the play used to put down a mutiny. Patrick Henry lifted his liberty-or-death line straight from Addison's script. And before the British hanged him, Nathan Hale, the American spy, wrote his own epitaph—"I only regret that I have but one life to lose for my country"—by cribbing Addison. ("What pity is it / That we can die but once to serve our country!")

The tragedy of the Roman Republic enabled a self-induced case of déjà vu. After reading a biography of Cicero in 1805, John Adams wrote, "I seem to read the history of all ages and nations in every page, and especially the history of our country for forty years past. Change the names and every anecdote will be applicable to us."

That must have been nerve-wracking. *Cato* was a tragedy, and so was the demise of the Roman Republic. Cato committed suicide at the end of the play—and at the end of his real life—and the bad guys did Cicero in a few years later. But all that classical nostalgia had a serious purpose. The American system was more than an experiment in political theory; it also attempted the most ambitious do-over in world history. The Revolution would let history repeat itself, with some major improvements.

The most important upgrade was an antidote for factionalism. What killed democracy in ancient Athens and destroyed the Roman Republic, they believed, was conflict between economic and social classes. Factionalism scared the Americans even more than kings did. So the founders established a system of checks and balances: The Senate would represent the aristocracy, being chosen by state legislatures. The "plebes," as the Romans called common citizens, would elect the House of Representatives. And both groups would choose the president. Each faction would keep the other out of mischief.

Which begs the question: what with all that checking and balancing, how could anything get done? Their answer lay in rhetoric. The new system would "refine and enlarge" public opinion, Hamilton said, "by passing them through the medium of a chosen body of citizens"—rhetorically trained citizens. The founders assumed that this natural aristocracy would comprise those with the best liberal education. "Liberal" meant free from dependence on others, and the liberal arts—especially rhetoric—were those that prepared students for their place at the top of the merit system. These gentlemen rhetoricians would compose an informal corps of politically neutral umpires. They would serve, Hamilton said, as a collective "impartial arbiter" among the classes.

The founders weren't starry-eyed about their republic. They knew that occasionally, inevitably, scum would rise to the surface. Hamilton even understood that political parties—which the founders equated with factions—might someday "infest" their republic. But he and his colleagues believed that the symptoms could be ameliorated by the combination of checks and balances and the "cool, candid" arbitration of the liberally educated professional class. Congress would serve as a "deliberative" body, Hamilton explained. Rhetoricians might be in the minority; but that was all right, so long as they held the swing votes; and being neutral by definition, they were bound to hold the swing votes.

The nation had no lack of rhetorically educated candidates. To get into Harvard in the 1700s, prospects had to prove their mastery of Cicero. John Jay read three of Cicero's orations as a requirement of admission to King's College (now Columbia). College students throughout the colonies held debates in which they pretended to be English Whigs debating ancient Greeks and Romans. Before he led New Jersey's delegation in Philadelphia, John Witherspoon was a professor of rhetoric and James Madison was one of his students.

Alas, the founders' classical education failed to prepare them for an enormous political irony: those same leaders who were supposed to counterbalance political parties—the enlightened, disinterested

▶ **Classic Hits**

SLAVES MADE THEM LIBERAL: While some of the founders disliked slavery, nearly all tolerated it, because it served what to them was a higher purpose. In a classical sense, slavery was consistent with republican values; after all, it had existed in every previous republic in history. The Romans had slaves. So did the Athenians. More important, slaves were part of the ancients' agricultural economy; they allowed the owners to live free of any interest—or as they put it, "liberally." Slavery's essential evil became a political reality only when the notion of disinterest faded.

few—wound up founding them. Each party, Federalist and Republican, rose to prevent the rise of the other. Each claimed not to be a faction at all; each vowed to *prevent* faction. Hamilton thought he was defending the rhetorical republic against the democratically inclined Jeffersonians, who, Hamilton thought, would encourage factionalism and prevent the election of a liberally educated aristocracy. The Jeffersonians defended the agrarian culture that the ancients had considered essential to personal independence. In fighting what they thought were threats to disinterested government—democracy and commercialism—both groups formed permanent competing interests.

Hamilton had originally thought of the American republic as an experiment that would test a hypothesis: whether people were capable of "establishing a good government from reflection and choice," or whether their politics were doomed to depend on "accident and force." By 1807, with the nation slipping further into factionalism, he had concluded that the experiment was a failure.

The political divisions brought a shocking collapse of civility. Newspapers in the early 1800s were packed with violent personal attacks and political sex scandals; editorials even went after saints like Ben Franklin and George Washington. Hamilton's dreaded "accident and force"—along with diatribe and personal attack—took the place of deliberation. Politics became mired in tribal language and fueled by a deep national division—not between social classes, as in Rome, but between sets of deeply held beliefs and values.

> ▸ **Persuasion Alert**
> Continuing my oration, I now come to the *proof* part. Some rhetoricians say you can merge the proof with *division*. I've done that as well.

The modern politician would have felt right at home.

You Can't Keep Good Rhetoric Down

Throughout this country's history, "values" have fostered occasional breakdowns in political debate, as citizens took sides around their ideals and formed irreconcilable tribes. When the abolition of slavery competed with states' rights, the result was civil war.

While the current division in values is not nearly so severe, tribes are forming nonetheless. In 2005, *Austin American-Statesman* reporter Bill Bishop found that the number of "landslide counties"—where more than 60 percent of residents voted for one party in presidential elections—had doubled since 1976. A majority of Americans now occupy these ideological bubbles.

Our tribal mind-set has destroyed what little faith we had in deliberative debate. Even as individuals, we think so little of argument that we outsource it. We delegate disagreement to professionals, handing off our arguments to lawyers, party hacks, radio hosts, H.R. departments, and bosses. We express our differences sociopathically, through anger and diatribe, extremism and dogmatism. Incivility smolders all around us, on our drives to work, in the supermarket, in the ways employers fire employees, on radio, television, and Capitol Hill.

But as you know, we make a mistake when we apply the label of "argument" to each nasty exchange. Invective betrays a *lack* of argument—a collapse of faith in persuasion and consensus.

It is no coincidence that red and blue America split apart just when moral issues began to dominate campaigns—not because one side *has* morals and the other lacks them, but because values cannot be the sole subject of deliberative argument. Of course, demonstrative language—code grooming and values talk—works to bring an audience together and make it identify with you and your point of view. But eventually a deliberative argument has to get—well, deliberative. Political issues such as stem cell research, abortion, and gay marriage deal with the Truth's black-and-white, not argument's gray. When politicians politicize morals and moralize politics, you have no decent argument. You have tribes. End of discussion.

On the other hand, deliberative argument acts as the great attractor of politics, the force that brings the extremes into its moderate orbit. The trick is to occupy the commonplace of politics, that Central Park of beliefs, and make it the persuader's own turf. You can't pull people toward your opinion until you walk right into the middle of their beliefs. And if that fails, you have to change your goal—promote an opinion that lies a little farther into their territory, or suggest an action that's not so big a step.

In other words, you have to be *virtuous*.

The Great Attractor

Remember Aristotle's definition of virtue:

> *A matter of character, concerned with choice, lying in a mean.*

The opinions of the most persuadable people tend to lie in the ideological center. Ideologues by definition can't be persuaded. But the number of those persuadable citizens—the swing voters—is getting shockingly small. If 269 Floridians had voted differently in the 2000 presidential election, Al Gore would have won. Just 269 out of 105 *million* people could have changed world history. Even in the 2008 election, which Obama won by a hefty margin, less than two percent of the electorate determined which way the swing states swung.

It's just as the American founders had predicted: when the country splits in two, a few independent-minded types hold the power to choose our leaders. But while Hamilton and Madison thought that those independents would be our best-educated, best-informed, rhetorically trained citizens, the opposite turns out to be true. Political scientists have found that voters who identify themselves as independents tend to be the *least* educated, least informed, and most easily manipulated by negative advertising and fear-mongering.

And the rest of us? We admire the politicians who preach values and stick to their guns. What happens when we so completely forget rhetoric that our definition of virtue becomes the opposite of Aristotle's? You get an anti-rhetorical nation, like the one we have now.

It's time to revive the founders' original republican experiment and create a new corps of rhetorically educated citizens. But we should do the founders one better. Education was a relatively scarce commodity in the eighteenth century; we can afford to educate the whole citizenry in rhetoric.

If I begin to sound like a rhetorical Pollyanna, take a look at high school and college curricula. Teachers are including rhetoric in an increasing number of courses. The AP English exam now has a rhetorical component. Colleges, led by the public land-grant universities, are doing their part; rhetoric has become the fastest-growing subject in higher education. Even at Harvard, rhetoric courses have slipped into the curriculum again,

through the expository writing program. Having spent
ten years of my career working for an Ivy League university—the most rhetorically intolerant place I know—
I find rhetoric's revival heartening. Rhetoric students
and professors are unlike their academic peers. For one
thing, you cannot offend them easily. I find it equally
hard to snow them. I have had dozens of them vet my
book manuscript; their comments, the toughest of any
readers, made me cringe. And they were dead on. I pity
any politicians who dare to appear before such audiences. What would
happen if we educated a few million more of these admirable citizens, and
if the rest of us continued to learn all we could of the art?

Why, we'd have a rhetorical culture: a mass exo-
dus of voters from political parties, since tribal politics
would seem very uncool. Politicians falling over one
another to prove their disinterest. Candidates forced
to speak intelligently, the way they do in rhetorically
minded Great Britain. No need for campaign finance
reform, because voters would see the trickery behind
the ads. Our best debaters would compete to perform
in America's number-one hit show on network television, *American Orator.* Car salesmen would find it
that much harder to seduce a customer. We would
actually start talking—and listening—to one another.
And Americans would hold their own against wine-
soaked Italians.

> **Persuasion Alert**
> This is a pretty
> informal version
> of the *refutation,*
> where I state my
> opponent's argu-
> ment, or an antic-
> ipated objection
> from the audi-
> ence, and smack
> it down.

> **Persuasion Alert**
> And now for the
> *peroration,* which
> can get emotional.
> A classic peroration
> describes a vision
> of the future; Martin
> Luther King used it
> in his "I Have a
> Dream" speech.

> **Meanings**
> The Greeks had a
> word for a person
> who didn't vote:
> *idiotes,* or "idiot."
> The person who
> lived an entirely pri-
> vate life, Aristotle
> said, was either a
> beast or a god.

Thank Kids for Arguing

All right, now I *am* talking like Pollyanna. Nonetheless, I invite you to help
foster the great rhetoric revival.

When you talk politics, and I devoutly hope you do, use all the tricks you
learned, including code language and emotional tools and other sneaky
stuff; but focus on the future. Insist that candidates for office use the "advantageous" as their chief topic: what's best for their constituents? Slam any

politician who claims to ignore the polls. He doesn't have to follow them slavishly, but public opinion is a democracy's ultimate boss. Ask any candidate who brags about sticking to his guns, "How's that going to fix the potholes or educate our children?" Insist on virtuous—rhetorically virtuous—leaders, the ones who make a beeline for the golden mean.

If you are a parent, talk to the school board about adding rhetoric to the curriculum as early as the seventh grade. (The Romans started them even younger.) Buy multiple copies of this book and distribute them to the English teachers in your schools. And raise your children rhetorically.

When I first learned rhetoric on my own, I unwittingly began to create a rhetorical environment at home, even when the children were little. I rattled on about Aristotle and Cicero and figures of speech, and I pointed out our own rhetorical tricks around the dinner table. I let the kids win an argument now and then, which gave them a growing incentive to become still more argumentative. They grew so fond of debate, in fact, that whenever we stayed in hotels and they got to watch television, they would debate it. Not *over* the television; with the TV itself.

> Why should I eat candy that *talks?*
> I bet that toy isn't as cool in real life.
> A doll that goes to the bathroom? I have a brother who does
> that.

It was as if I had given them advertising-immunization shots. But when the commentary extended to news and programming, I had to beg them for quiet. I still do, come to think of it. And as my children get older and more persuasive, I find myself losing more arguments than I win. They drive me crazy. They do me proud.

APPENDICES

▲

The Tools

I put rhetoric's techniques and concepts into categories that you will find most useful in day-to-day argument. That way you don't have to memorize dozens of terms and tools; just remember to

- Set your **goals** and the argument's **tense.**
- Think of whether you want to emphasize **character, logic,** or **emotion.**
- Make sure the **time** and the **medium** are ripe for persuasion.

When you draft a speech or presentation, keep Cicero's outline handy:

- **Introduction**
- **Narration**
- **Division**
- **Proof**
- **Refutation**
- **Conclusion**

If you have not yet read the rest of the book, much of this may not make sense. If you have read it, and the terms still give you trouble, refer to the glossary that follows. And if I still don't make sense after that, or if you want to delve deeper into the art, read the bibliography, Appendix IV.

Goals

PERSONAL GOAL: What you want from your audience.

AUDIENCE GOALS
> **Mood:** This is the easiest thing to change.
> **Mind:** A step up in difficulty from changing the mood.
> **Willingness to Act:** Hardest of all, because it requires an emotional commitment and identification with the action.

ISSUE CONTROL: Mastering argument's chief topics.
> **Blame:** Covers the past. Aristotle called this kind of argument **forensic.** Its chief topics are **guilt** and **innocence.**
> **Values:** Get argued in the present tense. This is **demonstrative** or tribal rhetoric. Chief topics: **praise** and **blame.**
> **Choice:** Deals with the future. This is deliberative argument, the rhetoric of politics. Its chief topic is the **advantageous—** what's best for the audience.

Ethos

This is argument by character—using your reputation or someone else's as the basis for argument. When you give a speech, play up your character— or what you want the audience to think it is. Its three chief aspects are **virtue, practical wisdom,** and **disinterest.**

DECORUM: Your ability to fit in with the audience's expectations of a trustworthy leader.
> **Code Grooming:** Using language unique to the audience.
> **Identity Strategy:** Getting an audience to identify with an action—to see the choice as one that helps define them as a group.
> **Irony:** Saying one thing to outsiders with a meaning revealed only to your group.

VIRTUE: The appearance of living up to your audience's values.
> **Bragging:** The straightforward, and least effective, way to enhance your virtue.

Witness Bragging: An endorsement by a third party, the more disinterested the better.

Tactical Flaw: A defect or mistake, intentionally revealed, that shows your rhetorical virtue.

Switching Sides: Appearing to have supported the powers that be all along.

Eddie Haskell Ploy: Throwing your support behind the inevitable to show off your virtue (you won't find the Eddie Haskell Ploy as such in rhetorical texts, but the concept appears frequently).

Logic-Free Values: Focusing on the individual values-words and commonplaces to bring a group together and get it to identify with you.

PRACTICAL WISDOM: *Phronesis* is the name Aristotle gave this rhetorical street savvy.

Showing off experience

Bending the rules

Appearing to take the middle course

DISINTEREST: Aristotle called this *eunoia*—an apparent willingness to sacrifice your own interests for the greater good.

Reluctant Conclusion: Appearing to have reached your conclusion only because of its overwhelming rightness.

Personal Sacrifice: Claiming that the choice will help your audience more than it will help you.

Dubitatio: Seeming doubtful of your own rhetorical skill.

LIAR DETECTOR: Techniques for judging a person's credibility.

Needs Test: Do the persuader's needs match your needs?

Comparable Experience: Has the persuader actually done what he's talking about?

Dodged Question: Ask who benefits from the choice. If you don't get a straight answer, don't trust that person's disinterest.

"That Depends" Filter: Instead of a one-size-fits-all choice, the persuader offers a solution tailored to you.

"Sussing" Ability: The persuader cuts to the chase of an issue.

Extremes: How does the persuader describe the opposing argument? How close is his middle-of-the-road to yours?
  Extremist Detector: An extremist will describe a moderate choice as extreme.
Virtue Yardstick: Does the persuader find the sweet spot between the extremes of your values?
Code Inoculation: Be aware of the terms that define the groups you belong to, and watch out when a persuader uses them.

Pathos

Argument by emotion is the seductive part of persuasion. *Pathos* can cause a mood change, make an audience more receptive to your logic, and give them an emotional commitment to your goal.

SYMPATHY: Registering concern for your audience's emotions.
  Oversympathizing: Exaggerated sympathy can make your audience feel ashamed of an emotion you want to change.

BELIEF: Aristotle said this is the key to emotion.
  Experience: Refer to the audience's own experience, or plant one in their heads; this is the past tense of belief.
    Storytelling: A way to give the audience a virtual experience.
  Expectation: Make an audience expect something good or bad, and the appropriate emotion will follow.

VOLUME CONTROL: Underplaying an emotion, or gradually increasing it so that the audience can feel it along with you.
  Simple Speech: Don't use fancy language when you get emotional.

UNANNOUNCED EMOTION: Avoid tipping off your audience in advance of a mood. They'll resist it.

PASSIVE VOICE: If you want to direct an audience's anger away from someone, imply that the action happened on its own. *The chair got broken,* not *Pablo broke the chair.*

BACKFIRE: You can calm an individual's emotion in advance by overplaying it yourself. This works especially well when you screw up and want to prevent the wrath of an authority.

PERSUASIVE EMOTIONS

> **Anger:** One of the most effective ways to rouse an audience to action. But it's a short-lived emotion.
>
>> *Belittlement Charge:* Show your opponent dissing your audience's desires. A belittled audience is an angry one, according to Aristotle.
>
> **Patriotism:** Attaches a choice or action to the audience's sense of group identity.
>
> **Emulation:** Emotional response to a role model. The greater your *ethos,* the more the audience will imitate you.
>
> **Humor:** A good calming device that can enhance your *ethos.*
>
>> *Urbane Humor:* Plays off a word or part of speech.
>>
>> *Wit:* Situational humor.
>>
>> *Facetious Humor:* Joke telling, a relatively ineffective form of persuasion.
>>
>> *Banter:* Snappy answers—works best in defense.

FIGURES OF SPEECH: You'll find the individual figures in the glossary. But here are the essential ways that you can create your own figures.

> **Cliché Twisting:** Using overworked language to your advantage.
>
>> *Literal Interpretation:* Reducing a cliché to absurdity by seeming to take it at face value.
>>
>> *Surprise Ending:* Starting a cliché as it's normally said, but ending it differently.
>>
>> *Reworking:* Switching words around in a cliché.
>
> **Word Swap:** Changing normal usage and grammar for effect.
>
>> *Chiasmus:* Creates a crisscross sentence.
>
> **Weighing Both Sides:** Comparing or contrasting opinions in order to define the issue.
>
>> *Either/Or Figure (dialysis):* Weighs each side equally.
>>
>> *Contrasting Figure (antithesis):* Favors one side over another.
>>
>> *Meaning-Change Figure (antistasis):* Repeats a word in a way that uses or defines it differently.

Editing Out Loud: Interrupting yourself or your opponent to correct something.

   Self-Correction Figure (metanoia): Lets you amplify an argument while seeming to be fair and accurate.

   Redefiner (correctio): Repeats the opponent's language and corrects it.

Volume Control: Amplifying or calming speech through figures.

   Litotes: Ironic understatement. Makes you seem cooler than your opponent.

   Climax: Uses overlapping words in successive phrases in a rhetorical crescendo.

Word Invention: Figures help you create new words or meanings from old words; they make you look clever.

   Verbing (anthimeria): Turns a noun into a verb or vice versa.

   "Like" Figure (parelcon): Strips a word of meaning and uses it as a pause or for emphasis.

Logos

Argument by logic. People like to think that all argument should be nothing *but* logic; but Aristotle said that when it comes to persuasion, rational speech needs emotion and character as well.

DEDUCTION: Applying a general principle to a particular matter.

   Enthymeme: A logic sandwich that contains deduction.

     We should [choice], because [commonplace]. Aristotle took formal logic's syllogism, stripped it down, and based it on a commonplace instead of a universal truth.

   Proof Spotter: A proof consists of examples or a premise. A premise usually begins with "because," or implies it.

   Commonplace: Any cliché, belief, or value that can serve as your audience's boiled-down public opinion. It's the starting point of your argument.

     Babbling: An audience's repetition of a word or idea; it often reveals a commonplace.

Rejection: Another good commonplace spotter. An audience will often use a commonplace when it rejects your argument.

Commonplace Label: Applying a commonplace to an idea, a proposal, or a piece of legislation as part of a definition strategy.

INDUCTION: Argument by example. It starts with the specific and moves to the general.

Fact, Comparison, Story: The three kinds of examples to use in inductive logic.

CONCESSION: Using your opponent's own argument to your advantage.

FRAMING: Shaping the bounds of an argument. This is a modern persuasive term; you won't find it in the classic rhetorics.

Framing Strategy:

1. Find the audience's commonplaces.
2. Define the issue broadly, appealing to the values of the widest audience.
3. Deal with the specific problem or choice, using the future tense.

Definition Strategy: Controlling the language used in an argument.

Term Change: Inserting your own language in place of your opponent's.

Redefinition: Accepting your opponent's terms while changing their connotation.

Definition Jujitsu: Using your opponent's language to attack him.

Definition Judo: Using terms that contrast with your opponent's, creating a context that makes him look bad.

LOGICAL FALLACIES: It's important to detect them, just as you should spot any kind of persuasive tactic used against you. Another reason to understand fallacious logic: you may want to use it yourself.

Bad Proof: The argument's commonplace or principle is
  unacceptable, or the examples are bad.

  False Comparison: Two things are similar, so they must be the
    same.

  All Natural Fallacy: Natural ingredients are good for you, so
    anything called "natural" is healthful. Also called the
    Fallacy of Association.

  Appeal to Popularity: Other kids get to do it, so why don't I?

  Hasty Generalization: Uses too few examples and interprets
    them too broadly.

  Misinterpreting the Evidence: Takes the exception and claims
    it proves the rule.

  Unit Fallacy: Does weird math with apples and oranges, often
    confusing the part for the whole.

  Fallacy of Ignorance: Claims that if something has not been
    proven, it must be false.

Bad Conclusion: We're given too many choices, or not enough,
  or the conclusion is irrelevant to the argument.

  Many Questions: Squashes two or more issues into a single one.

  False Dilemma: Offers the audience two choices when more
    actually exist.

  Fallacy of Antecedent: Assumes that this moment is identical
    to past, similar moments.

  Red Herring: Introduces an irrelevant issue to distract or
    confuse the audience.

  Straw Man: Sets up a different issue that's easier to argue.

Disconnect Between Proof and Conclusion: The proof stands up
  all right, but it fails to lead to the conclusion.

  Tautology: A logical redundancy; the proof and the
    conclusion are the same thing.

  Reductio ad absurdum: Takes the opponent's choice and
    reduces it to an absurdity.

  Slippery Slope: Predicts a series of dire events stemming from
    one choice.

  Post hoc ergo propter hoc: Assumes that if one thing follows
    another, the first thing caused the second one. I call this
    the **Chanticleer Fallacy**.

RHETORICAL FOULS: Mistakes or intentional offenses that stop an argument dead or make it fail to reach a consensus.

> **Switching Tenses Away from the Future:** It's fine to use the past or present, but deliberative argument depends on eventually discussing the future.
>
> **Inflexible Insistence on the Rules:** Using the voice of God, sticking to your guns, refusing to hear the other side.
>
> **Humiliation:** An argument that sets out only to debase someone, not to make a choice.
>
> **Innuendo:** A form of irony used to debase someone. It often plants an idea in the audience's head by denying it.
>
> **Threatening:** Rhetoricians call this *argumentum ad baculum*—argument by the stick. It denies the audience a choice.
>
> **Nasty Language or Signs**
>
> **Utter Stupidity**

Kairos

The Romans called it *occasio*, the art of seizing the occasion. *Kairos* depends on **timing** and the **medium**.

PERSUADABLE MOMENT: When the audience is ripest for your argument.

> **Moment Spotter:** Uncertain moods and beliefs—when minds are already beginning to change—signal a persuadable moment.
>
> **Perfect Audience: Receptive, attentive,** and **well disposed** toward you.
>
> **Audience Change:** If the current audience isn't ready for persuasion, seek another one. This is what market research is all about.

SENSES: The five senses are key to the proper medium.

> **Sight** is mostly *pathos* and *ethos*.
>
> **Sound** is the most **logical** sense.
>
> **Smell, taste,** and **touch** are almost purely **emotional**.

Speechmaking

INVENTION: The crafting part of a speech. Its tools are the tools of *logos*.

ARRANGEMENT: The organization of a speech.
> **Introduction**
> **Narration**
> **Proof**
> **Refutation**
> **Conclusion**

STYLE: Choice of words that make a speech attractive to the listener. The five virtues of style:
> **Proper Language**
> **Clarity**
> **Vividness**
> **Decorum**
> **Ornament**

MEMORY: The ability to speak without notes.

DELIVERY: The action of giving a speech.
> **Voice:** Should be loud enough for the room.
> **Gesture:** The eyes are key, even in a large room, because they lead your other facial muscles. Use few hand gestures in a formal speech.

▲

Glossary

accismus *(as-SIS-mus):* The figure of coyness. ("Oh, you shouldn't have.")

ad hominem *(ad HOM-in-em):* The character attack. Logicians and the argument-averse consider it a bad thing, but in rhetoric it's a necessity. *Ethos*, the appeal to character, needs a rebuttal in a real argument.

adianoeta *(ah-dee-ah-noh-EE-tah):* The figure of hidden meaning. ("I'm sure you wanted to do this in the worst way.")

a fortiori *(ah-for-tee-OR-ee):* The Mikey-likes-it! argument. If something less likely is true, then something more likely is bound to be true. Similarly, if you accomplished a difficult thing, you're more likely to accomplish an easier one.

anadiplosis *(an-a-di-PLO-sis):* A figure that builds one thought on top of another by taking the last word of a clause and using it to begin the next clause.

anaphora *(an-AH-phor-a):* A figure that repeats the first word in succeeding phrases or clauses. It works best in an emotional address before a crowd.

anthropomorphism *(an-thro-po-MOR-phism):* A logical fallacy—it attributes human traits to a non-human creature or object. Common to owners of pets.

antithesis *(an-TIH-the-sis):* The figure of contrasting ideas.

aporia *(a-POR-i-a):* Doubt or ignorance—feigned or real—used as a rhetorical device.

begging the question: Logicians know this as the fallacy of circular argument, or *tautology*. ("Bob says I'm trustworthy, and I can assure you that he tells the truth.") But in common usage it refers to speech that leaves out a beginning explanation.

Bushism: Fractured syntax and code words.

chiasmus *(kee-AZZ-muss):* The crisscross figure. ("Ask not what your country can do for you, ask what you can do for your country.")

circumlocution *(cir-cum-lo-CU-tion):* The rhetorical end run. It talks around an issue to avoid getting to the point.

concessio *(con-SESS-ee-o):* Concession, the jujitsu figure. You seem to agree with your opponent's point, only to use it to your advantage.

converse accident fallacy: A logical foul that uses a bad example to make a generalization.

deliberative rhetoric: One of three types of rhetorical persuasion (the other two are *forensic* and *demonstrative*). Deliberative rhetoric deals with argument about choices. It concerns itself with matters that affect the future; its chief topic, according to Aristotle, is the "advantageous"—what's best for the audience, family, company, community, or country. Without deliberative rhetoric, democracy is impossible.

demonstrative rhetoric: Persuasion that deals with values that bring a group together. It usually focuses on matters in the present, and its chief topic is right versus wrong. Most sermons—and too many political speeches—are demonstrative. (The other two forms of rhetoric are *deliberative* and *forensic*.)

dialectic: The purely logical debate of philosophers. Its purpose is to discover the truth through dialogue. Logical fallacies are verboten in dialectic. Rhetoric, on the other hand, allows them.

dialogismus *(die-a-log-IS-mus):* The dialogue figure. You quote a conversation as an example.

dialysis: The this-not-that figure. "Don't buy the shoes. Buy the colors." People take your wisdom more seriously if you put it cryptically; it's the idiot savant approach.

diazeugma *(die-a-ZOOG-ma):* The play-by-play figure. It uses a single subject to govern a succession of verbs.

disinterest: Freedom from special interests. (The technical name is *eunoia*.) One of the three traits of *ethos*. (The other two are *practical wisdom* and *virtue*.)

dubitatio *(du-bih-TAT-ee-o):* Feigned doubt about your ability to speak well. It's a personal form of *aporia*.

enargeia *(en-AR-gay-a):* The special effects of figures—vivid description that makes an audience believe something is taking place before their very eyes.

enthymeme *(EN-thih-meem):* Rhetoric's version of the syllogism. The enthymeme stakes a claim and then bases it on commonly accepted opinion. A little packet of logic, it can provide protein to an argument filled with emotion.

epergesis *(ep-er-GEE-sis):* The correction figure.

epideictic *(ep-i-DAKE-tic)* rhetoric: Aristotle's name for *demonstrative* rhetoric, speech that deals with values.

equivocation *(e-quiv-o-KAY-shon):* The language mask. It appears to say one thing while meaning the opposite. The Jesuits used it to trick the Inquisition without actually violating their beliefs.

eristic *(er-ISS-tick):* A competitive argument for the sake of argument.

ethos: Argument by character, one of the three "appeals"; the other two are *pathos* (argument by emotion) and *logos* (argument by logic).

eunoia: Aristotle's word for disinterest, one of the three characteristics of *ethos,* or argument by character. (The other two traits are *practical wisdom* and *virtue.*)

example: *Exemplum* in classical rhetoric. The foundation of inductive logic. Aristotle listed three kinds: fact, comparison, and "fable" or story.

forensic (legal) rhetoric: Argument that determines guilt or innocence. It focuses on the past. (The other two kinds of rhetoric are *deliberative* and *demonstrative.*)

homerism: The unabashed use of illogic, named after the immortal cartoon character in *The Simpsons.*

hypophora *(hy-PAH-phor-a):* A figure that asks a rhetorical question and then immediately answers it. The hypophora allows you to anticipate the audience's skepticism and nip it in the bud.

idiom *(ID-ee-om):* Inseparable words with a single meaning. Often mistaken for figures in general, the idiom is merely a kind of figure.

ignoratio elenchi *(ig-no-ROT-ee-o eh-LEN-chee):* The fallacy of proving the wrong conclusion.

innuendo: The technique of planting negative ideas in the audience's head.

jeremiad *(jer-e-MI-ad):* Prophecy of doom; also called *cataplexis.*

kairos *(KIE-ros):* The rhetorical art of seizing the occasion. It covers both timing and the appropriate medium.

leptologia *(lep-to-LO-gia):* See *quibbling.*

litotes *(li-TOE-tees):* The figure of ironic understatement, usually negative. ("We are not amused.")

logos: Argument by logic, one of the three "appeals"; the other two are argument by emotion *(pathos)* and argument by character *(ethos).*

metanoia *(met-a-NOI-a):* The self-editing figure. You stop to correct yourself with a stronger point.

metaphor *(MET-a-phor):* A figure that makes something represent something else. ("The moon is a balloon.")

metastasis *(met-AS-ta-sis):* A figure of thought that skips over an awkward matter. "Traffic was horrible. I got into a little fender-bender, no big deal, but I got you that shirt you wanted."

metonymy *(meh-TON-ih-mee):* A figure of swap. It makes a part stand for the whole, or vice versa. ("The throne" in reference to the queen, for example.) It can also use a cause to name an effect, or vice versa. The metonymy is one of the fundamental figures, along with *metaphor* and *synecdoche.*

neologism *(NEE-oh-loh-gism):* The newly minted word.

non sequitur *(non SEH-quit-ur):* The figure of irrelevance, a point that doesn't follow its predecessor. ("You know what your problem is? Whoa, did you see that car?")

onomatopoeia *(onna-motta-PEE-ah):* The noisemaker. This figure imitates a sound to name the sound. ("Kaboom!")

paradigm *(PAR-a-dime):* A rule that arises from examples. "Look at those maples turning colors; we must be getting into fall."

paralipsis *(pa-ra-LIP-sis):* A figure in which you mention something by saying you're not going to mention it. It makes you sound fairer than you are.

paradox: The contrary figure, an impossible pair. ("We had to destroy the village in order to save it.") The term's connotation has changed since ancient times, when it originally meant something contrary to public opinion or belief.

paraprosdokian *(pa-ra-proze-DOK-ee-an):* This figure attaches a surprise ending to a thought.

pathos: Argument by emotion, one of the three "appeals" of persuasion; the other two are argument by logic *(logos)* and argument by character *(ethos).*

periphrasis *(per-IH-phra-sis):* The speak-around figure. It uses a description as a name. Also known as *circumlocution.*

petitio principii *(pe-TIH-ee-o prin-CIH-pee-ee):* Begging the question; the fallacy of circular argument.

phronesis *(fro-NEE-sis):* Practical wisdom; street savvy. One of Aristotle's three traits of *ethos,* or argument by character. (The other two are *disinterest* and *virtue.*)

polysyndeton *(polly-SIN-de-ton):* A figure that links clauses with a repeated conjunction.

post hoc ergo propter hoc: The Chanticleer fallacy. A followed B; therefore, A caused B. ("My crowing makes the sun come up.")

practical wisdom: See *phronesis.*

prolepsis *(pro-LEP-sis):* A figure of thought that anticipates an opponent's or audience's objections.

prosopopoeia *(pro-so-po-PEE-uh):* The figure of personification. Ancient rhetoric teachers used the word to refer to school exercises in which students imitated real and imagined orators from history.

quibbling: Using careful language to obfuscate. ("That depends on what your definition of 'is' is.") The rhetorical term is *leptologia.*

red herring: The fallacy of distraction.

reductio ad absurdum: Taking an opponent's argument to its illogical conclusion. A fallacy in formal logic; in rhetoric, a great tool.

rhetoric: The art of persuasion. Aristotle listed three kinds of rhetoric: forensic (legal), which tries to prove guilt or innocence; demonstrative, which makes people believe in a community's values; and deliberative. This book deals mostly with deliberative rhetoric, the language of political persuasion; its main topic is the "advantageous"—what's best for an audience, community, or nation.

significatio *(sig-ni-fi-CAT-ee-o):* A benign form of innuendo that implies more than it says. "He's a stickler for detail," you say of an indecisive muddler.

slippery slope: The fallacy of dire consequences. It assumes that one choice will necessarily lead to a cascading series of bad choices.

solecism *(SOL-eh-sizm):* The figure of ignorance; a generic term for illogic, or bad grammar or syntax.

straw man fallacy: Instead of dealing with the actual issue, it attacks a weaker version of the argument.

syncrisis *(SIN-crih-sis):* A figure that reframes an argument by redefining it. "Not manipulation. *Instruction.*"

synecdoche *(sin-ECK-doe-kee):* The scale-changing figure. It swaps a genus for a species, or a species for a genus. ("Bluehairs"; "the word on the street.")

tautology *(taw-TAH-lo-gee):* The redundancy. It's often used in politics to mislead. Also known as *begging the question* or *petitio principii.*

yogiism *(YO-gee-ism):* The idiot savant figure, named after baseball great Yogi Berra. On the surface it's illogical, but it makes an odd sort of sense. ("You can observe a lot just by looking"—"Nobody goes there anymore. It's too crowded.")

▲

Chronology

B.C.

425 Gorgias, an itinerant Sophist, or professional rhetorician, wows Athens with his speechmaking.

385 Plato publishes *Gorgias,* an antirhetorical screed written in highly rhetorical language.

332 Aristotle publishes his *Rhetoric,* the greatest work on the subject ever written.

106 Birth of Marcus Tullius Cicero.

100 Birth of Caius Julius Caesar.

100 *Ad Herennium (For Herennius)* published. The most popular rhetoric textbook during the Middle Ages and early Renaissance. People attributed it to Cicero (and some still do), but he was a small boy when the book was written.

75 Cicero joins the Roman Senate.

63 Cicero, in his role as consul, puts down a major conspiracy by an aristocrat named Catiline.

59 Julius Caesar becomes a Roman consul.

55 Cicero writes *On the Orator (De Oratore),* his masterpiece.

48 Caesar becomes dictator of Rome.

46 Marcus Porcius Cato commits suicide; the thought of it would drive the American founders crazy.

44 Caesar assassinated.

43 Cicero killed.

A.D.

 93   A Spaniard named Quintilian writes a textbook on rhetoric that
      would be used through Shakespeare's time.

426   Augustine, who took early retirement as a rhetoric professor, writes
      On Christian Doctrine. It criticizes rhetoric while using its principles.

524   Boethius writes *The Consolation of Philosophy* while awaiting
      execution for treason. Promoting Christianity with classical
      rhetorical methods, the book becomes the most widely published
      in Europe.

630   Isidore of Seville, Europe's greatest scholar during the Middle
      Ages, writes *Etymologide,* the world's first encyclopedia. He
      introduces Aristotle to his fellow Spaniards and helps create the
      beginnings of representative government.

782   Alcuin of York teaches rhetoric to Charlemagne.

1444 George of Trebizond writes a rhetoric book and helps bring the
      classics to Europe. The Renaissance begins.

1512 Desiderius Erasmus, one of the greatest scholars of all time, writes
      De Copia (On Abundance), celebrating the richness of language.
      Erasmus discovered a number of ancient rhetorical manuscripts.

1555 Petrus Ramus, a French scholar, separates logical argument from
      rhetoric, reducing the discipline to one of style. The founders of
      Harvard were followers of Ramus, who was burned at the stake as
      a heretic.

1577 Henry Peacham publishes *The Garden of Eloquence,* which becomes
      the standard textbook for figures of speech. You can still buy it.

1776 Rhetorically trained Thomas Jefferson drafts the Declaration of
      Independence.

1787 Alexander Hamilton, James Madison, and John Jay write a series of
      letters to New York newspapers in favor of ratifying the Constitution.
      The letters, now called *The Federalist,* are a font of rhetorical
      principles.

1806 John Quincy Adams, a young U.S. senator, assumes the Boylston
      Chair of Rhetoric and Oratory at Harvard. The chair is now held
      by Jorie Graham, a poet.

1826 A young Massachusetts congressman named Daniel Webster
      delivers a eulogy for Thomas Jefferson and John Adams. The
      speech makes Webster a rhetorical superstar.

1860   Lincoln delivers a speech at Cooper Union in New York that
       propels him to the presidency.

1950   Rhetorician and literary critic Kenneth Burke publishes *A Rhetoric
       of Motives,* arguably the greatest work on the art of persuasion in
       more than a century. Burke introduces the idea of identity as a
       central tool in persuasion.

1958   Chaim Perelman, a Belgian legal scholar and a Jew who survived
       the Holocaust, poses a profound human question: How could
       people govern themselves when the chief intellectual tools of
       Perelman's time, science and logic and modern law, had failed
       to prevent war and Holocaust? Finding an answer in the art of
       persuasion, he writes an influential book, *The New Rhetoric.*

1962   Marshall McLuhan publishes *The Gutenberg Galaxy.* This Canadian
       rhetorician earns his fifteen minutes of fame by coining the
       commonplaces "The medium is the message" and "the global
       village." He helps revive rhetoric in academe. (I found the book
       entirely unreadable.)

1963   Martin Luther King Jr. delivers his "I Have a Dream" speech,
       brilliantly combining present-tense sermonizing rhetoric with a
       stirring vision of the future.

2006   The Rhetoric Society of America boasts "almost 1,000 members."

▲

Further Reading

People who want to immerse themselves in rhetoric will find the ancient stuff surprisingly easy to read, if a little dull in places. The modern guides are something else; the lack of good ones helped motivate me to write this book in the first place.

In fact, one of the best current resources is not a book but a Web site, grandly named "*Silva Rhetoricae,* The Forest of Rhetoric" (http://rhetoric.byu.edu). At the risk of overpromoting myself, my own site, "It Figures" (www.figarospeech.com), shows how rhetoric works in politics and the media.

Among the several hundred books on rhetoric that I have read over the years, I found the following the most useful and enjoyable.

A Handlist of Rhetorical Terms, by Richard A. Lanham. As Strunk and White's *Elements of Style* did for grammar, Lanham's well-organized and entertaining *Handlist* does for rhetoric. If you lack room on the shelf near your desk, toss Strunk and White and keep the *Handlist.* You'll find it infinitely more useful.

Encyclopedia of Rhetoric (Oxford University Press, 2001). Worth perusing in any library clever enough to order it. It has a wealth of articles covering all aspects of ancient and modern rhetoric, and everything in between. The material on Shakespeare's rhetoric is first-rate.

Classical Rhetoric for the Modern Student, by P. J. Corbett (Oxford University Press, 1990). The only thorough modern textbook extant. It suffers from the academic distaste for anything practical—Corbett wrote the book for composition students, and you will find little about rhetorical "delivery" or actual argument—but he dutifully leads you through the basic rhetorical principles.

The Art of Rhetoric, by Aristotle (Penguin, 1991). This is the rhetoric book that launched all the others, and it remains the art's fundamental textbook. Whenever I go back and reread passages that make no sense or seem irrelevant to modern life, I discover that the fault is mine, not Aristotle's. This book was his masterpiece, written late in life as a culmination of all his political and psychological knowledge. The bad news is you will not find it a page turner. Some scholars think that Aristotle's *Rhetoric* is merely a collection of his lecture notes, and that's how they read. But if you make the effort, you will uncover a truly uncanny work, one of the genuine classics.

Cicero, by Anthony Everitt (Random House, 2001). History's greatest orator wouldn't make a very good motion picture. At least, you would never see Russell Crowe playing him. For one thing, Cicero was a physical coward. His name meant "turnip seed" in Latin. And he failed to stop tyranny in Rome. But he was a central actor in some of the most interesting historical events of all time, perhaps history's greatest orator, and one of rhetoric's chief theoreticians. Everitt has written the most readable biography. He evokes the troubled times in Rome with novelistic flair, and helps us understand why the Romans considered rhetoric the highest of the liberal arts.

The Founders and the Classics, by Carl J. Richard (Harvard, 1994). Readers more interested in history than theory—especially those who find my history far-fetched—should get this book. Richard's short, readable romp through the founders' education shows their passion for the ancients better than any other book.

A Rhetoric of Motives, by Kenneth Burke (University of California, 1950). This brilliant, dense book is only for the rhetoric addict. Burke ranks as one of the leading philosophers and literary critics of the twentieth century. It is no exaggeration to call him the greatest rhetorical theorist since Augustine. But the book is slow going for the uninitiated.

▲

ACKNOWLEDGMENTS

There is something wonderfully paradoxical about writing a book on humanity's most social art while sitting alone in a cabin in Orange, New Hampshire. But I wasn't alone, as these acknowledgments will attest.

My wife comes first, and not in the commonplace way. When I told Dorothy Senior that I wanted to quit my job and write a book on rhetoric, she replied without irony, "I believe in you." As terrifying as those words were, without Dorothy's faith, her steady income, and her insightful criticism of my drafts, this book certainly would have been impossible. *I* would have been impossible.

My children, Dorothy Junior and George, supplied much of the dialogue in this book, and they showed stoicism beyond their years while I read chapters aloud, often repeatedly. They, too, caught important sins of omission and commission, and have made me (often against my will) the experienced debater I am today.

Cynthia Cannell, my agent, called me every few months for almost a decade to ask if I was ready to write the book, and won my heart yet again by selling it to a publisher. My editor, Rick Horgan, steered me with savvy wit and pushed me as no editor ever has. His assistant, Julian Pavia, provided brilliant line-by-line feedback on every draft and debated the finer philosophical points in scarily erudite e-mails.

Authors Jim Collins, Kristen Collins-Laine, Lisa Davis, Eugenie Shields, and Bob Sullivan dealt indispensable advice. Gina Barreca, a superb humorist and star faculty member at the University of Connecticut, saved me from miring myself in rhetorical jargon. Deborah Nelson and her AP English students at Lebanon High School, in New Hampshire, gave the manuscript its harshest, funniest comments. Thanks also to Sherry Chester, Jeremy Katz, Nat Reade, Steve Madden, and Kristen Fountain for their comments and advice. Jeff Shields, president and dean of Vermont Law School, helped me understand the ways that our judicial system cribs from rhetoric.

Harvard rhetoricians Luciana Herman and Stephen Larsen made me almost sorry I published articles about their university's attempt to kill rhetoric. They had their students read a draft as part of their course work, and their own comments were both helpful and heartening. Luci and Stephen were among dozens of rhetoricians at colleges across the country—too many to mention—who have helped me over the years. They have kept rhetoric alive just as the monks did in the Dark Ages.

Finally, the thousands of subscribers to Figarospeech.com, my rhetoric blog, sustain my faith in the art of persuasion. With a few million more figurists like you, we shall raise Aristotle, Isocrates, Cicero, Quintilian, Churchill, Burke, King, Madison, Lincoln, and Hamilton from the dead. Bless you all.

▲

INDEX

abortion, 102–103, 116–119
accismus, 209
Adams, John, 67, 288
Adams, John Quincy, xi, 314
Adaptation, 205
Addison, Joseph, 288
advantageous, the, 98, 121
Aeschylus, 250
Agnew, Spiro, 69
Ali, Muhammed, 234–235
Alice's Restaurant, 44
Allen, Woody, 218
amplification, 5
anadiplosis, 220–221
analogy, 209
anaphora, 211
anger, 86
Animal House, 5, 66–67
anthimeria, 222–224
antithesis, 5, 217–218
Antoinette, Marie, 74
AP English exam, 292
Apollo 13, 68
aporia, 51
Arctic National Wildlife Refuge, 178–178
argument by the stick, 85, 168–169
argument from strength, 7
argumentum ad baculum, see argument by the stick

argumentum a fortiori, see argument from strength
Aristophanes, 21, 91
Aristotle, 29, 46, 80–81, 84, 99, 119, 125–126, 131, 171, 176–177, 197, 219, 287
arrangement, 247, 249–252
asyndeton, 224
Athens, 77, 288
audience, 56
Augustine, Saint, 9, 23, 38, 426

backfire, 92
Behe, Michael, 91
belittlement, 86–87
Belushi, John, 66–67
Berra, Yogi, 16
Beverly Hillbillies, The, 204
blame, 27, 28
Bligh, William, 68
blogging, 241–242
book clubs, 247, 276–80
Boy Scouts, 81
bragging, 62
Breyer, Stephen, 183
Brown, Pat, 168
Buffon, comte de, 53
Burke, Kenneth, 47
Bush, George W., 19, 64, 69, 77, 99, 102, 112, 183, 193–198, 212, 217

Bush, Laura, 95
Bushisms, 193–198

Caesar, Julius, 4, 57
Caine Mutiny, The, 221
Calvin & Hobbes, 42, 222
capital punishment, 73
Carey, Mariah, 16
Carter, Jimmy, 51, 67, 74
casual Friday, 50, 51
Cato, 288–9, 313
Cato (Joseph Addison's play), 288
character, *see* ethos
Cheney, Dick, 16, 69
Chewbacca Defense, 149
chiasmus, 10, 215–217
Chironomia, 257
choice, 27, 28
Christian mass, 285
Christopher Marlowe, 287
Churchill, Winston, 96
Cicero, Marcus Tullius, 4, 6, 22, 39,
    49, 51, 56, 75, 83, 84, 94, 95, 123,
    240, 247–259, 260, 261, 276, 285–6,
    287, 313
clarity, 253
Clear Skies, 102
cliché, 101–102, 213–215, 278
Clinton, Bill, 58, 69, 108, 235
Cochran, Johnnie, 149
code language, 192–199, 203–207, 212,
    254, 280, 291
Columbia University, 289
commonplace, 4, 101–107, 126, 137,
    228–231
  books, 105
  label, 102
compassion, 85
concession, 3, 20, 21, 42, 96, 214,
    280–83
Constitution, U.S., 4, 287
Coolidge, Calvin, 95

Cooper Union speech, 76, 314
creationism, 91–92, 129

Dartmouth College, xi, 88, 257
Dartmouth College Case, 84
Dean, Howard, 16, 183
death penalty, 117
debate origin, 15
Declaration of Independence, 287
decorum, 44–55, 59, 240, 254, 275,
    279
deduction, 125–133
definition strategy, 108–120
deliberative argument, 33, 48, 107, 127
delivery, 247, 257
democracy, 29
Democrats, 29, 104–105, 112, 126
demonstrative rhetoric, 29, 33, 34, 183
dialectic, 27, 123, 155
dialogismus, 209
dialysis, 52, 217, 219, 286
diazeugma, 211
dirimens copulatio, 5, 277
disinterest, 56, 74, 172–175, 185–186
division, 250
Dole, Bob, 235
drug war, 81
dubitatio, 75–77, 256
Dukakis, Michael, 161–163

Ecclesiastes, 226, 232
Eddie Haskell Ploy, 64–65, 271
election campaigns, 99–100, 161–162,
    168, 193, 281–3
elections, 25, 104
e-mail, 239, 274
Emerson, Ralph Waldo, 247
Eminem, 48, 49
emotion:
    argument by, *see pathos*
    unannounced, 89
emulation, 86, 88

enargeia, see vividness
English literature, 5
Enron, 61
enthymeme, 6, 125–127, 140, 249
epergesis, 218
epideictic rhetoric, *see* demonstrative
    rhetoric
Erasmus, Desiderius, 123, 314
eristic, 19
esteem, 85
ethos, 38–78, 157
  word origin, 46
Everett, Edward, 259
examples (in inductive logic), 127
exordium, 252, 285
extremism, 177–180

facts, 109, 132, 275
fallacy, 137–154
  all natural, 139–140
  ambiguity, 139
  antecedent, of, 141
  appeal to authority, 157
  appeal to popularity, 140
  Chanticleer, *see post hoc ergo propter hoc*
  complex cause, 148
  false analogy, 142
  false dilemma, 148
  good money after bad, 159–160
  hasty generalization, 144–145
  ignorance, 145–146, 208
  many questions, 147–148
  misinterpreting the evidence, 144
  post hoc ergo propter hoc, 11, 151–152
  power, of, 156
  red herring, 149, 174
  reductio ad absurdum, 141
  slippery slope, 150
  straw man, 150
  tautology, 137–146
  unit, 142–143
Far Side, The, 195

Federalist, The, 72–73, 243
Federalists, 290
figarospeech.com, 11, 241–242
figures of speech, 208–235, 270
figures of thought, 212–225, 270
filmmaking, 102
flag burning, 87
Food Network, 8
Foreman, George, 16
forensic rhetoric, 29, 183
framing, 116
Franklin, Ben, 290
Freud, Sigmund, 94
Frost, Robert, 194

gesture, 238
Gettysburg Address, 259
gift giving, 243
Gladiator, 220
goals, 19, 272
God, 62, 240
Gone with the Wind, 47
Good Will Hunting, 81
Google, 105
Gore, Al, 69
Gospel of John, 123
Gottman, John, 15, 29
Great Britain, 293
gun control, 116, 151

Hamilton, Alexander, 72–73, 243, 287,
    289
Hamlet, 74
Harvard, xi, 289, 292
Haskell, Eddie, 64–65
Healthy Forests Initiative, 102
Henry, Patrick, 287–8
Hill, Anita, 164
Hilton, Paris, 237
Holmes, Sherlock, 126
Homer, 15, 181
Hoover, Herbert, 67, 74

House, 184
Hume, David, 3
humiliation, 166–168
humor, 81, 85, 94–97
   banter, 95–97
   facetious, 95
   urbane, 94
   wit, 95
Humphrey, Hubert, 235
Hurricane Katrina, 85
hyperbole, 209
hypocrisy, word origin, 257
hypophora, 39

identity strategy, 86, 191–207, 269
ideology, word origin, 207
idiom, 211, 215, 278
In Cold Blood, 83
inarguable, the, 36
incivility, 291
induction, 125–127, 275
innuendo, 167–168
instant messaging, 240–241
intelligent design, 91–92, 129–130
invention, 247
Iraq war, 69, 103, 159–160, 200
irony, 205–206, 213
Isocrates, 98
Italy, 285–6, 293
It's a Wonderful Life, 23

Jackson, Janet, 57
Jay, John, 72
Jefferson, Thomas, 105, 257, 287
Jesus, 57, 67
Job, 62
Jobs, Steve, 92
jokes, 81
Jonson, Ben, 121
journalism, 286
joy, 85
JumboTron, 237–238

kairos, 226–243, 272, 274
Kangaroo, Captain, 52
Kennedy, John F., 10
Kerry, John, 19, 100, 122, 198, 235
King James Bible, 210
King, Martin Luther, 234, 293, 315
Kissinger, Henry, 23, 24

labeling, 111
Lakoff, George, 182
landslide counties, 291
Law and Order, 29
Leahy, Pat, 16
l'esprit de l'escalier, 208
letter writing, 243
liberal arts, 289
liberal, origin, 72, 289
Lincoln, Abraham, 59, 75–76, 184, 259, 260
litotes, 57, 175, 220
Locke, John, 287
logic, *see logos*
logos, 38, 39, 40, 41, 45, 98–170
love, 85

Macaulay, Rose, 213–214
Machiavelli, Niccolò, 70
Madison, James, 72–73, 243, 289
magazines, 242
Manchurian Candidate, The, xi
Matrix, 4
McCain, John, 62–63
memory, 247, 255–257
Meriwether, Colyer, 133
metallage, 225
metaphor, 213
metonymy, 213
Middlebury College, 88
Milton, John, 137, 284
Mitterrand, François, 59
moderation, 177–180, 291–2
Mondale, Walter, 235

Monty Python, 169, 211
museums, 256
Music Man, The, 104
My Big Fat Greek Wedding, 285

Napier, Charles, 94
narration, 250
National Lampoon, 15
New Hampshire, 86, 249
newspapers, 242
Nixon, Richard, 23, 69, 74, 160, 168, 235
No Child Left Behind, 102
noise ordinances, 247–258

Obama, Barack, 260–269
occasion, *see kairos*
O'Connor, Sandra Day, 183
op ed, 243
ornament, 254
oxymoron, 209

Packwood, Bob, 53
paradigm, 131
paralipsis, 126
paraprosdokian, 161, 231
parelcon, 223
passive voice, 91
pathos, 38–45, 78–97
Patriot Act, 88, 106
patriotism, 86–87
Peacham, Henry, 79, 208
Peanuts, 168
Pelosi, Nancy, 183
perfume, 243
periphrasis, 112, 209–210
phronesis, *see* practical wisdom
Pitt, Brad, 28, 274
Plato, 15, 21
political correctness, 48
polysyndeton, 196
PowerPoint, 24, 53, 124, 238, 259, 274

practical wisdom, 56, 66–71, 181–188
praying, 240
premise, 125–127
prolepsis, 21
Protagoras, 80
push polls, 122, 128

Quintilian, 75–77, 314

race relations, 47
radio, 239
Ramus, Petrus, 158, 314
Ray, Dixie Lee, 93
Reagan, Ronald, 95, 258
recruiting, 184–185
redefining, 109–111
Redford, Robert, 274
refutation, 250, 292
relationships, 185–186
reluctant conclusion, 73
Republicans, 29, 104–105, 126, 290
Revolution, American, 87
rhetorical question, 209
Roberts, John, 95
Roman republic, 288
Royal Society, 286–7
Ruthless People, 82

Satan, 62
school prayer, 179
science, 91
seduction, 8, 9, 16, 21, 130
senses, 239–244
Shakespeare, William, 4, 114, 208, 222, 224, 252–253, 287
Shaw, Bernard, 161–162
Sheehan, Cindy, 217
Simlish, 194
Simpson, O. J., 83, 149
Simpsons, The, 16, 27, 34, 80, 83, 121, 131–132, 137, 139–140, 166–167, 171, 191, 218

skywriting, 238
slavery, 289
smoke signals, 243
snaps, 95
Socrates, 15
sophistry, 155
Sophists, 80, 155, 179, 313
South Beach Diet, The, 25
Spartans, 103
Stalin, Joseph, 228
stance, 108
Star Trek, 122–123, 161
status theory, *see* stance
Stehrwitt, 208
Stewart, Jimmy, 23
storytelling, 132–133, 250, 275
style, 247, 252–255, 287
syllogism, 123–124
sympathy, 43, 44
syncrisis, 4
synecdoche, 213

tactical flaw, 63
tautology, 137, 146
telephone, 242–243
television, 239
tenses, 28, 29, 30, 36
This Is Spinal Tap, 92
Thomas, Clarence, 164, 221
Thomas, Norman, 237
threat, 168–169
Three Stooges, 88
Thune, John, 174
Timex Ironman, 7
To Kill a Mockingbird, 59
topics, word origin, 101
tort reform, 112–113

Transamerica, 94
tribalism, 33
tropes, 213
trust, 75
truth, 27, 33, 137, 291
Tsongas, Paul, 235
Twain, Mark, 106

values, 27, 28, 36, 106, 273, 291
Venn diagram, 124
verbing, *see anthimeria*
Vietnam war, 160, 239
virtue, 56–65, 172, 176–180, 185–186,
    291–2
vividness, 253–254, 258, 269
voice control, 258
Vonnegut, Kurt, 169

Walton, Izaak, 44
Washington, George, 63, 287–8,
    290
Wayne, John, 94
Wayne's World, 110, 205
Webster, Daniel, 5, 83–84, 314
welfare, 281
Wieland, Christoph Martin, 72
Wilde, Oscar, 213–214
wit, 95
Witherspoon, John, 289
Wizard of Oz, 212
Wodehouse, P. G., 213–214
Wonkette, 241
World Trade Center attack, 89, 105

yogiism, 16, 159

Zeno, 154

PENGUIN HISTORY

THE ENGLISH YEAR

STEVE ROUD

This enthralling book will take you, month-by-month, day-by-day, through all the festivities of English life. From national celebrations such as New Year's Eve to regional customs such as the Padstow Hobby Horse procession, cheese rolling in Gloucestershire and Easter Monday bottle kicking in Leeds, it explains how they originated, what they mean and when they occur.

A fascinating guide to the richness of our heritage and the sometimes eccentric nature of life in England, *The English Year* offers a unique chronological view of our social customs and attitudes.

'The book is a delight, a fund of information' *The Times*

PENGUIN HISTORY

THE CRAFTSMAN
RICHARD SENNETT

Why do people work hard, and take pride in what they do? This book, a philosophically-minded enquiry into practical activity of many different kinds past and present, is about what happens when people try to do a good job. It asks us to think about the true meaning of skill in the 'skills society' and argues that pure competition is a poor way to achieve quality work. Sennett suggests, instead, that there is a craftsman in every human being.

The Craftsman shows how history has drawn fault-lines between craftsman and artist, maker and user, technique and expression, practice and theory, and that individuals' pride in their work, as well as modern society in general, suffers from these historical divisions. But the past lives of crafts and craftsmen show us ways of working (using tools, acquiring skills, thinking about materials) which provide rewarding alternative ways for people to utilise their talents. We need to recognize this if motivations are to be understood and lives made as fulfilling as possible.

'Richard Sennett is a prime observer of society ... one of his great strengths, the thing that makes his narrative so gripping, is the sheer range of his thinking and his brilliance in relating the past to the present' Fiona MacCarthy, *Guardian*

'A lifetime's learning has gone into this book ... Sennett writes beautifully' Roger Scruton, *Sunday Times*

PENGUIN LANGUAGE

THE STORIES OF ENGLISH
DAVID CRYSTAL

How did a language originally spoken by a few thousand Anglo-Saxons become one used by more than 1,500 million people? How have all the different versions of English evolved and changed? In this compelling global tour, David Crystal turns the traditional view of the history of the language on its head and tells the *real* stories of English that have never before been fully told.

'A spirited celebration . . . Crystal gives the story of English a new plot' *Guardian*

'Rejoices in dialects, argots and cants . . . enlightening – in a word, excellent' *Sunday Times*

'An exhilarating read . . . Crystal is a sort of latter-day Johnson' *The Times Higher Education Supplement*

'*The Stories of English* reads like an adventure story. Which, of course, it is' Roger McGough

'A marvellous book . . . for anyone who loves the English language(s) it will be a treasure-house' Philip Pullman

Steven Johnson

MIND WIDE OPEN
WHY YOU ARE WHAT YOU THINK

'Refreshingly personal ... endlessly fascinating' *Guardian*

In *Mind Wide Open* Steven Johnson takes us on a journey to the frontiers of brain science and reveals exactly how we're hard-wired to think and feel. Experimenting with the latest technology he discovers (among other things) that everything we do – from falling in love to forming a sentence – is caused by neurons firing and chemicals swirling around our heads; that there are gadgets which can enable us to control our own brainwaves; that everyone's mind, like their fingerprint, is unique; and that this can help us understand our own mental foibles - and see ourselves in a totally new way.

'Steven Johnson has an eye for the most interesting new ideas in this exploding field, and he explains them with insight and gusto' Steven Pinker

'As Steven Johnson explores his inner world ... we have a new sense of what it means to be human' *The New York Times*

AL FRANKEN

LIES AND THE LYING LIARS WHO TELL THEM: A FAIR AND BALANCED LOOK AT THE RIGHT

The No.1 International Bestseller

'The book that Fox News tried to prevent from being published. It's in-your-face ... acidic ... hilarious' *Observer*

Meet Al Franken, the man who's had Murdoch's media suing, conservatives up in arms and readers in hysterics over his exposure of right-wing politicians and pundits for what they really are: Liars. Lying, lying liars. Basically ... they make stuff up.

Join him as he trashes the untruthful, mauls the mendacious and bitch-slaps the bullshitters, proving how Bush and his fellow truth-twisters have told porkies over small matters like the election, their shady business connections and the war on terror. And how a 'neutral' American media spins those lies, with hysterical right-wing hacks, harpies and nutcases attacking all liberal thought. Al shoots them down by doing what they're incapable of: getting his facts straight.

'Wildly funny' *Time Out*

'Al Franken has helped to slay ... the biggest icons on the right ... and he's done it with humour' Michael Moore

'Fantastic' Ian Hislop

'Al Franken comically savages Murdoch's minions' *Guardian*

'Very funny ... Franken gets under the skin of his adversaries like no one else' *Independent*

PENGUIN REFERENCE

THE LORE OF THE LAND
WESTWOOD AND SIMPSON

Where can you find the 'Devil's footprints'?

What happened at the 'hangman's stone'?

Did Sweeney Todd, the demon barber of Fleet Street, really exist?

Where was King Arthur laid to rest?

Bringing together tales of hauntings, highwaymen, family curses and lovers' leaps, this magnificent guide will take you on a magical journey through England's legendary past.

'A real treasury' Philip Pullman

'A treasure-house of extraordinary tales, rooted in the wildly various and haunted landscapes of England' *Sunday Times*

'A fascinating county-by county guidebook to headless horsemen, bottomless pools, immured adulteresses and talking animals' *London Review of Books*

'Wonderful . . . Contains almost every myth, legend and ghost story ever told in England' Simon Hoggart, *Guardian*

PENGUIN PSYCHOLOGY

BLINK: THE POWER OF THINKING WITHOUT THINKING
MALCOLM GLADWELL

'Astonishing … *Blink* really does make you rethink the way you think' *Daily Mail*

An art expert sees a ten-million-dollar sculpture and instantly spots it's a fake. A marriage analyst knows within minutes whether a couple will stay together. A fire-fighter suddenly senses he has to get out of a blazing building …

This book is all about those moments when we 'know' something without knowing why. Malcolm Gladwell explores the phenomenon of 'blink', showing how a snap judgement can be far more effective than a cautious decision. By trusting your instincts, he reveals, you'll never think about thinking in the same way again …

OUTLIERS: THE STORY OF SUCCESS
MALCOLM GLADWELL

'Makes geniuses look a bit less special, and the rest of us a bit more so' *Time*

Why do some people achieve so much more than others? Can they lie so far out of the ordinary? What makes them exceptional?

In this provocative and inspiring book, Malcolm Gladwell looks at everyone from rock stars to professional athletes, software billionaires to scientific geniuses, to show that the story of success is far more surprising, and more fascinating, than we could ever have imagined. Gladwell reveals that success is as much about where we're from and what we do, as who we are – and that no one, not even a genius, ever makes it alone.

PENGUIN

TRAIN YOUR BRAIN
DR KAWASHIMA

Dr Kawashima's brain training will change your life ...

Do you ever find the simplest words or the most obvious names suddenly escape your mind for no apparent reason? Do you ever walk into a room and forget why you came in, or realize you don't know where you left your house keys just ten minutes ago? Is your memory getting steadily worse? Train Your Brain can turn back the clock ...

Like the body, the brain needs exercise. And Dr Ryuta Kawashima, world-renowned professor of neuroscience at Tohoku University, has dedicated his life to researching exactly how we can make our brains work better.

Here are his results – in a highly rewarding programme of carefully chosen, deceptively simple activities. Each day you fill in a worksheet of easy exercises and with weekly self-tests and a personal logbook you can track your progress. Taking just a few minutes a day over two months, you really can boost your brain power and creativity. We're so sure this will work that if your brain hasn't improved in sixty days – we'll give you your money back.

Join the Dr Kawashima revolution today.

PENGUIN SCIENCE

THE STUFF OF THOUGHT:
LANGUAGE AS A WINDOW INTO HUMAN NATURE
STEVEN PINKER

'Moments of genuine revelation and some very good jokes'
Mark Haddon, *Sunday Telegraph*

The Stuff of Thought is an exhilarating work of non-fiction. Surprising, thought-provoking and incredibly enjoyable, there is no other book like it – Steven Pinker will revolutionise the way you think about language. He analyses what words actually mean and how we use them, and he reveals what this can tell us about ourselves. He shows how we use space and motion as metaphors for more abstract ideas, and uncovers the deeper structures of human thought that have been shaped by evolutionary history. He also explores the emotional impact of language, from names to swear words, and shows us the full power that it can have over us. And, with this book, he also shows just how stimulating and entertaining language can be.

'Astonishingly readable' *Daily Telegraph*

'Perceptive, amusing and intelligent' *The Times*

'No one writes about language as clearly as Steven Pinker, and this is his best book yet' *Financial Times*

PENGUIN SCIENCE

THE BLANK SLATE STEVEN PINKER

'The best book on human nature that I or anyone else will ever read. Truly magnificent' Matt Ridley, *Sunday Telegraph*

'A passionate defence of the enduring power of human nature ... both life-affirming and deeply satisfying' Tim Lott, *Daily Telegraph*

'Brilliant ... enjoyable, informative, clear, humane' *New Scientist*

'If you think the nature/nurture debate has been resolved, you are wrong. It is about to be reignited with a vengeance ... this book is required reading' *Literary Review*

'Startling ... Pinker makes his main argument persuasively and with great verve ... This is a breath of air for a topic that has been politicized for too long' *Economist*

HOW THE MIND WORKS STEVEN PINKER

'Why do memories fade? Why do we lose our tempers? Why do fools fall in love? Pinker's objective in this erudite account is to explore the nature and history of the human mind' *Sunday Times*

'Witty popular science that you enjoy reading for the writing as well as for the science' *The New York Review of Books*

THE LANGUAGE INSTINCT STEVEN PINKER

'A marvellously readable book...illuminates every facet of human language: its biological origin, its uniqueness to humanity, its acquisition by children, its grammatical structure, the production and perception of speech, the pathology of language disorders and its unstoppable evolution' *Nature*

'An extremely valuable book, informative and well written' Noam Chomsky

'Brilliant ... Pinker describes every aspect of language, from the resolution of ambiguity to the way speech evolved ... he expounds difficult ideas with clarity, wit and polish' Stuart Sutherland, *Observer* know more

PENGUIN WRITERS' GUIDES

HOW TO PUNCTUATE
GEORGE DAVIDSON

HOW TO WRITE BETTER ENGLISH
ROBERT ALLEN

HOW TO WRITE EFFECTIVE EMAILS
R. L. TRASK

IMPROVE YOUR SPELLING
GEORGE DAVIDSON

WRITING FOR BUSINESS
CHRIS SHEVLIN

The Penguin Writers' Guides series provides authoritative, succinct and easy-to-follow guidance on specific aspects of written English. Whether you need to brush up your skills or get to grips with something for the first time, these invaluable guides will help you find the best way to communicate clearly and effectively.

Get your message across

www.penguin.com

He just wanted a decent book to read ...

Not too much to ask, is it? It was in 1935 when Allen Lane, Managing Director of Bodley Head Publishers, stood on a platform at Exeter railway station looking for something good to read on his journey back to London. His choice was limited to popular magazines and poor-quality paperbacks – the same choice faced every day by the vast majority of readers, few of whom could afford hardbacks. Lane's disappointment and subsequent anger at the range of books generally available led him to found a company – and change the world.

'We believed in the existence in this country of a vast reading public for intelligent books at a low price, and staked everything on it'
Sir Allen Lane, 1902–1970, founder of Penguin Books

The quality paperback had arrived – and not just in bookshops. Lane was adamant that his Penguins should appear in chain stores and tobacconists, and should cost no more than a packet of cigarettes.

Reading habits (and cigarette prices) have changed since 1935, but Penguin still believes in publishing the best books for everybody to enjoy. We still believe that good design costs no more than bad design, and we still believe that quality books published passionately and responsibly make the world a better place.

So wherever you see the little bird – whether it's on a piece of prize-winning literary fiction or a celebrity autobiography, political tour de force or historical masterpiece, a serial-killer thriller, reference book, world classic or a piece of pure escapism – you can bet that it represents the very best that the genre has to offer.

Whatever you like to read – trust Penguin.

read more
www.penguin.co.uk